DATE DUE			

GRENADA

Marxist Regimes Series

Series editor: Bogdan Szajkowski,
Department of Sociology, University College,
Cardiff

Ethiopia Peter Schwab
Romania Michael Shafir
Grenada Tony Thorndike

Further Titles

Afghanistan
Albania
Angola
Benin and The Congo
Bulgaria
Cape Verde, Guinea-Bissau and São Tomé and Príncipe
China
Cuba
Czechoslovakia
German Democratic Republic
Ghana
The Co-operative Republic of Guyana
Hungary
Kampuchea
Democratic People's Republic of Korea
Laos
Madagascar
Mongolia
Mozambique
Nicaragua
Poland
Soviet Union
Surinam
Vietnam
People's Democratic Republic of Yemen
Yugoslavia
Zimbabwe
Marxist State Governments in India
Marxist Local Governments in Western Europe and Japan
The Diversification of Communism
Comparative Analysis
Cumulative Index

GRENADA
Politics, Economics and Society

Tony Thorndike

Lynne Rienner Publishers, Inc.
Boulder, Colorado

© Tony Thorndike 1985

First published in the United States of America in 1985 by
Lynne Rienner Publishers, Inc.
948 North Street
Boulder, Colorado 80302

Library of Congress Cataloging in Publication Data

Thorndike, Tony.
  Grenada: politics, economics, and society.

  Bibliography: p.
  Includes index.
  1. Grenada—Economic conditions.   2. Grenada—Social conditions.
  3. Grenada—Politics and government.
  I. Title.
  HC156.5.Z7G848   1985   972.98´45   84-62665

ISBN 0-931477-08-5 (lib. bdg.)
ISBN 0-931477-09-3 (pbk.)

Printed and bound in Great Britain by
SRP Ltd., Exeter

Editor's Preface

The study of Marxist regimes has for many years been equated with the study of communist political systems. There were several historical and methodological reasons for this.

For many years it was not difficult to distinguish the eight regimes in Eastern Europe and four in Asia which resoundingly claimed adherence to the tenets of Marxism and more particularly to their Soviet interpretation—Marxism–Leninism. These regimes, variously called 'People's Republic', 'People's Democratic Republic', or 'Democratic Republic', claimed to have derived their inspiration from the Soviet Union to which, indeed, in the overwhelming number of cases they owed their establishment.

To many scholars and analysts these regimes represented a multiplication of and geographical extension of the 'Soviet model' and consequently of the Soviet sphere of influence. Although there were clearly substantial similarities between the Soviet Union and the people's democracies, especially in the initial phases of their development, these were often overstressed at the expense of noticing the differences between these political systems.

It took a few years for scholars to realize that generalizing the particular, i.e. applying the Soviet experience to other states ruled by elites which claimed to be guided by 'scientific socialism', was not good enough. The relative simplicity of the assumption of a cohesive communist bloc was questioned after the expulsion of Yugoslavia from the Communist Information Bureau in 1948 and in particular after the workers' riots in Poznań in 1956 and the Hungarian revolution of the same year. By the mid-1960s, the totalitarian model of communist politics, which until then had been very much in force, began to crumble. As some of these regimes articulated demands for a distinctive path of socialist development, many specialists studying these systems began to notice that the cohesiveness of the communist bloc was less apparent than had been claimed before.

Also by the mid-1960s, in the newly independent African states 'democratic' multi-party states were turning into one-party states or military dictatorships, thus questioning the inherent superiority of liberal democracy, capitalism and the values that went with it. Scholars now began to ponder on the simple contrast between multi-party democracy and a one-party totalitarian rule that had satisfied an earlier generation.

More importantly, however, by the beginning of that decade Cuba had a revolution without Soviet help, a revolution which subsequently became to many political elites in the Third World not only an inspiration but a clear military, political and ideological example to follow. Apart from its romantic appeal, to many nationalist movements the Cuban revolution also demonstrated a novel way of conducting and winning a nationalist, anti-imperialist war and accepting Marxism as the state ideology without a vanguard communist party. The Cuban precedent was subsequently followed in one respect or another by scores of regimes in the Third World who used the adoption of 'scientific socialism' tied to the tradition of Marxist thought as a form of mobilization, legitimation or association with the prestigious symbols and powerful high-status regimes such as the Soviet Union, China, Cuba and Vietnam.

Despite all these changes the study of Marxist regimes remains in its infancy and continues to be hampered by constant and not always pertinent comparison with the Soviet Union, thus somewhat blurring the important underlying common theme—the 'scientific theory' of the laws of development of human society and human history. This doctrine is claimed by the leadership of these regimes to consist of the discovery of objective causal relationships; it is used to analyse the contradictions which arise between goals and actuality in the pursuit of a common destiny. Thus the political elites of these countries have been and continue to be influenced in both their ideology and their political practice by Marxism more than any other current of social thought and political practice.

The growth in the number and global significance, as well as the ideological, political and economic impact, of Marxist regimes has presented scholars and students with an increasing challenge. In meeting this challenge, social scientists on both sides of the political divide have put forward a dazzling profusion of terms, models, programmes and varieties of interpretation. It is against the background of this profusion that the present comprehensive series on Marxist regimes is offered.

This collection of monographs is envisaged as a series of multi-disciplinary textbooks on the governments, politics, economics and society of these countries. Each of the monographs was prepared by a specialist on the country concerned. Thus, over fifty scholars from all over the world have contributed monographs which were based on first-hand knowledge. The geographical diversity of the authors, combined with the fact that as a group they represent many disciplines of social science, gives their individual analyses and the series as a whole an additional dimension.

Each of the scholars who contributed to this series was asked to analyse such topics as the political culture, the governmental structure, the ruling party, other mass organizations, party-state relations, the policy process, the economy, domestic and foreign relations, together with any features peculiar to the country under discussion.

This series does not aim at assigning authenticity or authority to any single one of the political systems included in it. It shows that, depending on a variety of historical, cultural, ethnic and political factors, the pursuit of goals derived from the tenets of Marxism has produced different political forms at different times and in different places. It also illustrates the rich diversity among these societies, where attempts to achieve a synthesis between goals derived from Marxism on the one hand, and national realities on the other, have often meant distinctive approaches and solutions to the problems of social, political and economic development.

University College   *Bogdan Szajkowski*
Cardiff

Contents

List of Figures

List of Tables

Acknowledgements

This book was made possible by the grant of sabbatical leave from the North Staffordshire Polytechnic and financial assistance from a variety of commercial and other sources. Particular gratitude is owed to Cable and Wireless PLC and Geest Industries Ltd. However, it must be made clear that neither they nor the other companies and trust funds who contributed either in grant or in kind are responsible for, or have in any way influenced, the approach taken in this study of the Grenadian revolutionary process and its conclusions.

Much encouragement and help was given by my good friends Tony Payne (Huddersfield Polytechnic) and Paul Sutton (University of Hull), with whom many happy hours have been spent discussing West Indian and Caribbean affairs, often in the depths of British winters. There were many other friends and colleagues who also took an active interest and to whom sincere thanks are due. Their number include Tony Bryan, Anselm Francis and Henry Gill (Institute of International Relations, Trinidad), George Danns and Clive Thomas (University of Guyana), Mike Erisman (Mercyhurst College, Erie, Pa.), Eddie Green (Institute of Economic and Social Research, Jamaica), Richard Hart (ex-Attorney General of the People's Revolutionary Government and currently of the University of Warwick), Phil Johnson (San Francisco State University), Vaughan Lewis (formerly of ISER, Jamaica, now Secretary-General of the Organization of Eastern Caribbean States), Frank Le Veness (St. John's University, New York), Barry Levine and Tony Maingot (Florida International University, Miami), Frank Manning (University of Western Ontario), Douglas Midgett (University of Iowa), Carl Parris (UWI, Trinidad), Carl Stone (UWI, Jamaica) and Marvin Will (University of Tulsa).

In Grenada, out of the many who gave information and offered valuable insights, particular thanks are due to Fennis and Kofi Augustine, George Brizan, Benedict Cuffee, Chris de Riggs, Francis Alexis, Basil Gahagan, Sir Eric Gairy, Bob Grant, Basil Harford, Alister and Cynthia Hughes, George Louison, Leslie Pierre, Kendrick Radix, Ray Smith and Winston Whyte. Fruitful discussions were also held with the two BBC correspondents on the island at the time, Christabel King and Nick Worrall, and the Representative of the Commission of the European Communities, Bob Visser. In England, more thanks are due to Fitzroy Ambursely, Rawle Boland, Roberto Espindola, Winston James and David Jessop, Director of the West India Committee, for their insights and interpretations. Regionally, I was able to draw upon the help of many other friends, notably Bobby Clarke (Barbados), Ralph Gonsalves and James Mitchell (St. Vincent), Tim Hector (Antigua), Lee Moore (St. Kitts), Trevor Munroe and Fr. Gerald McLaughlin (Jamaica), Assad Shoman and Said Musa (Belize), Cedric Grant, Cheddi and Janet Jagan and Rashleigh Jackson (Guyana) and Arthur ten Berge (Suriname). Their different and sometimes diametrically opposed political viewpoints were, to say the least, stimulating. I cannot forget the equally enjoyable times spent with members of the People's Revolutionary Government in happier times before the derailment of the revolution and, in some cases, before the insurrection. Special mention must be made of Bernard Coard. But both Unison Whiteman and Maurice Bishop also granted scarce time to see me on several occasions. Then there were the Grenadian people themselves, arguably one of the most hospitable in the world, who made me and my family very welcome.

Lastly, I thank my wife, Beryl. After entertaining a stream of visitors in Grenada, she then tolerated the long period of gestation and writing. Her tolerance ultimately made it all possible.

Tony Thorndike,
Stoke-on-Trent, 1985

Preface

This book is about a West Indian tragedy. It relates the story and analyses the genesis and process of a Marxist–Leninist revolution on the small island of Grenada which collapsed with a murderous implosion. Launched by an armed insurrection by the New Jewel Movement in March 1979, a constant search for Leninist orthodoxy in a hostile area ended four and a half years later with the killing of the Prime Minister of the People's Revolutionary Government (PRG), Maurice Bishop, several of his colleagues, and the wanton killing of numerous Grenadians. It paved the way for a United States-led invasion, whose troops were welcomed as rescuers by the bulk of the 90,000 population. Although militarily hurriedly put together, there was no doubt that it was politically well prepared and rehearsed.

These momentous and traumatic events and the insurrection remain of seminal political importance to the peoples of a region which, out of all the Third World, are the most deeply etched and shaped by colonialism. The insurrection threw down the gauntlet. The PRG challenged the status and all the political and social implications of economic dependency to which Grenada, in common with its neighbours in the Caribbean as a whole, had been assigned by circumstance and history. In doing so, it ushered in a period of hope and progressive policies which were to inspire many, not only in the region but also in distant places. But it also meant authoritarianism and political oppression, policies which were to cost the regime dear in terms of regional support. Worse, in the eyes of the colossus to the north, it meant a 'non-negotiable' foreign policy centred upon close economic and military relations with Cuba and thereafter with the Soviet bloc. This was intolerable to the United States: its hegemony and domination of the Caribbean Basin were threatened. Not only that, the Grenadian revolution coincided with a nationalistic renaissance which swept an America anxious to put the disgraces of Vietnam, Watergate and the Iranian Embassy hostages behind it, and to reassert its manifest destiny in its soft southern underbelly. The world watched as the Reagan Administration confronted a regime that became more radicalized and determined to resist with every turn of the screw. Invasion was always a threat. Indeed, invasions of Caribbean countries by the United States had been a feature of the region since 1898. Cuba, Haiti, the Dominican Republic and several states in Central America had seen American troops come and go. The invasion of Grenada, in conjunction with certain West Indian allies, broke new ground by confirming that the newly independent West Indian nations were subject to its political and economic direction and guidance. Political independence from Britain was, in other words, replaced by an all-embracing sphere of influence, the tenets of which will be, over time, just as politically and psychologically effective as the historically brutal experience of colonialism.

To attempt to record a revolution in a post-invasion atmosphere of suspicion, recrimination, harassment and bitterness was not easy. But oral evidence was clearly necessary. Some informants took risks in talking about their involvement in the revolution and the events that led to its derailment, their work and experiences and their impressions. There were also others who made themselves conspicuously available, whether in sympathy with the revolution or the opposite, and who related versions of events and offered interpretations which sometimes stretched credibility. Only through as much double-checking as possible could approximations of the truth be attempted. An earlier work (Payne, Sutton & Thorndike, 1984) was rapidly written in the aftermath of the invasion and did not have the benefit of such verification as might have been possible if there had been more time. Also, the Central Intelligence Agency, which became the warden of an extraordinary collection of captured documents of inestimable value to students of Marxist-Leninist affairs, released material as and when it was politically expedient to do so. Only by late 1984 was it estimated that all of the most significant had been published. Another difficulty was, at the time of writing, the impending trial of ex-Deputy Prime Minister Bernard Coard, his colleagues on the Central Committee and those soldiers of the People's Revolutionary Army allegedly involved in the killings of 19 October 1983. Some material had to be omitted for fear of prejudicing their defence. Where evidence given to the Preliminary Inquiry—which sought to determine whether there was a case of murder to answer—had been previously obtained through private conversation, careful editing was necessary. The trial will doubtless provide yet more insights either adding to, or disproving, the material in this work. Doubtless, there are others who worked for the revolution with extra or contradictory information.

What this analysis of the Grenadian revolution does not cover is discussion of the legality or otherwise of the invasion and the subsequent assumption of constitutional legitimacy and authority of the Governor-General. That was incorporated in the earlier jointly-authored work. Nor does it speculate on the trial and its outcome, beyond suggesting that it will chart areas of law as yet untried in the Commonwealth Caribbean and raise fundamental constitutional issues. The trial and the revolutionary experience as a whole will fuel debate and argument for years to come. There will also be a searching debate on the prospects for socialism in the West Indies and the wider Caribbean. Given concrete geographical reality and the socio-economic milieu, can the hopes and aspirations of the working-class masses in the region ever be fulfilled by socialism? And, above all, by what kind of socialism?

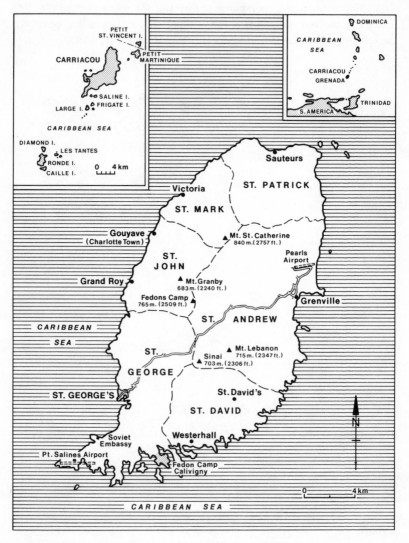

Grenada: parish boundaries

Basic Data

Official name	People's Revolutionary Government (13 March 1979 to 25 October 1983)
Population	89,088 (April 1981) plus approx. 1,800 armed forces and others not counted in census
Population density	264 per sq. km.
Population growth (% p.a.)	Less than 1
Urban population (%)	8 (1981)
Total labour force	33,607 (1981)
Life expectancy	70 (1978)
Infant death rate (per 1,000)	25 (1980)
Ethnic groups	Afro–West Indian (91%); Indian and Syrian-Lebanese (6%); White (3%)
Capital	St. George's (pop. 4,788)
Land area	344 sq. km (133 sq. miles), consisting of Grenada (297) and Carriacou and Petit Martinique (48)
Official language	English
Administrative division	Local government based on Grenada's parishes (St. Andrew's, St. David's, St. George's, St. John's, St. Mark's and St. Patrick's) ceased in 1969 but is retained for Carriacou and Petit Martinique
Membership of international organizations	CARICOM since 1973, UN and agencies since 1974, OECS in 1981
Foreign relations	Diplomatic and consular relations with 52 states. Eight resident missions: Brussels, Caracas, Havana, London, Moscow, New York, Toronto, Washington. Representatives of two countries were resident in St. George's: Cuba and Soviet Union; part-time representation for United Kingdom

Political structure
   Constitution   None approved
   Highest legislative body   Cabinet
   Highest executive body   Cabinet
   Prime Minister   Maurice Bishop
   Head of State   Queen Elizabeth II, represented by
                                   Governor-General Sir Paul Scoon

Food self-sufficiency (%)   72.5

Growth indicators (% p.a.)

	1979	1982
National Income*	2.1	5.5
Agriculture by value (exports)	19.6	−35.1
Food production	3.2	11.5

   * The post-PRG estimate was an average of 3% over 1979-82, falling to −2% in 1983.

Exports   US$19 million (1982)

Imports   US$57.2 million (1982)

Exports as % of GNP   38

Main exports   Bananas; cocoa; nutmeg and mace; fruit
                                 and vegetables; clothing; furniture; flour
                                 and wheat products

Main imports   Food grains; preserved foodstuffs; meat;
                                 consumer goods; vehicles; intermediate
                                 goods (fuel, raw materials, spare-parts and
                                 fertilizers); machinery and equipment

Destination of exports (%)   United Kingdom (36); Trinidad and
                                 Tobago (31); Netherlands and Belgium
                                 (15); East Caribbean (10); others (8)

Main trading partners   Canada; UK; Cuba; USA; Japan

Foreign debt   Approximately US$51m.

Foreign investment   US$89.8m. from public sources; US$2.1m.
                                 from private sources (1980-2)

Main natural resources   Excellent tourist potential

Ruling party   New Jewel Movement
Secretary-General   Vacant

Party membership

In October 1983 there were 350, consisting of 72 Full, 94 Candidates and 180 Applicants, 0.8% of adult population, and also 150 'Potential Applicants'

Armed forces

Approximately 1,800 in the People's Revolutionary Army (1982), 4.2% of adult population. Another 3,500 received instruction in the use of arms through the People's Militia, 1980-3.

Education and health
    School system

Primary school: seven years (5-12 age group) compulsory, enrolment 100%; Secondary school: four years (13-16 age group), enrolment 72%.

    Adult literacy (%)

90 (1982)

Economy
    Gross National Product
    GNP per capita
    Budget (expenditure)

US$54.6m. (1979); US$61.2m. (1982)
US$650 (1979); US$870 (1982)
Recurrent, US$25.6m, capital, US$38.5m (1982)

Defence expenditure as % of state budget

6 (not including military aid from Cuba, Soviet Union and North Korea).

Monetary unit

East Caribbean dollar. Fixed exchange with US$: US$ 1.00 equals EC$ 2.64

Main crops

Bananas, cocoa, nutmeg and spices, tropical fruits, vegetables, sugar, coffee

Land tenure

Average holding: 2 ha.

Main religions

Roman Catholic, Evangelical, Baptist

Road network

212 km. tarred; 230km. untarred

Airport

25 km. northeast of St. George's

Population Forecasting

The following population data are produced by Poptran, University of Wales at Cardiff Population Centre.

The age structure is derived from the 1981 census, and the birth and death rates from the Vital Registration System for the same year. A projection has not been made because the major component of demographic change at present is migration. At present (1985) net out-migration is of the order of 1.5–2.0 per cent per annum, thus approximately cancelling out natural population growth. Consequently, while the overall size will not have changed much between 1981 and 1985 it is likely that the age structure will have altered to some extent.

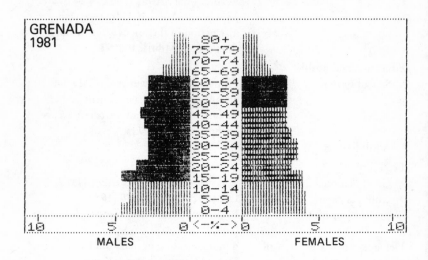

Projected Data for Grenada 1981

Total population ('000)	91,000
Males ('000)	44,000
Females ('000)	47,000
Crude birth rate	26.0
Crude death rate	8.0
Annual growth rate	1.8%
Under 15s	25.12%
Over 65s	10.55%
Women aged 15–49	24.12%
Doubling time	39 years
Population density	264 per sq. km.
Urban population	12,800

List of Abbreviations

ACLM	Antigua Caribbean Liberation Movement
CARICOM	Caribbean Community
CBI	Caribbean Basin Initiative
CC	Central Committee
CCC	Committee of Concerned Citizens
CDB	Caribbean Development Bank
CIA	Central Intelligence Agency
ECCA	East Caribbean Currency Authority
GFC	Grenada Farms Corporation
GMMWU	Grenada Manual and Mental Workers' Union
GNP	Grenada National Party
GULP	Grenada United Labour Party
JEWEL	Joint Endeavour for Welfare, Education and Liberation
LIAT	Leeward Islands Air Transport
MACE	Movement for Advancement of Community Effort
MAP	Movement for Assemblies of the People
NJAC	National Joint Action Committee
NJM	New Jewel Movement
NWO	National Women's Organization
NYO	National Youth Organization
OECS	Organization of Eastern Caribbean States
PRA	People's Revolutionary Army
PRG	People's Revolutionary Government
UWI	University of the West Indies
WIAS	West Indies Associated States
WPJ	Workers' Party of Jamaica

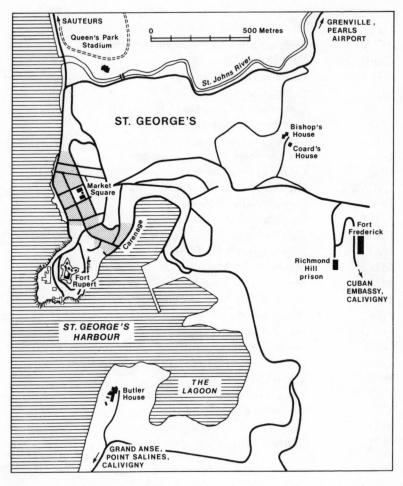

St. George's: simplified map

Part I
The Environment

1   The West Indian Condition

The Grenadian revolution, which lasted from March 1979 to its derailment in the wake of bitter internal division in October 1983, had a clear cornerstone. It was to challenge and change the deepseated and indelible impress of a past which had so fundamentally shaped the social, economic and political structure of the 133 square-mile island and the offshore Grenadine islands of Carriacou and Petit Martinique. This past had substantially determined the destiny of their 90,000 inhabitants. This historical experience is, therefore, critically important. The mould that it set—the West Indian condition—was common to all West Indian societies. It was to give these essentially black populations, particularly the English speaking, a distinctiveness that was to differentiate them in many ways from the remainder of their compatriots in the wider Third World. However, as events were eventually to unfold in all their tragedy, the Grenadian Marxist–Leninist revolutionaries of the New Jewel Movement, who inspired and directed the People's Revolutionary Government (PRG), discovered that the mould was too firm even to be cracked, let alone broken. Instead, it helped dictate the course of the bloody downfall of the revolution and its aftermath. But not only had this mould to be challenged; the revolution occurred in a geographical region beset by rising tensions. The survival of the Cuban revolution from 1959, despite constant and strenuous attempts by the United States to destroy it, had helped introduce Cold War tensions into an area traditionally considered America's exclusive sphere of influence. An alliance had grown between Grenada and Cuba, and the PRG's solidarity with other socialist countries offended both the tenets of the West Indian historical experience and American national interest. It was to prove a fatal combination.

Despite its short lifespan, the revolution deserves a prominent niche not only in Third World decolonization but also in Marxist theory and praxis. Grenada's very small size and population; strictly limited and underdeveloped resources; an entrenched class system with strong overtones of colour; an independent peasantry to whom land ownership was a high priority; a psychological dependency upon imported culture and values; and its strategic geo-political location: all combined to prompt a veteran West Indian Marxist,

Richard Hart, to label the experience 'the Improbable Revolution' (Hart, 1984, p. xi). But despite all the odds, popular power was established by revolutionary means. It also brought forth an extraordinary leader, Maurice Bishop. In time, he may perhaps be recognized as the most politically significant personality which the West Indies has ever produced.

The West Indies and the Caribbean

The islands and territories which collectively make up the West Indies form a distinctive social and cultural complex within the Caribbean Basin region. Originally colonized in the main by the British, the French and the Dutch, they stand in sharp contrast to the complex colonized by the Spanish. While the former is Black–West Indian–English/French, the other, comprising some 65 per cent of the population of the insular Caribbean, is White–Mestizo–Hispanic. As such, the inhabitants of Cuba, Puerto Rico and the Dominican Republic have close cultural ties with their Central and South American compatriots, just as the West Indian enclaves on the mainland—Belize, Guyana, Suriname and Guyane—share the cultural traditions of, say, Jamaica, Martinique, Trinidad and Grenada. Although distinctive, the two traditions are not mutually exclusive. Each shared exposure to a colonialism which was both qualitatively and quantitatively different from that experienced by other Third World societies, a critical factor being the brutal experience of slavery. None the less, the differences remain strong, and Grenada is wholly in the West Indian category. As such, any study of its historical and political experience must be placed firmly in the wider content of the West Indian condition.

Bonds and Fetters

The most important distinguishing feature of the West Indian historical experience was not just a prolonged exposure to European colonialism. A century and a half of slavery on a scale and harshness never before experienced in world history had not only destroyed indigenous culture; the notorious Middle Passage and slave auctions at its end also thoroughly undermined residual African consciousness. The descendants of those who survived had nothing to fall back upon but the values, assumptions and institutions of the colonial power. No wonder, then, that a deep-rooted state of mind—a pronounced form of psychological dependency—was the lasting legacy, later to be translated into modes of political outlook, activity and expression. Neither were the Indian (more properly called East Indian in the

Caribbean context) population immune. From the 1880s they had been imported as indentured labourers in considerable numbers, particularly to Trinidad and British Guiana (now Guyana), to alleviate labour shortages. These had become common following the emancipation of the slaves in the British Empire in 1834, and the subsequent disinclination of many Afro-West Indian field workers to continue plantation work. But the environmental mould which surrounded those they replaced slipped inexorably around them also.

By contrast, other Third World societies which had been, at least at elite level, transformed by colonialism, were able to revert to neo-traditional forms of culture, despite the elite's alienation from it. But in the West Indies, the European (and later North American) influence was so thorough that it could never be uprooted. Attempts to invoke the pre-slavery past by stressing the African heritage, such as by the black power movement of 1968–72, were doomed to failure. Even the one manifestation of cultural expression and identity associated with the Caribbean, that of Rastafarianism, looked to a wholly West Indian myth of African history for inspiration. The novelist V. S. Naipaul, a Trinidadian, mocked this 'mimicry', observing that even the revolutionaries of the PRG followed the pattern when they tried to build 'a socialist revolution on mimic forms' with all the imported apparatus, institutional and mental, of socialist political economies elsewhere (Naipaul, 1984, p. 23).

In essence, then, the model of behaviour, thought and action to be followed was always external. Not surprisingly, the result was an identity crisis. To David Lowenthal, this is central to any understanding of the West Indian psyche. 'A striking feature of West Indian identity is the low esteem with which it is locally held. West Indians at home often wish they were not West Indian . . . [and] . . . genuinely believe their identity can be altered. The wish is often realized in imagination; they easily persuade themselves they are something else (Lowenthal, 1972, p. 250). This permeates all levels of society: prestige and 'worth' are sought through identification with a superior concept of self-consciousness. 'Both Kingston [Jamaica] suburbanites', notes Lowenthal, 'and West Kingston Ras Tafari believe themselves citizens of another land'. Another perceived West Indians as 'an extreme example of the marginal man'. 'He constantly finds himself on the periphery of many systems, including his own, participating in them to a certain degree, yet never sure that he belongs to any of them' (Singham, 1968, p. 95). To be sure, this marginality helped make the transition to British or North American society a relatively easy one. But the mass emigration from the late 1940s not only robbed the fragile economies of their more dynamic manpower—

however much it relieved frustrations caused by land hunger and lack of opportunity—it also sapped the nurturing of a collective sense of ethnicity. That was to come only when, as coloured immigrants in London, Toronto or Brooklyn, they faced discrimination in lands they emulated and thought of as home. Of the idealists who travelled to Africa, not all found satisfaction. Colour apart, there appeared little in common after generations of diaspora.

To this fundamental phenomenon must be added the strong linkage between colour and class, or socio-economic status. This has had a very important political impact on party formation, constituency and policy, as much as in patterns of political behaviour. Over the years, miscegenation and the lasting heritage of slavery led to the evolution of a social structure with a heavy emphasis upon subtle graduations in pigmentation as a determinant of status. Put simply, the whiter the person, the higher the class. Although the correlation is by no means absolute, as those darker skinned with money or professional status can testify, it still clearly exists. The middle-class elites, commercial and bureaucratic, are in general noticeably of mixed race. By contrast, the working class, normally some 75 to 80 per cent of the population, is predominantly black. Between them lies a discernible divide. It is seen in levels of education and housing, type of diet, widely varying expectations and forms of religions, expression and affiliation, speech and dialect, attitudes to illegitimacy and marriage, and family structures. In summary, the gap is between those with 'worth' and those without. It is not too far-fetched to compare the divide to that observed in Britain in the inter-war period.

There is a habit of mind which thinks it . . . natural and desirable, that different sections of a community should be distinguished from each other by sharp differences of economic status, of environment, of education, and culture and habit of life . . . [and] regards with approval the social institutions and economic arrangements by which such differences are emphasised and enhanced. [Tawney, 1931, p. 49.]

West Indian Political Expression

It was in the political arena where, in most of the West Indian territories, the deeply segmented societies met. Confrontation had been made all the easier by the one major advantage enjoyed by West Indians over most other Third World societies, that of a modern world language, however much subjected to dialect on a class basis. It enabled political ideas and philosophies developed in Britain and Western Europe in particular to be easily transmitted, although not necessarily absorbed. Further, West Indian societies were not fettered by caste systems or tribalism. But the common use of

English as the sole language helped promote agreement on political aims, if not understanding, when political conditions permitted.

In very early days, the planters dominated the local legislatures until, one by one, each administration was transformed in the mid-nineteenth century by the British into Crown Colonies where London's fiat was undisputed. The planters had been highly reactionary, obdurate and ultimately, served no political purpose. When a very limited franchise, based on property ownership, was conceded after the First World War, the middle class monopolized what little political power was permitted them as 'representatives' by the Colonial Office. Their 'representational associations' did little for the ordinary people and their dependence upon gubernatorial whim was such that inclusion or exclusion from social gatherings at Government House became a matter of much discussion and heart-searching. However, unlike the former plantocracy, not all the middle class treated the black masses with cynical disregard. Some, such as Captain Cipriani in Trinidad and T. A. Marryshow in Grenada, stood up consistently for the 'bare-footed man' and encouraged him 'to better his lot'. But this lot became progressively worse as the interwar depression deepened. British—and middle-class—complacency was finally shattered by a series of strikes, riots and arson attacks, particularly upon sugar estates, beginning in St. Kitts in 1935.

The Imperial Parliament charged a Royal Commission under Lord Moyne's chairmanship to 'investigate social and economic conditions . . . and matters connected therewith, and to make recommendations'. The Moyne Report, as it became known, was ready by the outbreak of war in 1939. But its findings were so shocking that its publication was delayed until 1945 (West India Royal Commission, 1945), as it might have provoked a reaction highly damaging to the Imperial war effort. Grenada was, however, one of the few territories that escaped the destruction and unrest. Central to its recommendations was that, besides considerably increased aid and minimum wage rates, trade unions should be legalized and encouraged. However, it came down firmly against what its members termed 'extreme proposals' for self-government based upon universal suffrage; only a small increase in the elected 'unofficial' element was considered advisable.

The result was predictable. In most of the territories, trade unions of the black masses grew rapidly. Given the environment, they were inevitably political as wage concessions forced out of reluctant employers or the colonial government were subsumed in other, wider demands. Universal suffrage—commencing with Jamaica in 1944 and spreading to nearly all other territories by 1951—enabled trade unions to enter the formal political arena, acting as political parties. Some unions did not think it necessary to separate the bargaining unit from the representational for many years, such was the close identification. In general, political leaders with ambition had to have the backing of a union. It was, in essence, a short cut to power. The political parties that evolved in this fashion were, and in some of the smaller less developed islands still remain, loosely organized and with a strong element of spontaneity. The parties rarely depended upon a strong core of dues-paying members, for this was the union function. There were few, or no, cadres; again, they would be the union organizers. The union also provided the element of continuity. Such a party could only survive meaningfully in virtually constant crisis situations. In a small area, issues easily became politicized, highly charged and personalized. Scapegoats needed to be found, and blamed, on both sides. Rapidly, a strong personalist style of political leadership developed in the colonial atmosphere. The popular and charismatic leader of the masses was pitted against British officialdom and, more often as not, against the bureaucratic and commercial elites. Sometimes accused of being 'communists', the unions and their parties firmly regarded themselves as democratic-socialists. But their ideology was better described as 'labourism' or the improvement of labour within the existing society. No socialist reorganization was envisaged; rather, strategies such as state capitalism and 'industrialization by invitation' were promoted.

Along with this laborist position, strong anti-colonial and anti-upper-class senti-ments were expressed. The anti-colonial position was a comparative mild one—never really approaching revolutionary dimensions. It centered around a negotiated settlement of the issue of self-government (rather than independence) and the ending of the dominance of the planter class. [Henry, 1983, p. 297.]

Later, in the more developed territories, an indication of the extent of decolonization and growing political maturity was the diminishing impor-tance of personalism and unionism in party behaviour. The accession to power of George Chambers in Trinidad-Tobago exemplifies the trend, although in Jamaica Edward Seaga still relied on the support of a trade union and armed gangs to win the 1980 election over Michael Manley, who was similarly equipped but in addition has a charismatic personality. Dominica's Prime Minister, Eugenia Charles, on the other hand, used her charismatic qualities to the full in her victorious election campaign in the same year, achieved without any formal union association.

Faced with working-class politicization, the middle classes responded by forming 'respectable' political parties, in which personality, by contrast, counted for little, and the procedures were more routinized. But the class division in political activism was not absolute. Over time, many light-skinned politicians, beginning with Norman Manley in Jamaica, appreciated the new political reality and harnessed it (Munroe, 1972, pp. 36–42). They joined forces with unions and often assumed union-party leadership. Conversely, some of the new black leaders eventually distanced themselves from their power-base to join the middle class. Although politics thus afforded a means of social mobility for the ambitious, social acceptance was slow. It could be hastened by cautious emulation; however, 'political leaders who spring from the lower classes quickly come to display the same contempt for the masses, whether consciously or unconsciously, for indeed it is one of the marks of having achieved upper- or middle-class status' (Singham, 1968, p. 151). The most blatant was Eric Gairy (later Sir) of Grenada. From being a popular union leader in the 1950s championing the cause of the black Grenadian masses who, because the pre-war disturbances had passed them by, were ripe for politicization, he had a decade later become a byword for corruption and repression. By the 1960s and 1970s he, above all others, epitomized everything negative in the West Indian condition.

A Stillborn Nationalism

The lack of a widespread consciousness of West Indian identity led inevitably to low levels of national pride. After all, had not West Indian societies always been the responsibility of somebody else, whether slave owner or imperial power? The world was expected to look after them; aid was their right. The West Indies were poor and had to be helped. But 'relatively deprived' would be a more accurate term, for the comparison is with the United States and Canada, with Britain a poor second. They are by no means poor on the scale of, say, Haiti, Paraguay or Bangladesh. There are pockets of real poverty in Dominica, Grenada and parts of Guyana and Jamaica, but these are not common. Indeed, some islands, such as the Cayman Islands, have per capita incomes superior to many European states. The legacy of slavery was to one sociologist 'an emotional logic' of the historical experience.

West Indians see nothing amiss in calling upon other resources other than their own [for] 'they owe it to us'. . . . Never to deal, but always to be dealt with; never to move, but always to be moved . . . it is a world arranged by somebody else, and consequently an unfair world, unlikely to be improved by any efforts of one's own. [Thornton, 1960, pp. 118–20.]

From the early 1950s the tourist influx helped to perpetuate, and intensify, consumer values and rising expectations of a more materialist lifestyle. Tourist affluence and preference for imported food and services combined with the vicarious demands of relatives of those who had migrated to create ascendant ambitions. Notwithstanding the racial aspects of Caribbean tourism—white, rich visitors served by poor, black workers—hotel jobs at menial levels became much sought after, often at the cost of agriculture. West Indians, in their own estimation, were but branches of the same cultural tree as those from the colder north; not unnaturally, they wanted to be like them. Little consideration was given to the problem of tourist foreign exchange leakage—up to 80 cents in every tourist dollar—caused by foreign ownership of hotels and other facilities, imports and the lack of linkage with local agriculture and the lack of indigenous management. Rather, each territory tried to outdo the other in offering incentives for investment, anxious to diversify their little economies away from the poorly rewarded agricultural export sector.

The assumption of political independence—commencing in 1962 with Jamaica and Trinidad-Tobago within a month of each other—did little to reverse these presumptions. The smaller islands particularly sought independence ultimately to gain access to multilateral aid funds and to participate in international forums primarily concerned with economic development, rather than from an appreciation of its intrinsic worth. Indeed, to the astonishment of others in the Third World, offers of assistance after independence from unscrupulous organizations and individuals were often accepted with surprising *naïveté*. Their ideas about themselves bore little relationship to the real world situation in which they lived. In vain did Montserrat's Premier warn that 'we have bicycle societies with Cadillac tastes' (McIntyre, 1966, p. 1), and few were concerned at the extent of economic dependence in the region.

The Economic Dimension

What was originally envisaged for the Caribbean territories claimed by Britain was dramatically different from what eventually transpired. They were to be tropical versions of the North American settlements: white freeholders, with their indentured servants, would be self-sufficient and export tobacco, cotton and coffee to Britain. But this planned destiny was aborted by the transportation of convicts and rebels, few of whom were able to work in the hot sun, and within a short time, by slaves; for the mass production of sugar. Huge profits forced greater production and food plots became limited. Cheap food imports became the norm. The pattern was thereby set: a series of satellite economies from British Honduras (Belize) in the west to British Guiana to the east. None of the territories had the opportunity or ability to influence the price of their exports, whether sugar or, in the post-emancipation period, bananas, cocoa, spices and fruits. Of those territories fortunate enough to have mineral resources such as Jamaica and Guyana (and Suriname, the former Dutch Guiana) with their bauxite, and Trinidad with its oil, only the last had been able to exert some control over prices and the operations of the foreign-owned extractive and refining companies in the industry, and then only for a brief decade from 1973. Control over the cost of imports was similarly lacking. It became clear from the time of the first sugar exports to Europe that economic growth in the British Caribbean territories was virtually dependent upon external demand. For the great majority of the territories, such dependency was inevitably dictated by their small size and limited resources. But colonial policy deliberately accentuated the problem. Here, McIntyre's analytical dissection of dependency is useful. He distinguished between structural dependence caused by size and structure of the economy, which cannot be easily alleviated, and functional dependence. The latter arises from the impact of particular policies that are chosen. He made clear, however, that they were not mutually exclusive (McIntyre, 1966, p. 1). The deliberate neglect of domestic agriculture in favour of food imports so as to press all available land into sugar production, and the failure to diversify agriculture except in a few isolated instances owing to topography and climate, was an example *par excellence* of functional servitude. Through colonial protectionism, their products were destined only for Britain. Relief appeared on the horizon when the old merchantilist system, which sharply discriminated in favour of trade within the Empire, was dismantled with the ending of the sugar preference and the establishment of a wider-ranging free trade policy by a rapidly industrializing Britain. It was, however, revived in part in 1898 and reinforced in 1931 with the reimposition of imperial protectionism. The peak was reached in the war years and beyond, with the strict imposition of Sterling Area currency and trade controls to assure sources of cheap raw materials and foodstuffs to a beleaguered Britain.

The long-term effect of this was three-fold. First, it discouraged structural changes in the economy. Diversification was only possible if there was a market. But small size, topographical problems and lack of investment meant relative high-cost production. Dependence was thereby accentuated by the continuing need to secure protected markets and preferential trading agreements. The widespread consternation expressed by West Indian governments at the prospect of British membership of the European Economic Community was, fortunately in their view, assuaged by agreements with the Community via the Lomé Convention (1975) and the negotiation of special commodity quotas permitting continued access to the British market in particular. Second, the tradition of imported food became entrenched. While economic necessity forced the slaves' descendants to undertake some wage labour, very little food was grown beyond their immediate needs. By the 1880s, Canada had become the principal supplier of imported foodstuffs, and wheat, cod and apples became part of the staple diet. The middle and upper classes always displayed a high propensity to import, not only food but many other items which could be, or were, domestically produced. Emulation of foreign life-styles and preference for 'superior' products were only part of the reason. The commercial elites had dominated the import–export trade as commission agents from plantation days. They were powerfully entrenched in the economies and, not surprisingly, constantly stressed the importance of imports, literally their lifeblood. The profitability of trade attracted many Lebanese and Syrian merchants who emigrated to the West Indies in considerable numbers, particularly after 1945. Quickly assimilated into the West Indies' social structure, they and their colleagues in the Chambers of Commerce strongly supported the growth of the tourist industry. In itself, this boosted imports considerably; more critically it accelerated demand for North American-style food. By 1983, the foreign exchange bill for the English-speaking West Indies was unofficially calculated by the Caribbean Community (CARICOM), the regional trade organization which incorporated virtually all the territories, as US $60 million per year and rising (interviews with CARICOM Secretariat, Guyana, June 1984). Attempts to stem it, as in Jamaica in 1978–80 and in Guyana, helped spark off disturbances and political demonstrations.

The third result of merchantilism and protectionism was political and geographical insularity. Each territory dealt separately with Britain and most had their own administrations. The sea between them, far from being a highway, represented a barrier. A powerful particularist tradition grew, each planter-dominated oligarchic administration jealously safeguarding its privileges. Later, authoritarian Crown Colony government introduced in the late-nineteenth century helped perpetuate the process although the British made several valiant attempts to create administrative unions. As political parties emerged in the post-Moyne period, each leader contrived to dominate his little domain, wary of attempts to diminish his power base through forms of federation which would tend to concentrate power elsewhere. Although the small islands, in the main, gave their support to the most important British initiative in this direction, the West Indies Federation (1958–62), their enthusiasm waned with the insistence upon trade, aid and labour migration restrictions by the largest participants, Jamaica and Trinidad. Then, as now, public administration was a major source of employment at all levels and, therefore, of patronage.

The Federation finally collapsed in May 1962 amid bitter recrimination, as

Jamaica and Trinidad–Tobago went their own way. It left the smaller islands to find their own political salvation. Fortunately, economic necessity dictated the need for co-operation. A trade agreement severely restricted in scope and membership was initiated in 1965. This led to a wider grouping, the Caribbean Free Trade Association (CARIFTA) in 1968 and thereafter to the more ambitious CARICOM in 1973.

The Strategic Aspect

To the factors of small size, limited resources and psychological and economic dependence upon others must be added another distinguishing feature of Caribbean societies: their geo-political strategic significance. Quarrels over their possession were largely between Britain and France. But the Anglo–French settlement of 1815 brought only brief respite; by the 1840s, the colossus to the north, the newly emerging United States of America, had begun to apportion considerable importance to the Caribbean region.

The Federal government became increasingly concerned about America's southern boundary once war with Mexico had secured what became the south-west of the Union. It was neither secure from invasion or instability by an ocean, nor protected by a friendly ally. The declaration by President Monroe in 1823, which warned European powers not to attempt to annex territory in the western hemisphere in the aftermath of Spanish withdrawal, was enforceable only by the British navy. But, by mid-century, Britain and the United States were clearly rivals. Fortunately, a truce was signed in 1850. The Clayton–Bulmer treaty stipulated that neither would expand their existing rights, particularly in Central America, and that neither would enjoy exclusive rights over a planned trans-oceanic route through Nicaragua. By 1867, this had been broken by unilateral American action. In 1898, the United States served notice on Britain that it would not tolerate any action against Venezuela by British Guiana over the disputed Essequibo region. In the same year, war with Spain led to the annexation of Puerto Rico and the occupation of a newly independent Cuba. Such actions by an avowedly anti-colonialist country were rationalized by the doctrine of 'manifest destiny', whereby it was believed that Divine Providence had singled out the United States to fulfil a particular mission, that of spreading peace and prosperity initially westwards to the Pacific Ocean and then to the south. In reality,

Cuba emerged as a model for United States imperialism. American economic and political domination had been secured without the seizure of a colony. The United States could continue to boast its anti-colonial traditions and beliefs despite having transformed Cuba into a virtual dependency. 'Sphere of influence' became an internationally palatable euphemism for neo-colonialism. [Pearce, 1982, p. 10.]

As for Puerto Rico, it was an invaluable naval base: 'we need it as a station in the great American archipelago misnamed the West Indies', declared the *New York Times* (ibid.).

The creation of the Republic of Panama followed in 1903, which, as a client state, immediately signed a treaty with the United States leasing land 'in perpetuity' in order to construct the long-sought-after trans-oceanic canal. This was finally opened in 1914. To help protect it from the Atlantic approaches, the Danish Virgin Islands were purchased in 1917. In the meantime, armed interventions became commonplace in the Central American republics, Cuba and the Dominican Republic, normally when they defaulted on loan and interest payments. Trade and investment followed the flag, with huge sugar and banana plantations established by American corporations.

Britain's colonial empire was, by contrast, left untouched. But Britain had acknowledged its inferior position by withdrawing its forces during the Essequibo crisis. That did not, however, prevent suggestions circulating around Washington that the Lesser Antilles, the largely English-speaking chain from the Virgin Islands to Trinidad, should be annexed (Whitbeck, 1933, p. 26). They were finally scotched by President Franklin D. Roosevelt for economic and racial reasons, but not before Britain had become thoroughly enmeshed in Washington's strategic design through the Anglo-American agreement of 1940. In return for fifty elderly but urgently required warships for the Royal Navy, permission was granted by London for the construction and operation of a string of American Air Force bases from the Bahamas, through Antigua, St. Lucia and Trinidad to British Guiana. America saw this as essential since, by its potential entry into the Second World War, substantial amounts of oil from Trinidad and Venezuela could be shipped into the United States, together with bauxite and other products from the Caribbean. Convoy protection was necessary, as was protection for shipping using the Panama Canal.

In the postwar years, the United States relied upon its European allies to maintain security in their colonies or, in the case of France, its overseas *départements*. The Cuban revolution had heightened regional tensions which had to be contained. Their efforts in this regard were to be willingly supplemented as and when necessary by the United States. A notable example of Anglo-American collaboration in such circumstances was the removal from power of the Marxist regime of Cheddi Jagan in British Guiana in 1964, followed by new electoral arrangements to permit the accession to power of

Forbes Burnham, then regarded as more compliant to Washington's will. This paved the way to independence two years later. Not until 1980, when it was apparent that Britain was anxious to disengage from the area did the United States take a more direct interest, culminating in the invasion of Grenada in 1983. This extension of interest, particularly by the conservative administration of President Reagan, helped prompt the birth of a new geo-political concept, that of the 'Caribbean Basin', incorporating *all* the terri-tories around the rim of the Caribbean Sea. However, the United States never assumed responsibility for the high-priced exports of the Common-wealth Caribbean. Instead, its citizens quickly made the area a favoured tourist destination. By 1982, 60 per cent of all tourists to the English-speak-ing islands were from the United States, with a further 6 per cent from Canada (*Caribbean Tourism Statistical Report 1983*: by comparison, 11 per cent originated from Europe). It was in this sector that American investment pro-ceeded apace. Apart from any other considerations to this industry and its investors, political stability was an absolute necessity.

Whereas Britain was quick to resent American intrusion into the Middle East and, later, into what it regarded with France as Europe's interests in tropical Africa, it had no qualms over the West Indies. Despite protests from its former progeny, it appeared determined to disengage as quickly as diplomatic niceties would allow. It disregarded the strong Anglo-West Indian links built up over centuries, reinforced by the presence of a million Britons of West Indian descent in its population. It had for long neglected the area economically, starting with a deep reluctance to force the backward-looking and rapacious plantocracy to help develop the territories they and their forebears had skilfully exploited. Nobody in 1917 had disagreed with Prime Minister Lloyd George's description of the West Indian colonies as 'the slums of Empire' (Williams, 1970, p. 443). Later and more enlightened attitudes by the British Treasury admittedly alleviated the distress experi-enced by the most destitute. Sometimes the aid was of more benefit to the more affluent, such as with the construction of prestigious schools and the University of the West Indies. By the 1980s, the Foreign and Commonwealth Office made clear that, the Grenadian revolution notwithstanding, the Caribbean was of marginal importance in its foreign policy (House of Commons, Foreign Affairs Committee, 1982, p. 2). Further, when it had to respond to the rising tensions in the area, it uncritically supported the United States at virtually every turn. No wonder one observer characterized British policy as being set 'in an unimaginative and distinctly conservative mould' (Payne, 1984, p. 94). Paradoxically, it was only after the collapse of the Grenadian revolution that any thought was given to long-term strategy in the region, as opposed to piecemeal aid policy. Within a week of the American invasion, British High Commission staff in Grenada increased from one half-week diplomat to four on full-time duty, with ancillary personnel!

The great majority of West Indians welcomed the greater involvement of the United States in their affairs. As a source of largesse and economic development, Washington was far more attractive a prospect than an increasingly parsimonious Britain. From the time of the 1940 agreement, which created unprecedented employment opportunities, American investment carried an image of prosperity, especially for the black masses. The elites—the commercial and bureaucratic as well as the political—welcomed the role of protector which the United States assumed for their polities. Inured to their history, they applauded the plea of Dominica's Prime Minister Eugenia Charles to the American Ambassador to the Eastern Caribbean in 1980. 'The US presence in our region is not enough', she insisted. 'We are not in your backyard, we are your front door, and you should help us to keep it open' (*New Chronicle*, 28 July 1980). To Prime Minister Vere Bird of Antigua-Barbuda, a 'strong US eagle' was needed as a 'protector' of the 'little birds' of the Eastern Caribbean in particular (*Caribbean Contact*, April 1982). Together with several other West Indian political leaders, both he and Miss Charles were to endorse enthusiastically the United States' invasion of Grenada and to participate in it. The inevitable result was that American political and economic interests and preferences were widely served. A political climate was reinforced whereby attempts to challenge the United States' hegemony and the stranglehold of the deep-seated state of psychological and economic dependency in the Caribbean became increasingly difficult and, ultimately, virtually impossible. The architects of the Cuban revolution had successfully forged a separate, socialist path which, from 1961, had become closely associated with the Soviet Union, a development undoubtedly fostered by American intransigence. Those who in later years were to challenge American hegemony, notably Michael Manley of Jamaica, Forbes Burnham, the Sandinista junta in Nicaragua and Maurice Bishop and his fellow Grenadian revolutionaries, received short shrift. Against all, various methods of destabilization and diplomatic and commercial isolation were attempted with varying degrees of success. In Manley's case, the severe shortages of essential imports that resulted were a contributory factor in his electoral defeat in October 1980. The message from Washington was indeed clear to what became colloquially dubbed as its 'backyard'.

The Challenge to Come

The West Indian condition seemed to be destined for posterity. Only Cuba appeared to forge a different path. Resisting American imperialism, its educational and social advances were outstanding. Partially inspired by its example, an intellectually-based challenge, which became increasingly influenced by Marxism–Leninism, was mounted in the late-1960s finding fertile soil in which to grow. It was eventually to lead to the Grenadian revolution.

2   A Revolutionary Challenge

The first challenge to the deep-rooted values and socio-economic and political assumptions of the West Indian condition came with the formation of the New World group of economists and other social scientists at the University of the West Indies. Included in their number were Havelock Brewster, Alastair McIntyre—the future Deputy Secretary-General of the United Nations Conference on Trade and Development (UNCTAD), Orlando Patterson, Courtney Blackman and Clive Thomas. They and others in the movement first analysed and then offered prescriptions for reform of the neocolonial political and economic system in which they lived and worked. They were critical of the 'industry by invitation' model, first shaped by the doyen of West Indian economists, Arthur Lewis, in 1950 (Lewis, 1950), and which had been enthusiastically adopted by Luis Muñoz Marín, the Governor of Puerto Rico. Their argument was that greater welfare spending and nationally orientated development programmes and capitalist enterprises were possible through regional co-operation. The legacy of the defunct West Indies Federation might have been politically bitter; but lessons had been learnt and new attempts at economic co-operation had to be forged. Political will to do so, they argued, would be facilitated by greater public support through the greater involvement of the lower strata of the population in decision making at all levels, and by an assertion of cultural decolonization.

Rastafarianism and Black Power

Some of their ideas were to be institutionalized with the eventual evolution of the Caribbean Community (CARICOM) in 1973. As a form of regional co-operation, it worked for the rationalization and promotion of production. But their more populist prescriptions were partially paralleled by Rastafarianism. A messianic religion *par excellence* of the oppressed, it promised redemption to those in poverty or suffering severe psychological stress. Its adherents were exiled in 'Babylon', whose forces represented 'dread' oppression. Africa, on the other hand, signified freedom, symbolized by Ethiopia and its imperial ruler, Haile Selassie or Ras Tafari. The appeal of Africa was not new. In Jamaica, and later in New York, the activities of Marcus Garvey in particular in the early decades of this century had attracted attention although his contribution was not to be fully appreciated until later.

Rastafarianism spawned in the West Kingston slums from the 1930s, appealing to the depressed *lumpenproletariat*. Thirty years on, it spread to the West Indies as a whole and later, to the West Indian diaspora. As an Afro-West Indian cult, it provided for many young people a sense of identity and purpose rather than a religious experience. Further, as it was not welcomed in many parts, membership was an act of defiance. But it stressed self-sufficiency and anti-materialism, as much as racial distinctiveness. Inevitably, it became associated with the black power movement. An off-shoot of the 'freedom marches' and the anti-racist campaigns in the American Deep South in the early 1960s, this swept through the region from 1968. Racial pride and identification were aggressively asserted, centring upon the slogan that 'Black is Beautiful'. It inspired many West Indians to travel to Africa, to Ghana and Nigeria in particular, although some were shocked to find little commonality there with themselves. Other manifestations included 'roots food', 'Afro' hairstyles and the spasmodic appearance on school curricula of Caribbean literature and history.

Politically, it reached its height with widespread disturbances in the Trinidadian capital, Port of Spain, in April 1970. But these were inevitably bound up with internal Trinidadian political issues; none the less, its scale occasioned a careful offshore naval watch by American and British warships. Not unexpectedly, the demonstrations encountered ethnic division in Trinidad—for it was first and foremost an Afro- rather than an Indo-Caribbean phenomenon. It was also ideologically sterile. Cultural pride was insufficient by itself. For substantial progress to be made in alleviating the lot of the working masses, of whatever ethnic background or creed, socialism and socialist policies had to be adopted as guiding principles. One black power activist, the Grenadian Michael X (né Little) was especially active and influential on a popular level, although he was to be later executed for a ritual murder. The link between socialism and race was an obvious one: the dispossessed were almost wholly black. To Stokely Carmichael, the American leader of the Black Panthers, the association was clear. Those who advocated socialism stood for 'the economic rights and political moral dignity' of the 'black masses'. 'Castro', he announced, 'is the blackest man I know' (*Time*, 12 May 1967). Walter Rodney, perhaps the most influential Marxist historian that the region had produced, gave the link with socialism a firm intellectual stamp. Underdevelopment and imperialism were indisputably coupled with racial discrimination. He defined black power as 'a movement and an ideology springing from the reality of oppression of black peoples by whites within the imperialist world as a whole'. The West Indies, he argued, had always been part of white capitalist society and progressively exploited. It followed that black power meant 'three closely related things: (i) the break with imperialism which is historically white racist; (ii) the assumption of power of the black masses in the islands; (iii) the cultural reconstruction of the society in the image of the blacks' (Rodney, 1969, p. 28). He was at pains, however, not to exclude Indians and whites. They would have the 'basic rights of all individuals' but 'no privileges to exploit Africans'. Completely new attitudes on their part were required: 'what we most object to is the current image of a multi-racial society living in harmony—that is a myth designed to justify the exploitation suffered by the blackest of our population, at the hands of the lighter-skinned groups' (p. 29). It was therefore 'the duty' of progressive black intellectuals to identify with the suffering masses and be their servants. Failure to do so would lead to 'a black intellectual bourgeoisie trying by devious methods' to inhibit the rise of 'challenging leaders and champions of the proletariat from the grass roots of the trade unions, and thus ensuring and enhancing the circulation of the intellectual elite' (p. 32). The Marxist notion of class as primary actor and class struggle as the principal dynamic was thus reformulated for West Indian conditions. Whatever the emphasis upon colour, the central issue was socialism.

He found ready support from the growing number of intellectuals who had taken advantage of rapidly expanding opportunities in higher education. Many had gone to Britain or North American universities. There, their convictions had been hardened during the turbulent years of American civil rights campaigns and anti-Vietnam protests, and by exposure to racism. Those at the University of the West Indies' Jamaican campus had also been radicalized, not only by their own interpretation and development of New World philosophy but also by Rodney's expulsion by the Jamaican government in 1968 which triggered prolonged student unrest. To the consternation of the government, the unrest rapidly spread to the slum areas of Kingston, many of whose *lumpenproletariat* slum dwellers had seen in Rodney's philosophy and teaching a hope for the future. The 'Rodney riots' may have been inspired by his black power advocacy, but they primarily expressed the growing social and economic deprivation of the dispossessed urban poor: the target was the property of the non-black economic elite (Payne, 1983, pp. 172–3). Thus ideological, racial and economic factors combined. Nationalism in the region was forced to turn from politics to economics. The agenda of Jamaican politics slowly began to change and other West Indian political systems reluctantly followed.

Until his death by assassination in June 1980 in his native Guyana in circumstances which seemed beyond reasonable doubt to implicate Burnham's government, Rodney continued to provide inspiration. His intellectual colleagues took up his mantle after 1968 and determined that the fetters of the past had to be broken. They saw oppression, imperialism and servitude in the West Indies in a far wider context, just as their forebears had done. They were inspired by such West Indian intellectuals as Ras Makonnen, George Padmore, and C. L. R. James who had travelled widely after the First World War, advocating socialist solutions for the plight of the negro as part of the Pan Africanist cause. They readily echoed Makonnen who, in his old age, recollected that 'we were able to see the worker, the struggle of the proletariat much more clearly (in England) than across the Atlantic' (Robinson, 1983, p. 345). Like these earlier stalwarts of socialism, the later aspirants to power had firm middle-class backgrounds. But they identified unambiguously with the black masses. They were as sharply critical of 'bourgeois nationalists' and 'idealists' as they were of traditional party structures and leadership. These 'bourgeois nationalists' had been labelled 'cuckoo politicians' by a New World political sociologist (Singham, 1965, pp. 23–33). They loudly proclaimed their presence, like the bird in a cuckoo-clock, clad with the symbolic trappings of power, but served little real purpose as the real power lay in imperialist hands.

The Noncapitalist Way

Caribbean Marxism was, by their activism, reborn. It had been virtually lost to the region, except in Guyana, with the voluntary exile of such thinkers as C. L. R. James and Richard Hart, victims of Cold War hysteria some two decades before. To the new generation, the objective reality of under-development and arrested cultural growth led them to consider seriously the prospects offered by the theory of noncapitalist development. It had impeccable Marxist antecedents. Its critical feature was, as first outlined to a sceptical Moscow meeting of Communist and Workers' Parties in 1960, the circumvention of the capitalist stage in the transition to socialism. Lenin himself had suggested it—'with the aid of the proletariat of the advanced countries, backward countries can go over to the Soviet system . . . without having passed through the capitalist stage' (Lenin, 1962, p. 244)—but it was left to the eminent Soviet scholar R. Ulyanovsky to detail the path. As it developed as a doctrine in the late 1960s, Soviet ideologues had the potential socialist transformation of the newly emergent African states foremost in mind. However, much of it was incorporated into the 'Declaration of Havana', approved by the Conference of Communist Workers' Parties in Havana in 1975. It reached the Caribbean by this route.

Ulyanovsky posited three stages: decolonization and 'the shaping' of the noncapitalist way; national-democratic transformations; and socialist society. Whereas the last could only be considered 'largely in tentative terms and indeed, was only one of the possible prospects for development', the first two could be mapped out fairly rigorously, drawing upon the experience of such socialist-orientated countries as Guinea and Tanzania.

The first stage, the 'starting point', was not political independence as such but rather the subsequent radical swing in social processes towards 'the socialist prospect'. In his words, it was 'the triumph of the national liberation (anti-imperialist) revolution, going hand in hand with the establishment of a revolutionary-democratic dictatorship' (Ulyanovsky, 1974, p. 446). This initial stage resulted from the contradictions inherent in post-colonial development, arising from popular desires for multi-sectoral development pitted against continued exploitation by foreign-owned and domestic capitalist institutions. Socio-economic structures 'implanted' by colonialism had to be eroded by the development of state industrial enterprises, farming co-operatives and new crops and products. The activity of foreign monopolies had to be limited, but some guarantees given regarding their property. State planning would encourage private initiative but within an established framework which would promote the public sector to the point where it became dominant. This, together with industrialization, would create an urban proletariat and undermine urban social relations; similarly, agrarian reform and stratification of the peasantry would undermine traditional rural social structures. All communal traditions and anti-Europeanism, stemming from reactions by the dispossessed to foreign-owned plantation systems, had to be exploited and developed. The national intelligentsia would grow, as would the bourgeoisie, but no one social section or class could claim leadership without a 'solid alliance of all anti-imperialist forces'. The government, therefore, should be a coalition of progressive forces. Foreign trade (and domestic wholesaling) had to be controlled and, despite a continued heavy reliance upon world capitalist markets, ties with socialist countries would be a fundamental prerequisite, as would attempts at regional co-ordination of anti-imperialist activities.

The stage of national democracy is 'the turning point of noncapitalist development'. Arising from the growing convergence of anti-colonialism and anti-capitalism, it is characterized by 'sharpening contradictions between the socialist and capitalist tendencies of development in every sphere of life in the developing countries and a fierce struggle between the social forces involved' (Andreyev, 1974, p. 92). Post-colonial economic ties and structures now become 'intensively disintegrated' and foreign policy ties assume greater importance. Despite the initial unprofitability of state industrial and other enterprises, the process must be regarded as inexorable. Foreign-owned operations become increasingly 'confronted' by the new reality. The national bourgeoisie, he counselled, will take advantage of decolonization to fill lucrative positions vacated by the colonial bureaucracy and will occupy those sectors of the economy once dominated by foreign capital. These, and the 'comprador bourgeoisie', whose livelihood continues to depend upon colla-boration with such capital and monopoly interests, will resist socialist policies but must be firmly controlled. But at this stage they must not be eliminated.

The dualism of the economy makes for the dualism of the social structure of the liberated countries. In this period, the political activity and organisation of the working class are enhanced, the toiling masses of peasants are consolidated, and the rivalry between the democratically-minded intelligentsia and the national bour-geoisie in the struggle for power is ever more acute. [Ibid., p. 93.]

Considerable emphasis was put upon the role of the national intelligentsia in the transformation process. Because of the very limited proletarian strata, it would normally be expected to be of middle-class origin. But they 'embody' the tendency of 'democratic orientation'. The intelligentsia must, however, form a vanguard section advocating and working for 'deep-going social transformations' in the working people's interests. It must also be capable of giving expression to working-class aspirations by encouraging national culture and pride, and by realizing the potentialities of workers and peasants through working with them in a 'joint struggle' to advance socialist transfor-mation.

However, Ulyanovsky darkly warned that, under the pressure of the 'bourgeois environment', the material attractions of international imperial-ism and, in many cases, personal background, some of the national intelli-gentsia would inevitably be tempted not only to deviate but to ally with the national bourgeoisie and frustrate class struggle and the revolutionary process. This counter-revolutionary tendency should be countered by all available means, as 'bloc formation' with foreign imperialist circles and 'domestic reactionary elements' would spell disaster for working-class aspira-tions. This process would mean, he forecast, that socialist-oriented countries would suffer a period of crises, plots, vacillation and policy revisions; in short, 'aggravated social contradictions' (Solodivonikov & Bogoslovsky, 1975, p. 102). It would also mean pessimism and despondency at the long and intense struggle against those whose tendency to vacillation was well known. Those who expected rapid and fundamental improvement of their lot would be disappointed; they were 'psychologically unprepared' for such traitorous and unpatriotic acts, and were a ready target for intensified imperialist propaganda. This would seek to blame shortcomings and mistakes by socialist-orientated countries on noncapitalism, instead of on the colonial legacy and imperialist destabilization. But help would be available through the deepening of relations with socialist countries. Vacillation in foreign policy, while expected, would gradually ease with the 'qualitative change' involved in strengthening alliances with progressive forces elsewhere, both for mutual benefit and as a mark of solidarity. Slowly, principles of equality would be achieved in relations with capitalist states. The efforts involved in 'walking the tightrope' between the opposing systems would become easier in time as other socialist and socialist-orientated states offered mutual support and solidarity in the 'principled' anti-imperialist struggle.

The Revolutionary Blueprint

The theory of noncapitalist development was seized upon by West Indian intellectuals. Ralph Gonsalves of St. Vincent argued that it could be 'creatively applied' where capitalism was underdeveloped as it had 'its roots in the science of historical materialism'. It was an alternative to capitalism and not a separate social formation halfway between that and socialism. He advocated a 'broad class alliance' to realize it, involving 'the proletariat, the semi-proletarian masses, the revolutionary or democratic strata of the petty-bourgeoisie (including the peasantry) and even the progressive patriotic elements of the emerging national bourgeoisie'. In line with the theoretical framework, this would govern through a 'revolutionary-democratic or national-democratic state which links up itself increasingly with the forces of world socialism' (Gonsalves, 1981, pp. 2–14).

The contradictions inherent in the theory were recognized but set aside. This was not only because it was realized that the transition period to socialism would be a long one, but also because the establishment of the People's Revolutionary Government in Grenada, guided as it was to be by the thesis, would provide a unique opportunity to discover its potentialities and constraints in political reality. Primary among these contradictions was that already outlined by Ulyanovsky, the tendency of the national intelligentsia to vacillate in its commitment to socialism. It would have to constitute the dominant force in the class alliance as progressive elements of the working class and peasantry were, in West Indian circumstances, pitifully few. This threat could only be met by careful construction of Leninist party organization, methods of self-criticism and study and unambiguous political commitment in all spheres of life and work. These measures would also leaven the second contradiction: that those progressive elements of the national bourgeoisie in the class alliance would be working for their own extinction as they strove for socialism and the dictatorship of the proletariat. As for the third, the necessity for state planning in tiny, 'open' economies heavily dependent upon world trade, subject to debilitating price fluctuations and with currencies pegged to the American dollar, the initial solution was the help and solidarity which the socialist countries could, and presumably would, offer. This solidarity (and possible military help) would help the aspirant state to socialism to meet the onslaught of American imperialism, angry that a perceived 'strategic breach' had been torn in its regional defence net.

But there was no answer readily available, other than sensitivity, to C. Y. Thomas's criticism of the theory. In the class alliance outlined by Gonsalves, he warned that the tendency of the intelligentsia would be 'to see themselves as arbiters and the only real representatives of the national interest' (Thomas, 1978, pp. 24–5). This, he argued, all too frequently resulted in the institutionalization of a military-bureaucratic authoritarian state with only lip-service being paid to workers' and peasants' interests and aspirations. It was but one step to corruption when non-accountability prevailed: no doubt he had his homeland, Guyana, in mind. Neither was any answer available to a wholly West Indian contradiction, and one relating to the Eastern Caribbean in general and to Grenada in particular. Land ownership after Emancipation was equated with freedom. A land-owning peasantry had grown up to whom the sociology of property was no academic concept. In sharp contrast to traditional African societies, there was no tradition of communal land tenure, save in one very small island of 1,100 inhabitants, Barbuda (Lowenthal & Clarke, 1980).

This final contradiction subsumed a wider one which indicated that the noncapitalist way model was politically and historically inappropriate for West Indian societies. The theory assumes the existence of largely pre-capitalist economies and societies; the West Indies clearly do not meet that criterion (Ambursley & Cohen, 1983, pp. 6–9). Neither was there evidence of violent antagonism between the lower and middle stratum, nor any apparent potential for it. Rather, there was the unappealing and negative prospect of ethnic strife between working-class communities of African and Indian origin, especially in Guyana.

The Rat Island Meeting

The first indication of regional action by intellectual socialists was a meeting organized at Rat Island, off St. Lucia, in mid-1970. It was called in the aftermath of the Trinidadian disturbances, which had been echoed in a few other islands although in very muted forms, such as that involving Maurice Bishop in the Grenadian capital, St. George's, in May 1970. The agenda was to review the situation and the potentiality for socialism, and to discuss future strategy. It was decided to create a series of 'forums', or discussion groups, with associated newssheets of the same title, in as many territories as possible and with public involvement. Forms of 'popular democracy' were discussed, the participants being anxious to break away from the traditional hierarchical and patronage-ridden party structures. Indeed, they eschewed the notion of forming political parties as such. Further, there was no 'grand strategy' planned or discussed, as later alleged by those assuming that the genesis of the Grenadian revolution, aided by Cuban 'subversion', was to be found in its deliberations (*Washington Post*, 30 November 1983). Clearly, however, Marxist theories predominated—Trevor Munroe of Jamaica, the later leader of the Workers' Party of Jamaica, being particularly influential (interviews with G. Odlum, April 1976 and March 1984). When the various governments and the British and French colonial authorities learnt of the meeting—largely because of indiscreet statements by the Trinidad delegates of the National Joint Action Committee (NJAC)—some invitees were prevented from attending. For instance, Tim Hector of the Afro-Caribbean Liberation Front of Antigua (later renamed the Antigua-Caribbean Liberation Front as black power died away) was detained en route, in Martinique.

As agreed, 'FORUMS' were established in St. Vincent, Dominica, St. Lucia and Grenada. Equivalent groups appeared in Antigua, Montserrat and Jamaica. The NJAC was already *in situ* in Trinidad, albeit already racked with dissention: its indiscretion about the Rat Island meeting had been deliberate, its leader Geddes Grainger (who later renamed himself Makandal Daaga) being angry that its Marxist element had already deserted it in protest at the negative and crude expression of its black power philosophy (interview with NJAC, February 1984). In Guyana, the Marxist People's Progressive Party led by Cheddi and Janet Jagan regarded itself as fulfilling the role. But, despite the initial reservation of the Rat Island participants, the formation of political parties became a necessity to promote the struggle. Some went through various manifestations and mergers—Grenada's amongst them—but nearly all remained very small with strictly limited electoral appeal. The exceptions were Jamaica, where a constantly deteriorating economic situation after 1975–6 could be, and was, skilfully exploited by Munroe. But, above all, there was Grenada. The evolution of what was to become the New Jewel Movement was, however, due to the highly specific political circumstances of that island, summarized as Gairyism, which were not present elsewhere.

3   The Road to Gairyism

Early Years

Although Grenada and the Grenadines were first sighted for Europe by Columbus during his third voyage in 1498, when he gave the name Conception to Grenada, the indigenous Carib race was left in undisturbed possession for over a century. Two hundred-and-eight British colonists landed in 1609 but were forced off after a few months by the Caribs. A similar fate met a French expedition in 1638. But the Caribs' defeat was inevitable as, within a few years, many covetous eyes were cast in Grenada's direction. The French landed again in 1650 and, after establishing a settlement near what is now the capital, St. George's, proceeded to wipe out the natives. No quarter was given by either side, and the bloody extermination ended when the forty remaining Caribs leapt over a cliff, rather than be sold into slavery or slaughtered. The name of the nearby villages, Sauteurs, or 'leapers', bears witness to this defiance. Within twenty-five years, commencing around 1675, the first black slaves were introduced.

The three sugar estates of 1701 with their 525 slaves swelled to eighty-three estates and 12,000 Africans by 1753; by 1705, St. George's (then called Port Louis) was founded. Besides sugar, there were coffee, cocoa, indigo and tobacco to be profitably exported. This prosperity, however, abruptly ended with war between France and Britain. In 1763, Grenada was ceded to Britain but 1779 saw its recapture by the French. Relations between the two European communities seriously deteriorated with discriminatory laws being applied to the British settlers, in sharp contrast to the treatment of the French during British rule. After four years, in 1783, Grenada was restored to the British Crown and strong pressure was put upon the colonial government to remove all religious and other privileges from the French colonists. By 1793, the Catholic church lost virtually all its political rights; the slaves, by now mostly converted to that faith, refused to participate in the services of the Established, i.e., Anglican, Church. Tolerance might have saved Grenada from the disaster that was to come, for the reverberations of the French and Haitian revolutions were to go hand in hand with religious grievances.

From their Guadeloupe headquarters, the revolutionaries led by the Commissioner of the National Convention, Victor Hugues, planned Grenada's recapture through subversion and insurrection. An edict of 1792 had declared the equality of all races. Taking advantage of British unpreparedness and an exceptionally inept Governor, a rebellion broke out in March 1795, marked by a bloody sacking of Grenville. Led by a coloured French planter, Julien Fedon, more and more slaves were attracted to 'the alluring temptations which were held out to them, of participating in the property of their plundered masters, and the flattering promises of total emancipation' (Devas, 1964, p. 110). For two years, Fedon's forces held most of the island—except for St. George's and the south—taking advantage of the extraordinarily poor military leadership of the British. The Spanish government in Trinidad gave assistance but to no avail; finally, in June 1796, Fedon's army was defeated, but only after the British formed a battalion of trusted slaves, the Black Rangers, despite the protests of the beleaguered planters. Fedon was later venerated as a national hero by the People's Revolutionary Government, as a campaigner for slaves' rights. But no slaves were ever formally freed. His brief reign, although marked by considerable bravery and military skill, was a bloody one. Those who opposed him met the same fate as nearly all his British prisoners—execution. The British exacted their revenge, with mass hangings of the leading rebels—although Fedon was never found—and the deportation of many to Santo Domingo. French power on Grenada was completely destroyed and all that now remains of this part of Grenada's heritage are French place and family names, and some elements of French inheritance laws.

Under restored British rule, the slave trade continued to the point that, when it was abolished within the British Empire in 1807, no anxiety was expressed in Grenada as by then slaves had been plentifully supplied. Indeed, many were profitably re-exported to Trinidad. Close links with that island had begun in 1783 when Spain finally permitted immigration from Grenada and other islands, a process that has continued to the present day. At Emancipation in 1834, 23,600 toiled in the sun. Thereafter, Grenada fell into a gentle economic decline. In contrast to some less physically endowed islands, Grenada's mountainous interior and thick bush beckoned many former slaves who refused continued plantation work. A largely independent peasantry developed as the planters faced both falling sugar prices, caused by beet sugar production in Europe and the loss of tariff privileges, and labour shortages. In 1848, wage reductions following a sharp fall in the London sugar price triggered revolt, as did unemployment and destitution for returning soldiers in 1920, who attempted to burn down St. George's. Grenada's open economy meant very considerable susceptibility to external economic pressures; those of the interwar years prompted two Grenadians, Uriah 'Buzz' Butler and T. Albert Marryshow, to take political action. Like Fedon, they were to be acclaimed by the PRG as precursors of development and national pride and to be emulated. But their strengths and weaknesses had been carefully analysed by the New Jewel Movement leadership, well before the insurrection in 1979 which brought them to power. Valuable lessons were learnt.

Although born within a decade of each other, Butler in 1897 and Marryshow in 1887, their backgrounds were remarkably different and their paths rarely crossed. Butler, a superb orator, was of working-class origin and a self-taught man. After serving in the British army from 1914 to 1918, he migrated in 1921 to Trinidad, attracted like so many of his countrymen by the prospect of work in the oil fields. Before economic circumstances forced his move, however, he helped found the Grenada Union of Returned Soldiers and was closely involved in the 1920 riots. Soon becoming the workers' spokesman, he became a full-time political activist after an industrial accident in 1929 which made further manual work impossible. Working first with Cipriani, he formed his own party in 1936, the British Empire Workers and Citizen Home Rule Party, after accusing Cipriani of lip service to the cause of the black masses. Whether his agitation helped precipitate the widespread disturbances in Trinidad in mid-1937 is open to question. The British certainly thought so and attempted to arrest him just as a strike, organized by him, broke out. A bloody clash, with fatalities, ushered in the riots. Going into hiding for three months and successfully evading 2,000 British troops detailed to find him, his influence and prestige in the West Indies became firmly guaranteed.

Butler's popularity was such that he could have hidden anywhere in the island. There are still hundreds if not thousands who are alive today to testify to this fact. Butler symbolized the fate of the poor workers and citizens of the Colony. He was a national hero. [Obika, 1984, p. 56.]

Giving himself up to testify before a Commission of Inquiry, he was later imprisoned. But his actions helped publicize the appalling conditions suffered by the working class. The riots elsewhere in the British West Indies led to much of his evidence being given subsequently to the Moyne Commission. He founded the Oilfield Workers' Trade Union and was elected to the Legislative Council. But his idiosyncratic behaviour and sometimes domineering manner led to political isolation and even a period of imprisonment by the independent government of Trinidad–Tobago. None the less, his seminal role in the development of trade unionism in the Caribbean was recognized well before his death in 1977. To Prime Minister Williams, however, the 'real problem' was that Butler

proved inadequate to the task either of forming a political party or of organizing the oilfield workers, and whilst his popularity was undoubted and was fully deserved . . . he proved as inadequate as Cipriani had proved before him in the sense of mobilizing the mass movement that he had helped to develop and guiding it along inevitable organizational channels for the capture of that power when it had been captured. [Williams, 1972, pp. 164–5.]

By contrast, Marryshow was born to a middle-class family and remained in Grenada. A journalist, debater and essayist, he put his considerable intellectual versatility to the service of the black masses. But, although highly respected, his career was marked by ambivalences. He was instrumental in founding the Representational Government Association in 1917, seeing representative government—although not independence—as the key to social and political advance, a standpoint constantly reiterated in his newspaper, *The West Indian*. He attacked the racialist tenets of European civilization and looked forward to a future African renaissance. But he insisted that there was no race problem in Grenada, or in the West Indies as a whole. Campaigning hard for Legislative Council representation, he tended to ignore the Executive Council, where the real power lay. Although he criticized the extent of 'unofficial' representation permitted the Grenada Legislative Council in the 1925 constitution (although he welcomed the elective principle which the British conceded), his election to the Council seemed to him an opportunity to work for progress from within government. Constantly fighting the impotence of the elected members on the Council against the Governor who was 'packing the nominated side with a number of gramophones who merely said what he wished them to', he became steadily more radical, declaring himself socialist in 1933. The need for racial, i.e., black, pride was essential. 'We must learn to love our race first, just like other people do, and love others next. We should no more desire to be black Englishmen than Englishmen desire to be recognized as white negroes' (Emmanuel, 1978, p. 91).

On the advice of the British Labour Party, contact with which profoundly influenced Marryshow, he helped form the Grenadian Workingmen's Association (GWA) in 1930–1 out of the Grenada Labour Party formed a year earlier, in 1929. Although he wanted it to be multi-class in membership and programme, it was ignored by the elites. Demands for universal suffrage and the full legislation of trade-union activities fell on deaf ears, not only those of the British, although they helped establish a minimum wage. But the GWA failed to become an enduring political party. Not only was Marryshow singularly ill-equipped to lead the working class, he constantly lectured them that it was their own fault that they were not organized. Although the GWA's only foray into the arena of mass protest was successful—a peaceful demonstration against higher customs duties—it petered out for want of leadership and mass support, particularly in the countryside, 'the bulk of its adherents [being] disgruntled members of the slowly growing lower middle stratum of lower-paid civil servants, commercial clerks, teachers and the like' (ibid., p. 102). Later, it was not his efforts that brought about universal suffrage in 1951, that being determined by events outside Grenada. Further, his radicalism diminished and he was unable to grasp the political significance of the growing trade-union movement in the 1940s. He died in 1958, just as the ill-starred West Indies Federation was being launched, believing that his dream of a self-governing Grenadian jewel within a West Indian crown had at last been realized.

The Emergence of the Grenadian Peasantry

Marryshow's career might have been different if Grenada had suffered the same degree of deprivation and demonstrations that marked the other West Indian territories in the 1930s. That it did not was substantially due to the gradual development after Emancipation of the independent peasantry. Although the break-up of many estates and the ready availability of land were essential pre-requisites, a major impetus by 1856 was provided by the displacement of sugar by cocoa as the main crop. Nutmeg and its outer-covering, mace, also became important exports. Tree crops, as with bananas in the mid-twentieth century, were eminently suitable for small-scale peasant cultivation. By 1843, 1,360 freeholders—5 per cent of the population—worked and owned farms of two and a half acres or less; 1881 saw 3,000 (8 per cent). By 1911, there were 6,332 (11 per cent) (Knight, 1946, p. 43), and 12,924 in 1930 (20 per cent) (Brizan, 1979, p. 6). Full-time farmers totalled 8,202 (9 per cent) in 1981. However, it was estimated in 1982 that agriculture sustained 36 per cent of the population, excluding those in marketing, processing and transportation. The average farm size was 4.2 acres, and over two-thirds of all farmers were part-timers (Government of Grenada, 1982, pp. 19–20).

This development was first made possible by the 'contract out' system, which was established soon after Emancipation. In return for land, ex-slaves had to grow cocoa for the owners, their 'provision crops'—yams and other foodstuffs—being inter-planted with the cocoa to shade the young trees. When the trees were about to bear, in the fifth year, loans to the landowner would be made by the merchants, the trees being collateral. Most of these loans would be passed on to the growers, the 'contractors', at a fixed rate per tree. Many used the money to purchase land and later to diversify into nutmegs. The contractors also had first call on estate employment. This combination of wage labour and own-account farming prompted the development of the concept of 'agro-proletarians' (Frucht, 1967), or 'proto-peasantry' (Brizan, 1979, p. 13), particularly apt since two-thirds of the part-time peasantry in 1981 were engaged in wage labour occupations other than estate work. The introduction of bananas on a large scale, after a disastrous hurricane in 1955 destroyed much of the cocoa crop, gave an impetus to self-employment. Nevertheless, although 98 per cent of farmers worked 53 per cent of the agricultural land with two-thirds occupying only two acres, a mere 1.45 per cent had 44.68 per cent of the acreage, often of a superior quality and location. Many peasants had, furthermore, fragmented holdings due to archaic inheritance laws, and even the more prosperous found credit difficult to obtain. Nationally, despite the widening of owner-ship and encouragement of food growing, a large food import bill remains. In 1960, the value of imported food was 1.5 times the value of food produced locally; by 1980, this had only slightly fallen to 1.3 times (Government of Grenada, 1981), although a greater improvement was masked by a highly profitable trade with Trinidad in fruit and vegetables that had developed in the 1970s.

The peasant system, as it evolved, promoted a degree of pride and inde-pendence not met elsewhere in the West Indies, except to a certain extent in St. Vincent and Jamaica. It certainly prevented a drift from the land as happened in those islands more suited geographically than Grenada for sugar cultivation, such as Antigua and Barbados. The availability of food for the black masses from their plots, and the much more favourable prices for cocoa compared to sugar, mitigated the general effects of the world-wide Depres-sion. The 'contract-out' system had also perpetuated a more paternalistic relationship between estate owner and worker than existed on the sugar islands, although handouts were rare. But underlying resentment was wide-spread. They were on the fringe of society and amazingly, wage rates were the same, sometimes lower, in 1938 as a century before (Government of Grenada, 1938, pp. 7–8). As a landowner, the peasant resented those who had a call on his produce; as a wage labourer, he was angry at the low rate of pay; as a pro-ducer, he had very little control over the workings of the marketing boards, who were dominated by the interests of the plantation owners and the merchants. Often acting in collusion, these elites were, like the bureaucrats in the faraway government, observably of the same class. Although there was little foreign absentee ownership of land—in sharp contrast to other islands—the plantocracy left much land idle which they refused to sell. Despite the peasant system, therefore, the potential for rural trade unionism was very considerable.

Notwithstanding the lack of disturbances, that of 1938 being wholly in St. George's and under Marryshow's restraining influence, the recommendations of the Moyne Commission applied to Grenada as much as any other West

Indian territory. It recommended greater representation on the grounds that social and economic advance were inseparable from constitutional reform. But local control through a majority of unofficial members in both the Legislative and Executive Councils was ruled out as incompatible with the retention of official reserve powers, which were 'essential' in the absence of self-government. That was, in effect, a coded reference to the need to maintain control over local finance to prevent alleged irresponsible spending by elected members (West India Royal Commission, 1945, p. 310). Although the concessions were few, the working atmosphere in the two Councils was much improved owing to a far greater sense of tact and enlightenment by British officials, led from the top by Governor Sir Arthur Grimble (1942–8), than hitherto had been the case. But Marryshow's demands for universal suffrage were neither supported by the British nor by the conservative and complacent middle-class representatives who shared the elected benches with him. In the words of a contemporary observer, they, the employers and the merchants 'have created a further image of themselves and believe that they know best what is good for the people; workers are children, irresponsible, indolent, and prodigal, who prefer leisure and fun to worthy material goals.' The 'power of decision', he reported, 'is a monopoly of the "better" classes' and the basis of a 'stable society and well being for the workers' (Rottenberg, 1955, p. 53). Such attitudes were wholly expressive of the class divide. The result was that

political goals and style were set within certain fundamental British-colonial values such as imperial loyalty, the myth of racial harmony, a respect for British institutions and acceptance of gradualist evolution to higher constitutional status and, generally, a disposition to accept that the 'uncultured' black strata were unqualified for rights of political participation and representation. [Emmanuel, 1978, p. 104.]

In this still stifling atmosphere, there was to be little change for five years. Weak attempts at establishing trade unions, all urban based, were made and reluctantly recognized. Membership was small but some minor wage agreements were negotiated, the planters and merchants having little excuse given the relatively high prices Grenada's produce was fetching in a war-torn Europe. More importantly, following Moyne's recommendations, the 'feudalist' system of remuneration with its array of non-monetary forms of income was replaced by the 'capitalist' system, employees receiving all their income in cash, leaving them to make separate contractual arrangements with the owners regarding the use of estate plots. By such action, the old symbiotic relationship between the two, planter and employee, was broken, making the potential for union organization all the greater. The lack of it forced the government eventually to strengthen minimum wage legislation, albeit after much hesitation, on the advice of the newly appointed Labour Adviser, a post again owning its existence to Moyne.

By 1950, the Grenadian masses stood in sharp contrast to those of neighbouring islands. There, influenced by the struggles of the previous fifteen years, dynamic and charismatic labour leaders had emerged, such as Vere Bird, Robert Bradshaw (St. Kitts) and Ebenezer Joshua (St. Vincent). Marryshow, in his retreat from socialism, instead advocated a benign plantocracy whose administration of 'human kindness' would soothe the 'mass despair' of the black workers. He also echoed the insistence of the Colonial Office and the local middle class upon the divorce of trade unionism from political activity. He was sadly out of touch with reality as this was clearly impossible in the circumstances of the West Indies. Social, economic and political subjugation could not be separated. The stage was set for this to be made clear in Grenada.

'Hurricane Gairy'

The catalyst was the return to Grenada of Eric Matthew Gairy from work overseas. He was born in 1922 near Grenville to what he described as 'decent poor' parents, his father a poorly paid black foreman on an estate, his mother a deeply religious maid. After a spell as a primary 'student-teacher', he left for Trinidad in 1941 to help construct the new United States Air Force base. On its completion, he moved to Aruba. Working as a clerk in the oilfields, he became involved in union activities to the extent that he lost his job. While there, he met Marryshow, who regularly visited the large Grenadian community. Gairy became interested in the affairs of his homeland and decided to return. He first attracted attention by successfully claiming compensation for some tenant farmers wrongly evicted from an estate. Word spread of his ability and, in July 1950, he registered the Grenada Manual and Mental Workers' Union (GMMWU). He plunged immediately into work amongst the rural workers; by August, GMMWU claimed a following of 27,000. 'I organized more people in one year than any other man in the West Indies', he later claimed (Singham, 1968, p. 153). The first target was the sugar industry. Demanding a 50 per cent increase, a strike was called. Before that was settled (at 25 per cent), a strike of *all* agricultural workers had been organized.

The elites were totally unprepared for the sudden outbreak, revealing their almost total ignorance of the pent-up hostility of the people. The employers responded by not recognizing the GMMWU, insisting that they would deal only with the small existing urban-based unions who shared their concern of this newly emergent and destabilizing force. Gairy replied by calling a general strike, by now involving public works' labourers. His was an inevitable victory, for the settlement reached on agricultural pay with the nonrepresentative unions stipulated a zero increase in minimum wage, with bonuses paid depending upon the price of cocoa. A small increase indeed followed but, coinciding with Gairy's demands, the world price fell and most of the bonus was lost. By February 1951, 5,000 agricultural and 1,500 public works' labourers were idle. Lasting a month, the strike was an overwhelming success. The elites—and the colonial government—played into his hands, giving it a political form by declaring a State of Emergency, and by ordering his arrest and deportation to Carriacou by British naval forces.

He represented a 'communist conspiracy' and the planter class openly carried weapons with police connivance. Violence and arson broke out, and he was greeted by large crowds on his release. Solidarity rallies were held in Jamaica and Trinidad. The power of the old planter class had been irrevocably broken in what, in retrospect, was the critical turning point in Grenada's history. In short, as a visiting anthropologist observed,

In such a social structure, violence is done to planter class values if workers lay claim to equality in the bargaining process, if workers share in the making of economic decisions, and if their bargaining representatives are, like themselves, black and of working class origin . . . The violent, personal tones in which the planters refer to the union leaders indicates that they are concerned with something a good deal more fundamental than wage demands. [Rottenberg, 1955, p. 54.]

Even after his release, the planters and other employers refused to negotiate with him. Instead, the Labour Adviser, with the Governor's support, broke the deadlock. A new wage agreement was signed and Wages Councils established. The messianic Gairy was in complete control of the situation, to the extent that, as demonstrations continued despite heavy police reinforcement, the Governor was forced to ask him to make a nationwide broadcast appeal for calm. It was a memorable speech. He made it clear that 'when I say stop I mean stop . . . for everyone has that love for "Uncle Gairy" . . . who will turn you down completely [if wrongdoing continued]. So join me now those of you listening', he ended, 'let's say "no more violence" three times together: "No more violence, No more violence, No more violence", Thank you' (Jacobs & Jacobs, 1980, pp. 57–8). The riots ended and work resumed again. He styled himself 'the little black boy' who, 'knowing his onions', had forced 'the upper brackets' to deal with him. This was literally true: his objective had not been to organize a revolution to topple the government. Once the agreements were signed, he took what seemed to him the most practical course, that of co-operating closely with the government to obtain more concessions from the employers for his members. But this also entailed social recognition by the elite, and none gave the slightest indication that he would be socially acceptable.

The elites were to have no respite. The politicization of the masses was to be permanent and reinforced by the introduction of universal suffrage. The Grenada Legislature had agreed to this in May 1950 by removing the literacy test after pressure from the Colonial Office. It was anxious to further the development of the impending West Indies Federation: to do so, the constitutional provisions of the smaller islands had to be brought up to those of the larger. It was a move that they later greatly regretted for Gairy exploited it to the full. He fashioned a political party out of the union in the by now well-established West Indian tradition. Originally called the Grenada People's Party, the party was soon renamed the Grenada United Labour Party (GULP). It went on to win the 1951 general election, with 64 per cent of the vote and six of the eight Legislative Council seats. Later, GULP lost only two of the six general elections that followed until it was overthrown by the 1979 insurrection, although victories in the final two, 1972 and 1976, involved highly dubious methods.

From the start, and indeed until it was overthrown, the GULP lacked organization. It was Gairy's creature: loyalty at the constituency level was to him, not to the constituency member or candidate. There was no 'inner circle' executive responsible for policy: each branch chairman, such as existed, and each Legislative Council member, was heavily dependent upon the leader's personal support to maintain his position. Gairy was convinced that his natural abilities as a political leader and later, Divine protection, was sufficient to sustain the GULP and his own power. In summary, 'His party was at best a faction, and he maintained coalitions with individuals only as long as they continued to support him personally and unquestionably' (Singham, 1968, p. 264). For example, when one of his followers, Council member L. C. J. Thomas, built up his own constituency organization, Gairy expelled him from the party.

Control was maintained through meetings. Fully realizing the critical importance of the union base of the party, regular business meetings were held with union cadres, who assumed party responsibilities as and when necessary. Relatively formal, Gairy conducted meetings in a sombre manner, reviewing all the local problems and any personal or political difficulties facing the activists. Beforehand, he would personally interview local people who had specific grievances; certainly any party supporter who wanted a decision or action had to see him. Where factional disputes existed, his stand was normally neutral, seeing everybody involved personally and stressing the need for unity. Failure to unite and to agree, he always warned, would mean drastic action by him. When in St. George's, he always made himself available, where possible, to rural supporters and others who wanted to see him. Although the business meetings brought a measure of routinization and bureaucratization, the party always kept its personalist character. As time went on, and learning from subsequent elections and reductions in the GULP's share of the popular vote, the party came to assume a separate identification from the union although links remained very close. It was then necessary to construct a greater degree of organization (interviews with E. M. Gairy, January 1977, March 1984). A further spur was the development of sources of finance apart from union dues, specifically for the party. The British administration strongly encouraged the break-up of otherwise idle estates and their division into lots for sale to prospective peasants. At the same time, during the 1950s and 1960s, many Grenadians, including a number of East Indian origin, purchased substantial areas of land with overseas earnings, as the old white and coloured plantocracy sharply reduced in size. Collectively known as 'black planters', they donated large sums to the GULP, as well as to other parties, as a form of insurance. Other landowners gave gifts in kind such as food and rent-free facilities for rural rallies, or 'fêtes'. These were a regular occurrence, Gairy using them as much for the opportunity to give speeches as social occasions combined with business meetings. Considerable amounts were spent on transportation, food and drink: at one fête in Grand Bras village in 1977, thirty-six buses were used (many owners donating them free of charge) to transport about 1,000 supporters, and over EC$7,500 (US$2,840) was spent on food and entertainment.

By such methods, the GULP showed that it was not a mass party. Gairy had many supporters personally committed to him but not controlled by him. This critically important feature of Gairyism was made plainer by his relationship with the masses at large specially organized open-air meetings. In a seminal work, Singham characterized these encounters as being between a 'hero' and a 'crowd', a characterization that was to enter the political lexicon. Gairy's charisma was the basis of his 'ability to mesmerize crowds and channel their emotions for short periods of time'; for their part, the masses participated in the political process through these meetings 'as members of a crowd rather than as a movement', responding to numerous biblical references, hymn singing and answering rhetorical questions. Those in the crowd did not see in the party 'an institution which provided *sustained* psychological support for their values, beliefs and attitude' (my italics), but they none the less turned to Gairy to give answers to collective frustrations and resentments and so provide a structure of order to their perspective on life. In summary, 'the crowd was propagandized rather than politicized' (Singham, 1968, pp. 190–3). There was also his mysticism to consider. This was to develop markedly in the later stages of his political career before his eventual downfall. In a country so devoted to Christianity, it was taken seriously. In one famous instance, in 1952, he called upon God to send a sign that He favoured a strike.

That night there was a downpour, heavy even by Grenadian standards. The road between St. George's and Gouyave was blocked by fallen rock, which many regarded as a sign of divine support . . . The Public Works Department tackled this roadblock with unusual energy. With Gairy's divine sign, and a wave of awe sweeping Grenada, police took up protective positions. [Smith, 1965, p. 290.]

Within the confines of the colonial constitution (ministerial government was not introduced until 1959), he worked energetically to promote land reform, greater security for tenant farmers and better credit facilities. The cocoa and nutmeg marketing boards, whose members were elected by the big farmers and planters, were replaced by bodies with nominees of his choosing in the interests of his followers.

In the absence of proper planning, there was little progress to show for his efforts. He kept up the atmosphere of crisis by threatening, and organizing, a number of strikes. But he ignored the urban workers, whose disruptive power was far greater than their numbers would suggest. They were controlled by Derek Knight. It was only much later that Gairy allied himself with Knight, who was to become the GULP government's Attorney-General. The estate owners responded by forming the Grenada Agriculturalists' Union, who undercut Gairy by voluntarily offering wage increases. Oblivious of these weaknesses, Gairy made reckless demands and put himself above the law: he refused to submit the annual accounts of the GMMWU; to acquire a driver's licence and to submit tax returns. Successfully prosecuted, his support ebbed; in the 1954 election, the GULP again won six seats but with only 46 per cent of the votes cast. His power further declined with a boom in the economy following the introduction of banana cultivation on a substantial scale, profitability of which at the time was high. Widespread emigration of the unskilled to Trinidad and Britain took members away (Tobias, 1980, p. 43), and rival unions sprang up capturing others. Through a new lifestyle and a rapidly developing sartorial elegance, he visibly removed himself from the membership. But he was still socially ostracized by the elite, despite the careful cultivation of what passed as an 'upper-class accent'.

The election of September 1957 was a disaster: although winning 44 per cent of the votes cast, the GULP won only two seats. The victor was the Grenada National Party (GNP), led by lawyer Herbert Blaize, from Carriacou. It represented the by now shaken middle class and had been formed the previous year. A far more organized party than the GULP, it made determined attempts to appeal to the working class but had few adherents outside St. George's. Gairy had responded by leading a steel band through a GNP meeting for which he was successfully convicted, disenfranchised for five years and deprived of his seat. Rapidly assuming martyr status, he used the period to weed out those who doubted his leadership, to reorganize the GMMWU as the Grenada Workers Union, and to select a new crop of loyal candidates for the 1961 elections. The GULP won eight of the ten seats with 55 per cent of the vote, a GULP member standing in for Gairy in his constituency. The government, now headed by a Jamaican-born Administrator, J. M. Lloyd (Grenada was now a unit of the West Indies Federation), faced a popular leader who, from his house, acted as if he was Chief Minister, let alone a member of the Legislature. He named his ministers and 'government policy' was regularly announced by him from St. George's market square. Eventually, pressure was such that Lloyd was forced to lift the ban; by April 1961, Gairy *was* Chief Minister. He nursed a deep grudge against Lloyd, whom he saw as being responsible for his disenfranchisement. Within a short time, Gairy was accused of corruption and administrative irregularities, after having massively increased taxes to remove the need for Federal subsidy and therefore close scrutiny of Grenada's financial affairs. Expensive refurbishment of the official residence was 'squandermania', an accusation that was to stick forever. He insisted that, as the head of a popularly elected government, he had to live in 'dignity'. As for corruption, the difficulty was one of definition. Certainly 'accepted administrative practice' had been bypassed 'to get', in his words, 'Grenada moving', but it was admitted there were no actual breaches of the law. At its heart lay a struggle, as before, between the black masses and a coloured middle-class bureaucratic elite who conceived it 'as their clear duty to protect public funds from what they consider illegitimate encroachment by the politicians' (Singham, 1968, p. 234). He bullied them and they responded with forms of bureaucratic sabotage, such as by withholding files. In an atmosphere highly charged with class tension, it was forgotten that many of the 'irregularities' had until then been considered normal practice.

The clamour was such that by early 1962, Lloyd formally announced a Commission of Inquiry. Gairy saw this as another personal attack by Lloyd and mounted a highly vituperative campaign against him. The result was a foregone conclusion: Gairy's government was dismissed and the constitution suspended (*Report of the Commission of Inquiry*, 1962). The commercial and bureaucratic elites, whose collaboration had for long, in their view, kept the Grenadian political system in equilibrium, were victorious over a maverick politician who refused to accept a narrow definition of the role assigned to him by them. But, once again, he became a martyr and readily assumed he could win the September 1962 election. However, the campaign was dominated by the question of Grenada's political future after the collapse of the West Indies Federation a few months before, a debate for which Gairy was ill-prepared. The small East Caribbean islands, except Grenada, searched for another federal solution amongst themselves, the so-called 'Little Eight'. Blaize advocated union with Trinidad, a notion which Dr Williams, Trinidad's Prime Minister, did little at the time to discourage. Gairy was equivocal over the issue, arguing that more discussion was needed. He failed to capture the popular mood. Winning 46 per cent of the vote, the GULP won only four seats. But as events quickly showed, the results of Grenada's overtures to Trinidad were, as Gairy forecast, a total failure. He campaigned on 'the GNP fraud' for the 1967 elections and, as Blaize's administration had done little to respond to working-class demands in the interests of efficient and account-able administration, the GULP swept back to power with seven of the ten seats. By this time Gairy faced little restraint for a few months previously, a new 'associated statehood' constitution had been ushered in by the 1967 West Indies Act. Designed to offer a political future to the remnants of the second attempt to federate, which broke down with the independence of Barbados in 1965, it granted 'internal independence', to each island, leaving only defence and foreign affairs as British responsibilities (Broderick, 1968). Gairy denounced it before the United Nations as just another manifestation of British colonialism.

Firmly back in power, his policies became increasingly exploitative. The 'little black boy' with the self-styled Robin Hood image steadily distanced himself, socially and politically, from the working class. His powers of patronage reaped a rich harvest. The middle classes became, in effect, dependent upon him, their political loyalty (and financial kickbacks) purchased through import licences and monopolies, tax concessions and many legal and illegal incentives. His strong encouragement of tourism brought in foreign multinational companies with whom local capitalists made rapid and profitable links. Only occasionally did his links with international trade unionism result in positive benefits, as with the funding by the American Musicians' Union of the luxury Spice Island Inn. In all other spheres, he made clear that he was pro-capitalist. 'We are supporting employers', he announced, 'we are supporting industrialists to the fullest.'

(Jacobs & Jacobs, 1980, p. 66.) Anti-labour legislation was passed and his erstwhile base, the Grenada Workers' Union, became just another source of patronage and revenue. There were no meaningful negotiations as Gairy told the employers what to pay. Funds were syphoned off and workers lost pension and other benefits. Employers were also ordered to recognize the union, even if their workers preferred another. Victimization of those who opposed him—employer, landowner, worker and peasant alike—became widespread. Women who refused sexual favours were particularly suscept-ible. Public sector investment and expenditure fell dramatically, and roads and schools fell into disrepair. Health standards declined sharply. Inter-nationally, sinister links were forged with the fascist regime of Chile; military aid was despatched by General Pinochet, and in their new uniforms, the Grenada Defence Force became known as the 'Green Beasts' and the 'Iguanas'.

It was not, however, the 'Green Beasts' which were to catch world atten-tion. Opponents soon suffered from a new weapon: in the aftermath of the black power rally in May 1970—events later were to show it was of con-siderable political importance—he made public the existence of special 'police aides'. Recruited from what he admitted were 'the toughest and roughest roughnecks', they had been gradually and covertly assembled since 1967 as a reserve force answerable only to him. Christened the 'Mongoose Gang', they worked with another, smaller group called 'The Night Ambush Squad'. Together, they soon terrorized those who voiced opposition. Repression was justified in terms of anti-communism and Divine wisdom. The latter became part and parcel of his interest in the occult, which was to become a near obsession. It incorporated Unidentified Flying Objects and other cosmic phenomena; when discussed by him on the world stage, he rapidly became the object of derision.

The meaningful contribution and the impactful and efficacious thrust we make in matters of Regional and International proportions could not have been possible without God's Inspiration, His Protection and Guidance . . . It was through Divine Inspiration, that we raised in the United Nations the concept of the universality of God . . . [and] that I was motivated to install, on the most prominent site over-looking our capital city, a large Holy Cross . . . [and] that Grenada raised at the United Nations the question of the occurrence of strange and seemingly inexplic-able psychic and related phenomena which continue to baffle man . . . Many persons who heard my address might have considered my presentation as being somewhat extraneous . . . [Searle, 1983a, pp. 10–11.]

Politics and the cosmos became inextricably linked, and *obeah* and other superstitions were encouraged. His brothels and night-clubs—which he had slowly accumulated since the early 1960s—came to display colourful cosmic insignia.

Everyman knows in his heart that God seeks out the wrongdoer, the atheist, the communist, and all those who challenge Divine Providence. Certain evil persons in our beloved island wearing sheep's clothing and who go in the night preaching hate and deception among our people cannot fool God. The wrath of God will surely visit them, even as I speak now, but we shall shed no tears for them. They will disappear, as others before them. [Government of Grenada, July 1978.]

Just before independence in 1974, an official prayer had to be read out in all schools.

Have mercy upon our Prime Minister Designate, Eric Matthew Gairy, remove from him all dark evil and negative conditions that may be around him; an evil force that may try to tie him down or weigh him down or burden him in any way or tend to prevent him to perform his obligations more promptly and more effectively. Save him from all danger and all malice, jealousy and hate of his enemies. Save him from their arms, weapons and whatever plots and schemes they may formulate against him . . . [Government of Grenada, 1974, p. 2.]

He had successfully exploited the grievances of the common people in 1951 and set Grenada upon a new course. Twenty years on, he had betrayed most of his promises and failed to realize that the world, including Grenada, had moved ahead. He was an anachronism, and dismissed the growing youthful resistance as beneath his, and God's, contempt. A laughing stock in the Caribbean, he became blind to his image, and to much else in his *naïveté* and susceptibilities. It was to prove disastrous to him.

Part II
The Revolution

4   The New Jewel Arises

The black power movement had reached its apogee just as Maurice Bishop returned to his native Grenada in February 1970. Born in Aruba of Grenadian middle-class parents, he had kinship links to the influential La Grenade family. He had travelled to London in late 1963 to study law. Qualifying in 1966, he had been Chairman of the West Indian Students Society of London University, had co-founded a legal aid clinic for West Indians in the heavily immigrant-populated district of Notting Hill and was an active member of the Campaign Against Racial Discrimination. His activism followed earlier work in Grenada. After being Head Boy of the Catholic Presentation College in St. George's, he had, months before his departure, organized The Assembly of Youth After Truth. Even at that early stage, he was known to be a good speaker with a magnetic personality. He returned via Trinidad and experienced the tension which was building up. Very soon after the April disturbances in Port of Spain, he helped lead a solidarity demonstration of some 300 in St. George's the following month, although the slogans concentrated far more on the need for jobs. Gairy responded with his 'police aides', backed up by an Emergency Powers Act which gave him wide powers. He was dismissive of the demonstrators: 'these irresponsive malcontents,' he complained, 'these disgruntled political frustrates coming from abroad, coming here, metaphorically and literally hot and sweaty, and shouting "Power to the People!" ' (Government of Grenada, 3 May 1970).

Bishop attended the Rat Island meeting a few weeks later and, as planned, established FORUM. But it lasted less than a year. Clearly, a mass-based organization was needed to advance political change; research and discussion of Grenada's socio-economic problems was not enough. Accordingly, the 'Movement for the Advancement of Community Effort' (MACE) was formed in early 1972, but its work was limited to St. George's. Bishop was joined in MACE by another lawyer, Kendrick Radix, with whom he had formed a legal partnership aimed especially at assisting victims of Gairyism. The event that precipitated the formation of MACE was the ferocious dispersal of a small demonstration of thirty nurses who were protesting at the bad conditions at St. George's hospital. They had been joined by others, notably the trade unions and the GNP; twenty-two were arrested and successfully defended. Bishop and Radix were also, on occasion, joined by Bernard Coard. He had returned from North American and British universities to teach international relations in, successively, the Jamaican and Trinidadian campuses of the University of the West Indies. Born in St. George's in 1944 of middle-class parents (his father was a civil servant), he had been a secondary school teacher before leaving for Boston. He had become a convinced Marxist while away and had married an equally fervent ideologue, Phyllis Evans, when teaching in Jamaica. His political work began in London and centred upon racism in schools. His book, *How the West Indian Child is Made Educationally Sub-Normal in the British School System* became required reading for many trainee teachers in the future PRG.

Other groups were also formed. In St. George's, the Committee of Concerned Citizens (CCC) brought together the young commercial elite who saw little prospect of the GNP successfully combating Gairy. A quite different constituency supported JEWEL, the 'Joint Endeavour for Welfare, Education and Liberation'. Led by an economics teacher, Unison Whiteman, who had been a former GNP candidate, it was formed soon after the February 1972 elections which reconfirmed Gairy in power. Based in the rural area of St. David's, its centre was a farming co-operative involving youths, some of whom had become Rastafarians. Within weeks, the CCC and MACE combined to form the 'Movement for Assemblies of the People' (MAP). Although, like JEWEL, its political programme was imprecise, it made clear its objective of 'participatory democracy'—the outlines of which had been touched upon at Rat Island—whereby the inherited adversarial partisan system of Westminster would be replaced by 'people's assemblies'. The *ujamaa* experiment in Tanzania was foremost in mind. Mass participation in decision-making, Bishop stressed, was central. 'Politics where you live and politics where you work' was the aim, and 'elections in the sense of elections we now know would be replaced by Assemblies at different levels'. In this scheme, a National Assembly would be composed of nominated representatives from lower level elective assemblies in villages and workplaces. The National Assembly would elect a Council as an executive body, members of which would chair committees composed of lower level assembly members to head and oversee the work of government departments. In this way, Grenadians were later assured, the deep divisions and victimization of the people found under the party system would be removed. (New Jewel Movement, 1973, p. 3). The JEWEL was also engaged in political action. In late 1972, a British landowner blocked access through his estate at La Sagesse to a public beach. As Gairy did nothing, the local people turned to JEWEL for help. A 'people's trial' was held which 'convicted' the owner and the newly built fences were torn down. Clearly, JEWEL had shown its mobilizing potential. The concept also owed much to C. L. R. James (James, 1977, pp. 174–82). To Bishop, decentralizing government in favour of the black masses was an institutional bridge between black power and socialism.

Foundation of the New Jewel

Several months after the La Sagesse incident, the two groups merged in March 1973 to form the New Jewel Movement. By doing so, the urban and the rural sectors were linked. One of its first acts was to stage a successful three-day demonstration against Gairy after a NJM member, Jeremiah Richardson, was killed by a policeman in Grenville. Pearls airport was closed and a state of siege descended upon St. Andrew's parish. The wider base of the NJM and its clear commitment to political action attracted working-class activists such as George Louison, Hudson Austin and Selwyn Strachan. As a youth leader, Louison brought with him several enthusiastic youths who were later to form the core of the first NJM mass organization, the National Youth Organization (NYO). Jacqueline Creft, a teacher, also undertook an active recruitment role among her colleagues.

In its early days, the NJM was not self-consciously Marxist. It was, however, without doubt uncompromisingly socialist in general outlook. Imperialist activities the world over were condemned and ideas about how to rid Grenadians of their oppressors circulated. Concrete proposals based upon the noncapitalist thesis were to come afterwards. A later commentary argued that its 'principal socialist character' was its 'cardinal commitment' to democratic centralism, or inner-party democracy where issues are debated and where decisions are taken by the highest body, representing the majority, and binding on all lower bodies (Jacobs & Jacobs, 1980, p. 81). This attributed too much political sophistication to the party at that stage. Their number was small and they were closely knit socially and politically. All were involved in policy and decision making and any suggestion or hint of elitism was firmly suppressed. But there was no party decision-making structure. 'Consensus' was the key and discussions were interminable; the size of the Political Bureau—sixteen— did not help and much time and effort was wasted (interview with U. Whiteman, May 1979). But the party was galvanized into action and thrust into headlines in the region and beyond by the independence crisis.

'Independence Sellout'

The issue of independence was the catalyst that united opposition to Gairy. He had from 1969 voiced his dissatisfaction with associated statehood, calling it 'this sop of a system'. The problem facing him was that section 10 (1) of the West Indies Act stipulated a popular referendum involving a two-thirds majority, in addition to a similar vote of approval in the Legislature, should an 'associate' wish to proceed to independence without British consent. This condition could be waived if the 'associates' formed a federation amongst themselves or with another, independent, state. These hurdles were designed by the Colonial Office drafters who saw the constitutional arrangements to be long term, and to arrest attempts by what were perceived as small and economically non-viable islands from becoming sources of international instability and permanent mendicants. But the opportunity given to surmount the barriers was an attempt to persuade the United Nations, and its Anti-Colonialism Committee, that it was a genuine exercise in decolonization.

Neither the United Nations nor Gairy accepted these arguments. Far from independence being an economic burden, Gairy argued that it would open doors to international financial institutions and aid donors, who would not deal directly with legally dependent countries. 'Independence will support Grenada', he boasted, 'the people of Grenada do not have to support independence'. Further, independence was Grenada's right and, in common with all leaders of the other Associated States who later followed Grenada's example, he refused a referendum. Other British colonies with less advanced constitutions—he particularly singled out the Bahamas—had no such obligation. In any event, referendums were not only highly unusual in the metropolitan mother country; in the highly politicized and segmented societies of the British West Indies, it would be impossible to isolate the issue from others. Defeat could well prove mortal. Accordingly, he sought independence first through another attempt to federate with Trinidad-Tobago. Prime Minister Eric Williams sidestepped his initiative by suggesting that the Associated States should themselves federate first. He went ahead, also involving Guyana, but met resistance and apathy. Finally, he advocated a union with St. Vincent and St. Lucia but that met a similar fate (Government of Grenada, 1969). This avenue closed, he decided to ask Britain to use its discretionary powers under the Act to terminate unilaterally the association agreement. Fortunately, the Act's drafters had included this provision (section 10.2) for Britain's own protection. By 1972, Britain had realized that association had not facilitated withdrawal from the area. Rather, it meant, in practical political terms, that it had responsibilities without effective power to execute them. The 'threshold of viability', which had been so much in the minds of the constitution makers only five years previously, was no longer considered important. When, therefore, Gairy approached the British government on the matter in early 1972, he was informed that if an election was won on a manifesto advocating independence, then a formal request for Britain to use its discretionary powers would be sympathetically considered (Jacobs, 1974, p. 22).

In fact, the GULP manifesto, of April 1972, issued just two days prior to polling, made scant reference to it. Therefore, when Gairy announced that he would request independence without a referendum, protests were immediate. The GNP and its allies, the Employer's Federation and the Chamber of Commerce, argued that Grenada's precarious and mismanaged economy could never support independence. Anti-Gairy trade unions, the Civil Service associations and the churches feared that independence would remove the last vestige of colonial control over Gairy's excesses; to the NJM, independence under Gairy meant that the opportunity to develop a national identity and higher standards of living, which independence would be expected to promote, would be lost. His approach to Britain was, it claimed, 'an opportunist move to strengthen the grip of tyranny and oppression' (*The New Jewel*, 18 May 1973). In May 1973, while Gairy and Blaize argued at the constitutional conference in London, the NJM matched its words by deeds. A People's Convention on Independence was convened in Seamoon, near Grenville, attended by over 10,000, which demanded popular consultation on the proposed constitution. Strikes broke out and petitions were despatched to an unsympathetic British Foreign and Commonwealth Office (Thorndike, 1974, p. 63). Unknown to the Grenadians, the British Cabinet had earlier that year commissioned a study by its Policy Review Staff to assess, through a cost-benefit analysis, the options open to Britain for the future of its dependencies. It came down firmly in favour of accelerated decolonization.

The NJM's activities soon attracted media attention outside Grenada, particularly after a well-publicized BBC film on the crisis. It published a *Manifesto* in late 1973, 'We'll Be Free in '73', which listed a 'Statement of Principles'.

1. People's participation, people's politics, people's democracy.
2. People's cooperatives for the collective development of the people.
3. Health care based on need.
4. Full development of the people's talents, abilities and culture.
5. Full control as a people of our own natural resources.
6. Employment for all.
7. A decent standard of living for every family.
8. Freedom of expression and religion.
9. The liberation of black and oppressed peoples throughout the world.
10. A united people . . . a new society . . . a just society.

These principles were to form the basis of many of the 'principled positions' of the People's Revolutionary Government. Designed to have national appeal, mention of socialism or of overtly socialist policies was mute. After all, there was not only the relatively ideologically underdeveloped working class to consider, but also the middle strata. But Grenadians were warned that

When a government ceases to serve the people and instead steals from and exploits the people at every turn, the people are entitled to dissolve it and replace it by any means necessary. Very few people in Grenada today believe that it would be possible for power to be transferred from the corrupt Gairy regime by means of an election . . . The NJM proposes to hold in the near future a National Congress of the People to work out the best strategy for taking power. [New Jewel Movement, 1973, p. 12.]

The National Congress never took place, but a 'People's Congress' did as the *Manifesto* reached the streets. The independence crisis deepened. Thousands attended the Congress at which Gairy was 'convicted' of twenty-seven crimes. Designs for his resignation within a fortnight were backed up with threats of a general strike. Gairy responded by urging his police aides (led by Maurice's cousin, Willie Bishop) to 'cinderize' his opponents. Plans for the strike were set in motion and on Sunday, 18 November, the NJM leadership travelled to Grenville to discuss strategy. Maurice Bishop, Radix, Whiteman, Austin, Strachan and Simon Daniel were arrested and severely beaten by the Mongoose Gang. 'Bloody Sunday', as it came to be known, united virtually all sections of the population against Gairy. Although all those attacked recovered, Bishop suffered from double vision from that time on due to severe head injuries. While the NJM leaders languished in prison, a coalition of middle-class groups, trade unions and churches formed the 'Committee of 22' or more formally, the National Unity Council. It called a strike on 19 November and demanded that Gairy authorize an investigation of the Grenville beatings and to arrest those responsible. Gairy agreed to an investigation, appointing Sir Herbert Duffus, a Jamaican judge, to head a Commission of Inquiry, and the strike collapsed after a week.

By the year's end, the NJM leaders were released on bail. They and the party supported the Committee of 22 but efforts to join it were rebuffed on the grounds that the Committee was 'non-political', at least in the partisan sense (interview with R. Smith, June 1974). In the meantime, Gairy had refused to disband his police aides. On New Year's Day 1974, the long awaited national strike began. Lasting three weeks, it was marked by continuous protests and reprisals by Gairy's forces. As one NJM member remarked, 'Tension fills the air and everywhere the dreaded secret police, their clubs, rifles and axe handles at the ready, stand poised to break the people's will. In that struggle, a new people is born' (*The New Jewel*, 11 January 1974). Tension intensified with the gunning down by the police aides of Maurice Bishop's father, Rupert Bishop, on 'Bloody Monday', 21 January. He had been standing in the doorway of the Seamen's Union office on the Careenage, the inner harbour of St. George's, protecting a group of women and children. From that moment, the struggle changed in nature. Up to then, the Committee of 22 wanted reform of the political and economic system within the Westminster and mixed economy framework. The NJM seized the initiative and more revolutionary demands were made. Although few overseas had any respect for Gairy, alarm bells rang. Britain responded to Gairy's plea for money to pay the police and civil servants, treasury coffers being virtually empty. An 'advance instalment' of £100,000 from the £2.5 million independence gift earmarked for Grenada was given, and US$2 million of loans arrived from Jamaica, Trinidad and Guyana. More importantly, just as the strike had depleted all fuel stocks and left other commodities in critically short supply, the Seamen and Waterfront Workers' Union, headed by GNP activist Eric Pierre, called off its action even though days before it had received very considerable financial support from other unions in the region and elsewhere. The reason was the offer of mediation by the Caribbean Congress of Labour at the instigation of the anti-communist and allegedly CIA-funded American Institute for Free Labor Development, the 'research and training' branch of the American trade-union federation.

Although other sections of the economy were still on strike, Independence Day—7 February 1974—proceeded as planned. It was marked with the arrest of the NJM leaders and the burning of Bishop's house. As one bemused reporter later remembered,

Shortly before midnight, we assembled on the battlements of Fort George, overlooking the harbour for the lowering of the Union Jack. On the roof before us stood an escort of British bluejackets ... Under our feet, quite literally, sat the opposition: safely locked up in their cells following the afternoon round-up. Gairy made a preposterous speech in which he declared, 'We are now completely free, liberated, independent. In spite of a wicked, malicious, obstructive, destructive minority of noise-making self-publicists, God has heard our prayers. God has been merciful. God has triumphed.' A British sailor sealed the occasion by blowing the last post before the navy marched away to the quayside. With huge sighs of relief, ... we, the British, had knowingly delivered Grenada into the hands of a lunatic. If there was a society clearly destined for misery as an independent state, it was the tiny pimple of Grenada. [Hastings, 1983.]

Revolutionary Foundations

After independence, only strong regional pressure forced the publication of the *Duffus Report*, which catalogued the brutality of the Mongooses, who had been joined by some policemen. But far from disbanding his aides as urged by Duffus, Gairy expanded their number and appointed one Inspector Belmar, particularly cited for his brutality, a government minister! The economy never fully recovered in the remaining years before the revolution, its problems made worse by the effects of the world oil crisis of 1973-4. A period of stagnation set in, and then decline. Public utilities were particularly affected: rural water supplies in many areas literally dried up. Infant mortality reached 29.5 per 1,000 live births and on occasion, rural dispensaries ran out of medicines, even aspirins, and linen. Functional literacy slipped to 40 per cent and lack of maintenance caused several schools to close. Textbooks became virtually non-existent. Land compulsorily acquired from opponents was no longer redistributed to peasant supporters but became inefficiently run state farms. Marketing Boards were controlled by GULP members and 'administrative costs' rapidly increased at the expense of the peasants. More anti-worker laws were passed: eleven categories of workers became subjected to strike bans during 1977 and 1978. By 1979, less than 30 per cent of the remaining workforce was unionized and unemployment climbed to 49 per cent. This effectively disguised a 69 per cent rate for women and an extra-ordinary 80 per cent for young people under twenty-three years (Joseph, 1981, p. 16). The British government was able to insist upon the placement of a British Treasury official in the Treasury, ostensibly to supervise the expenditure of the £2.5 million gift. The overall situation was one clearly exploitable by the NJM.

The March to Marxism

The first party institution, the Political Bureau, had been established in September 1973, formalizing what had been until then a steering committee comprised of the most active members. After independence, the party suffered increased repression. In the name of anti-communism, its paper, *The New Jewel*, then edited by Selwyn Strachan, was banned. It was thereafter printed secretly, much reliance in particular being put upon market women to sell it from underneath their baskets. Inexorably, the party edged to more radical positions and a streamlined structure to combat Gairy all the more efficiently. Ideologically, the tenets of the noncapitalist path were more fully explored. It was 'the most appropriate intermediate option', permitting 'the mobilization of diverse social elements in the movement towards national liberation and change'. Given the objective socio-economic conditions of Grenada, any move 'directly to scientific socialism was ultra-leftist and idealistic'. But 'scientific socialist principles were applied to analysis and assessment of the objective reality', recalled a Bureau member (interview with G. Louison, November 1983). Marxist methodology and terminology became commonplace and Leninist principles studied and followed.

Intensive internal discussions in March and April 1974 led first to the confirmation that the NJM was a strictly vanguard party. To realize this, membership criteria were strengthened to ensure an elitist, select and dedicated pool of cadres. Second, in May the Political Bureau was reduced in size to nine, and those whose commitment appeared less than total were obliged to leave. Third, parish-based support groups were established, each being the responsibility of a Bureau member, who additionally were given wider functional duties. The working-class activists strongly supported this process of transformation. They had had little exposure to black power; rather they saw socialism as the only practical policy to relieve the lot of their class, and made up in enthusiasm what they lacked in education. Finally, in mid-1975, the Bureau formally confirmed, in secret, that the NJM was a Marxist-Leninist party. Elitist membership would be implemented by mass organizations designed to mobilize the people and to create linkages with, and popular support for, the party. Strachan later recalled the evolution to revolutionary socialism.

[The NJM] started off as what we would call a revolutionary party, a revolutionary democratic party. We never called ourselves socialist at the beginning . . . As we got more and more mature, we were able to work out a clearer ideological position. It didn't come artificially, it was the result of struggle, in a concrete way . . . Lots of organizations started off as Black Power Organizations in the Caribbean . . . but as the struggle developed and they became more clear on the situation, they were able to settle into a permanent trend as to how society should go, what form the struggle should take. We went through that process also. [Bishop, 1982a, pp. 21-2.]

Several members resigned as a result. They had worked for the NJM in the belief that once it had defeated Gairy, it would be reformist and pro-Western—in short, a social-democratic party. Prominent amongst them was George Brizan. A popular teacher, he was a centrist. Soon after his defection, he established *The People's Tribune* and, until the 1979 insurrection, utilized his inside knowledge of the NJM to criticize it constantly. They were, he thundered, 'the minority Communist element'. Nothing but 'upstarts' and 'parasites', they fed upon 'the foundations laid by dedicated builders. . . . Like worms, their activities would destroy Jewel or bring it into disrepute if the more stable elements fail to assert themselves' (*The People's Tribune*, September 1978, p. 7). But he did not realize that the departure of himself and others made the 'minority'—if there ever was one—into virtually the whole. *The New Jewel* vigorously responded to his charges, denigrating 'his lack of principled positions and desertion from scientific socialism' (*The New Jewel*, 18 January 1978). Once the NJM assumed power, however, Brizan escaped detention by becoming strictly non-political.

It was clear that major targets of Brizan were Bernard and Phyllis Coard. Coard had resigned his university post to return to Grenada in September 1976, in time to campaign successfully in the general election scheduled for the following December. From his Trinidad base he had undoubtedly influenced the transition to Marxism–Leninism. Henceforth, his presence ensured that the process would deepen. Brizan was instrumental in making public the existence within the party of the Organization for Research, Education and Liberation (OREL), which he labelled 'Wh-orel'. This had emerged in early 1975 from a small radical youth group, the Joint Organization for Youth (JOY), formed three years earlier by Basil Gahagan and Liam James. They were also the founders of OREL, announcing it as a forum within the party for those who considered themselves revolutionary socialists. Neither age nor experience mattered. It soon superseded its youthful parent and became, despite the original aim, a select group. The Coards joined it very soon after their return, and because of Bernard's university and political experience, he became the 'study guide'. His energy and enthusiasm inevitably led to him assuming leadership and to OREL exercising an influential role.

But criticism, often in relatively open meetings, of those NJM members considered not fully committed to the revolutionary cause, embarrassed and angered many. Coard was ultimately threatened with expulsion in late 1977 unless OREL was disbanded, on the official grounds that 'a party within a party' was inconsistent with Leninist principles. A compromise was eventually reached. OREL would be disbanded on the condition that a more Leninist structure would be introduced. From this agreement came the foundation of the Organizing Committee in February 1978. This assumed responsibility for everyday decisions and the monitoring of members' work and activities. It rapidly became the party executive (interview with U. Whiteman, May 1981). However, the spirit of OREL lived on in the form of an informal pressure group with fluctuating membership right up to the time of the revolution's collapse. It normally met in Coard's house, as before, to study Marxist texts and undertake self-criticism. But to guard against any accusation of factionalism, the meetings were publicized among the membership (interview with B. Gahagan, June 1984).

The length of time taken to institutionalize the party, both in the pre-insurrection period and after, was symptomatic of a sometimes casual attitude to formal organization and the routinization of business held by the leadership. Coard was particularly critical. The general pattern was to act first and routinize later, a manner of operating not dissimilar to that of West Indian political leaders of the orthodox mould. It was, of course, due mostly to the very small numbers involved who, in constant contact, never felt formality to be necessary. They had discarded a lot of unwanted ideological baggage, such as the nihilism of black power philosophy, the vague idealism associated with Tanzanian socialism and the mysticism of Rastafarianism, and that seemed enough. The mass organizations also grew in a haphazard manner. Although the National Youth Organization (NYO) and the National Women's Organization (NWO) preceded the insurrection, there was no carefully thought-out plan of action. The NYO had no firm organizational structure until 1980, and NWO membership was firmly elitist until the end of that year. By 1976, however, the party regarded itself as well established. Bishop claimed that it had the support of half of the country (*Advocate News*, 14 January 1978), but that was clearly exaggerated. However, it was undoubtedly benefiting from the massive rise in secondary school education, 56.1 per cent during the period 1946–70, and the increase in the urban-based working class. Conversely, Gairy's peasant base had eroded: in the same period, there had been a 30.3 per cent drop in the agricultural work force (Jacobs & Jacobs, 1980, p. 81). The NJM accordingly decided to widen its appeal through participation in the December 1976 elections. It was seen as being as much a strategic move as a tactic.

The People's Alliance

Despite its aversion to elections within the established political system, there were five clear benefits to be gained by participation. First and foremost, elected office was the key to legitimacy in the eyes of the country generally and of the middle class in particular. The second advantage was that it provided a legitimate forum from which to articulate party policy and so help construct a national political consciousness. The third followed: their views would be heard beyond Grenada. Fourth was the hope that it would win more seats than the GNP and, as the new 'Official Opposition', would eliminate the party of the capitalist superstructure. Lastly, it was calculated that NJM participation in the House of Assembly would enable it to show its democratic nature and demonstrate how bourgeois democracy was abused under the guise of Westminster constitutionality.

Accordingly, the People's Alliance was forged with the GNP and a newly formed party representing the business community, the United People's Party (UPP). The UPP had originally been founded by a businessman, Leslie Pierre, exasperated by the GNP's ineffectualness in combatting Gairyism. Winston Whyte, a young and articulate businessman who had been one of the very few effective GULP ministers following his election in 1969, assumed its leadership. The Alliance manifesto, largely drafted by Brizan, was essentially reformist. Forty-eight per cent of the votes and six seats were finally won despite blatant electoral fraud. Three were won by NJM candidates, including Bishop (named Leader of the Opposition) and Coard, two by the GNP and one by Whyte. There was no doubt that the NJM had begun to attract middle-class support. In some ways they suffered more from Gairyism than did the peasantry. They fretted at the state of the economy on which their prosperity largely depended, and the absence of respectable and efficient government which would attract foreign investment and fulfil the ideals of public administration bequested by the British.

It was not long before the NJM publicized its view of 'the caricature of democracy' in which it was working. The House of Assembly, it charged,

had degenerated into a theatrical act with Gairy as the leading actor. For the government, the object of their control of Parliament was to hurl personal invective, ridicule the Opposition, kill debate by giving insufficient notice of bills, while denying the Opposition the use of the radio. [*Trinidad and Tobago Review*, May 1979, p. 19.]

By mid-1977, however, the Alliance existed only on paper and in votes in the House of Assembly and the Senate. Whyte, in particular, objected to 'NJM domination' and 'extremism'; he found a ready echo in Blaize. They helped spread rumours that the 'Jewel Boys' were responsible for at least two of the five assassinations of alleged Gairy opponents attributed to the Mongoose Gang. This did not prevent a sharp increase in grassroots support for the NJM as victimization increased. Bishop's stature as a speaker and leader was an undoubted fact. Deep splits in the police force and the Defence Force were exploited by the party, which began to develop an armed clandestine wing. In early 1978, it decided to infiltrate the trade unions. Although some NJM members established themselves in executive positions, some prominent unionists, such as Fred Grant of the Technical and Allied Workers Union, needed little incentive to follow the NJM's industrial relations policies as pressures intensified. Some of his members, and those in the civil service, were refused salary increases recommended by the Salaries Revision Committee. Their protests and threat of a strike were met by a warning that Gairy 'could not guarantee' the safety of their leaders: in short, they risked death. A new union was formed, taking advantage of the by now widespread opposition to Gairy among those in the middle classes who did not owe their living to him. The Bankers' and General Workers' Union under Fitzroy Bain called a strike of Barclays Bank employees in February 1979 which was violently suppressed by the Mongooses.

It was painfully obvious that established procedures of political change were completely ineffectual, a fact which both the GNP and UPP realized but could do nothing about. As a peasant NJM member recalled,

And so the thing went from strength to strength. And when we contested the elections, we see definitely that there was no way out because Gairy had ripped it so to speak and we could do nothing. So it came that we see election was useless, that it was depending on some of those persons like Blaize and so on who are useless. So there is only one way out: pull the bull back by its horns. [EPICA Task Force, 1982, p. 50.]

By early 1979, Gairy had united the bulk of the population against him, notwithstanding barriers of colour and class. Moreover, a radical alternative to electoral change grew increasingly acceptable to many. The inevitable end was in sight.

5 Insurrection and Reaction

The insurrection in the early hours of 13 March 1979 came as a complete surprise to Grenadians and the world. Armed with weapons mainly smuggled in from the United States in oildrums, about forty to forty-five members of the embryonic People's Revolutionary Army (PRA), led by Hudson Austin, attacked the Defence Force barracks at True Blue. Within the twelve hours, and at the cost of three deaths (one of which, a civilian, was accidental), the final police station surrendered and the Provisional (later People's) Revolutionary Government was proclaimed. The secrecy of its planning depended upon strong Leninist discipline within the Political Bureau. As Coard later explained,

[It was] forced upon us by the making of our newspaper illegal, by the refusal of permission to use loudspeakers, by the refusal to permit us to hold public meetings, to demonstrate and so on. The other side of that coin was that it forced us to be a disciplined, organized, tightly knit security-concious party, so that it was therefore possible in the circumstances to call upon people, day and night to respond to the call. [*Caribbean Sun*, April/May 1979, p. 22.]

The insurrection had been precipitated by a warning from NJM informants within the police and Defence Force that Gairy had given instructions for the arrest of the party leadership during a visit that he was to make to the United Nations. Ostensibly, it was to attend a Conference on the International Year of the Child but his main purpose was to lobby the Secretary-General and the UN's Use of Outer Space Committee on the need for a UN Agency to investigate UFOs. It was alleged that cells had been prepared and that even execution was possible. The leadership went into hiding once Gairy had departed. But there was indecisiveness. The four (Bishop, Coard, Austin and another) entrusted with the decision were evenly divided. Louison was added and, at four a.m., he broke the deadlock by voting with Coard and Austin in favour of action (Hart, 1984, p. xxiii). Messages were flashed to the insurgents and to the Parish support groups; the latter were warned to expect action. Once the Defence Force had been neutralized, the revolutionary forces seized the radio station to mobilize NJM supporters and the people. By late afternoon, the police and army had been disarmed as there were many pro-Gairyites in their ranks. Although many policemen were retained, the new security forces were to be indistinguishable from the regime as a whole.

The Sovereign Will of the People

The response was astonishing and fully justified the PRG's claim that the revolution was legitimized by the clearly expressed will of the people.

Crowds of people descended on the police stations around the country, armed with implements such as crude knives and cutlasses. Citizens helped the PRA soldiers capture members of Gairy's secret police and the Mongoose Gang. Squads of volunteers patrolled the island to maintain order and guard against counter-revolutionary activity... Telephone workers blocked all overseas calls... people lent their vehicles to transport men and arms, while women cooked vast quantities of food for the revolutionary forces. [EPICA Task Force, 1982, p. 55.]

That night saw an island-wide carnival atmosphere. Bishop had broadcast that morning over the newly named Radio Free Grenada. The insurrection heralded a new future but what was immediately required was national unity.

People of Grenada, this revolution is for work, for food, for decent housing and health services, and for a bright future for our children and great-children. The benefit of the revolution will be given to everyone regardless of political opinion or which political party they support. Let us all unite as one. Let me assure all supporters of the former Gairy government that they will not be injured in any way ... so long as they do not offer violence to our government. In closing, let me assure the people of Grenada that all democratic freedoms, including freedom of elections, religions and political opinion, will be fully restored to the people. [Marcus & Taber, 1983, pp. 24–5.]

Five days later, the People's Revolutionary Government was officially proclaimed to an enthusiastic crowd of 25,000—the largest ever seen in Grenada—at a rally at the Queen's Park Stadium in St. George's. Maurice Bishop was declared Prime Minister with Bernard Coard as Minister of Finance; the title of Deputy Prime Minister was to be assumed later. The news that Gairy had conceded defeat from his New York hotel suite met a roar of approval. However, although Bishop talked of 'revolution', most Grenadians took this to mean reform. They were encouraged in this belief by the official *Declaration of the Grenada Revolution*, which served as a preamble to the first ten 'People's Laws'. These were proclaimed and acclaimed by some 15,000 people at a later rally at Seamoon, on 25 March.

WHEREAS constitutional government in Grenada has been interrupted as a consequence of the violations and abuses of democracy committed by the administration of Eric Matthew Gairy under the guise of constitutionality;
AND WHEREAS the people of Grenada have expelled the above Gairy from office together with all his Ministers and have appointed in their stead a People's

Revolutionary Government for the time being to manage the affairs of Grenada as the Trustees and Executors of the Sovereign powers and rights of the people and have empowered the said People's Revolutionary Government to issue such Laws, Orders, Rules and Regulations and to do all things as it may deem necessary for the restoration and preservation of the Peace, Order and Good Government of Grenada;

AND WHEREAS the People's Revolutionary Government pledges to return to constitutional rule at an early opportunity and to appoint a Consultative Assembly to consult with all the people for the purpose of the establishment of a new Constitution which will reflect the wishes and aspirations of all the people of Grenada. That new Constitution will be submitted for popular approval in a referendum . . .;

AND WHEREAS during this period of transition the People's Revolutionary Government pledges to observe the fundamental rights and freedoms of our people subject to certain measures necessary to:

(i)   The maintenance of stability, peace, order and good government;

(ii) The final eradication of Gairyism; and

(iii) The protection of the People's Revolution;

AND WHEREAS on the morning of March 13th 1979 the people of Grenada in the exercise of their sovereignty overthrew the regime of Eric Gairy. This sovereign act of necessity involved the suspension of The Grenada Constitution Order 1973 . . . [Bishop, 1979, pp. 1–2.]

The need for a 'transition period' and the suspension of the constitution pending its replacement was readily accepted. So was the formal establishment of the PRA with powers of arrest (People's Law no. 7), the imposition of imprisonment without trial, or 'preventive detention'—albeit subject to appeal to a preventive detention Tribunal (People's Law no. 8)—and the promulgation of laws through 'oral declaration and/or publication on Radio Free Grenada by the Prime Minister or in the official *Gazette* under the hand of the Prime Minister' (People's Law no. 10). Not only would these apply for a short period but most people thought that the new constitution would be little changed bar the inclusion of provisions designed to prevent a return to a Gairy-like dictatorship; and that elections would follow, the whole process being over in a matter of months. There is no doubt that if such had taken place, the NJM would have decisively won virtually every seat, and probably would have been unopposed in most constituencies.

There was also a not far-fetched fear that the new regime was threatened by a possible Gairy-led mercenary counter-attack. Gairy and his Attorney-General, Derek Knight (who escaped in a yacht), had deposited considerable sums in American banks which could be used for such a purpose. Bishop asked for military assistance from Grenada's traditional allies, Britain, Canada and the United States, but to no avail. Guyana, however, responded.

Arms were sent and training facilities in Guyana made quickly available. Cuba, recalling its own experience, was also not slow to realize the danger. Links had already been built up with visits to some of the NJM leadership: within a few weeks of the insurrection, a Cuban cargo ship unloaded arms at the darkened port, fulfilling an arms agreement. Three further arms agreements were signed with Cuba, the Soviet Union and North Korea between 1980 and 1983. Only those with Cuba included military advisers. While few in Grenada were ignorant of the agreements, none outside the NJM leadership and top command of the PRA knew of their extent.

The Overseas Reaction

The timing of the insurrection and the known pro-Cuban sympathies of the revolutionaries, together with rumours of the arrival of Cuban arms, produced a decidedly mixed reaction, ranging from guarded hostility and apprehension to outright congratulations. Although closely linked in many minds, suggestions of a pre-arranged conspiracy directed by Havana were not developed as no evidence whatsoever existed. Different countries' reactions tended to stress one or the other. Whereas, for instance, many of Grenada's Commonwealth Caribbean partners were concerned more about constitutional issues and the danger of insurrection becoming a precedent, the United States was exercised far more about the Cold War implications, seeing Cuba as a Soviet surrogate interfering in what it regarded as its exclusive sphere of influence. Foreign reaction was crucially important to the regime from the time of its birth. Although the initial responses were undoubtedly influential and instructive, reaction to the revolution as it eventually evolved became critical in determining its direction and, eventually, its very fate. It was foreign reaction which led the PRG to arm itself heavily, perceiving that only a vigilant revolutionary Grenada could be secure. It failed, however, to realize that defence does not necessarily lead to security; and given Grenada's geo-political position and the values and assumptions of its neighbours and traditional trading partners, attempts to bolster defence through arms, military advisers and defiant statements served only to increase its insecurity in what was perceived as a hostile world.

There were four groups of states closely interested in the Grenadian revolutionary experiment: the West Indies or more specifically, the Commonwealth Caribbean; the United States and Britain; Cuba and the Soviet Union; and the hemispheric middle powers, Canada, Mexico, Venezuela and—through its West Indian *départements*, France.

The Commonwealth Caribbean

While there was universal relief at the removal of a regional embarrassment, there was by no means a united response by Grenada's Commonwealth Caribbean colleagues. None, however, could ignore the clear endorsement of the insurrection by the great majority of Grenadians. But neither could they ignore unconstitutionalism and the threat to their own polities that this represented.

Relations between the various territories of the Commonwealth Caribbean, the former British West Indies, have been pockmarked by dissent. Indeed, two dramatically contrasting faces have been shown to the world. On one hand, there is the clear underlying sense of brotherhood impressed by a long and common experience of British colonialism, but stopping well short of constituting a West Indian nation. This relationship underpins CARICOM, perhaps the most successful of Third World attempts at integration and cooperation. But there is always a potential for fratricidal division. This paradox has been apparent since earliest times. Attempts by the British to achieve closer union, culminating in the West Indies Federation, fell victim to it. However, between the former associated states—Antigua, St. Kitts-Nevis, Dominica, St. Lucia, St. Vincent and Grenada, together with colonial Montserrat—there exists a more urgent need for cooperation as all are tiny islands vulnerable to the vicissitudes of international economics and politics. They had formed a cooperative association in 1966, the West Indian (Associated States) Council of Ministers (WIAS), with a Secretariat in St. Lucia. An economic arm, the Eastern Caribbean Common Market, was based in Antigua from 1968. In 1981 they were reorganized as the Organization of Eastern Caribbean States (OECS), each Prime Minister (or Premier in Montserrat's case) being chairperson in rotation. Grenada is not only a member of both CARICOM and the OECS but also of other regional organs, notably the Caribbean Development Bank (CDB) based in Barbados, and the East Caribbean Central Bank (ECCB) in St. Kitts. The latter was created in October 1983 as the successor to the former East Caribbean Currency Authority (ECCA) and supplies a US dollar-pegged common currency, the East Caribbean dollar (EC$), to all OECS members. After the débâcle of federation, no pretensions to supra-nationality are given or hinted at in any of these institutions. None the less, they express in institutional terms a complex web of economic, political and social relationships that exist between all the varied constituents.

When they received news of the NJM takeover, only Jamaica and Guyana immediately welcomed it; indeed, Bishop later remarked that they were the first to respond to his government's call for assistance and diplomatic support (Bishop, 1982, pp. 111 and 129). This was not surprising since, in Jamaica's case, Prime Minister Michael Manley had since 1974 espoused an ideology of democratic socialism, many social and economic policies of which paralleled those of the new PRG. Forbes Burnham of Guyana, for his part, had established what he and his followers termed a Co-operative Socialist Republic in 1970 although it was far more imagined than real. In contrast, Trinidad's position was lukewarm at most. Stating that it was not its practice to issue statements of formal recognition—'we recognize countries, not governments . . . we are not telling Grenada what to do or what not to do', said its Minister for CARICOM affairs—it refused to receive official PRG delegations although 'officially diplomatic relations continue' (*Caribbean Contact*, June 1980).

Grenada's WIAS colleagues and Barbados occupied the other end of the spectrum, that of disapproval and, to some extent, fear. This was rather over-dramatically expressed by a London-based journal.

[The insurrection] is still striking terror into the hearts of the smaller island governments . . . nearly all (of whom) have come out against the coup, seeing it, especially because of their own small size, as a threatening example to their own leftists with whom Bishop, as a regional human rights lawyer, had close personal relations. [*Latin America Political Report*, 23 March 1979.]

In other words, their vulnerability to takeovers by determined and organized revolutionary activists was suddenly exposed. Further, they feared that recognition would serve to legitimize future insurrections. Hence, at two emergency WIAS meetings, a decision to refuse recognition was reached. But it came to nought. Only Dominica and St. Lucia were independent states; the others as associated states remained reliant on Britain to conduct their external affairs. At a stroke, therefore, they recognized the PRG when Britain did so two weeks after the takeover. All their other attempts to isolate Grenada failed, such as the attempt to prevent LIAT, the regional airline in which the WIAS members had shareholdings, from landing there. St. Vincent's Premier Milton Cato proposed an East Caribbean police force on permanent standby to stamp out future outbreaks of revolutionary insurrection, but none were prepared to foot the bill or find terms of reference acceptable to regional, and world, public and legal opinion. Prime Minister John Compton of St. Lucia demanded British intervention. In the end, they only delayed an issue to Grenada of EC$3 million new banknotes from ECCA.

Their fear of a virus overlaid a deeper concern: the insurrection violated hallowed constitutional rules. Barbados took the initiative and called an emergency meeting of foreign ministers of the independent members of CARICOM. Prime Minister Tom Adams proposed a constitutional formula to regularize the changeover. Bishop would be appointed a minister of the GULP government by Gairy's deputy, Herbert Preudhomme, after which Preudhomme would resign (he was actually in prison at the time). The Governor-General—specifically recognized as Head of State by the PRG by virtue of People's Law no. 3—would then appoint Bishop as Prime Minister. In turn, Bishop would choose a 'cabinet' of the remaining five members of the opposition, i.e. including Blaize and Whyte, and two former GULP ministers. That CARICOM felt impelled to meet to consider a takeover in one of its members, let alone this extraordinary scheme, underscores the uniqueness of the institution in the Third World. A similar meeting of, for instance, the Organization of African Unity or Organization of American States (OAS) can hardly be imagined. It finally decided on recognition, helped by assurances allegedly made by Bishop that elections would be held shortly (Government of Barbados, *Debates*, 1983, p. 51).

Bishop cursorily dismissed it. 'Those who are making the loudest noises', he laughed, 'have the most to fear from their own people.' Perhaps recognizing that he had misjudged the situation, Adams later admitted 'that we were prepared to overlook the means by which this [Gairy's] regime was ended' as 'many of us were so glad' to be rid of him (ibid.). But it did not end there as Barbados and its neighbours felt increasingly threatened when left-wing parties, which openly admired the PRG, assumed power following elections in St. Lucia and Dominica. When their leaders met with Bishop a few months later, banners at a solidarity rally openly proclaimed 'St. Vincent next' (*The Guardian*, 19 November 1979). What went largely unreported, however, was the deportation to St. Vincent for trial of several Rastafarian youths who had been involved in a minor uprising on Union Island, the most southerly of the Vincentian Grenadines. They had fled to neighbouring Carriacou once a police contingent from Barbados arrived in response to a call for assistance from Milton Cato. Bishop refused them asylum, fearing condemnation on a scale which would seriously threaten the fledgling regime's security. Fortunately, regional attention had been diverted to a scandal in Antigua, whose government was amongst the most pro-American. ACLM leader Tim Hector had established that a mysterious company, the Space Research Corporation, was using Antigua to test ballistic shells and as a shipping point for the South African armed forces. There was also the close collaboration between the PRG and Cuba to consider. In short, established values were under threat. This feeling appeared reinforced by the signing of the 'Declaration of St. George's' later in the year by Bishop, George Odlum (Deputy Prime Minister of St. Lucia) and Oliver Seraphine who headed Dominica's government. It set 'popular democracy, respect for the rights of workers, and social and economic justice for the masses' as the cornerstone of their domestic policies. Imperialism was roundly denounced and non-alignment in foreign affairs praised. All travel restrictions between their three countries were removed as a concrete symbol of solidarity ('Declaration of St. George's', 1979, pp. 32–4).

The PRG made no attempt to allay these fears. Although it reaffirmed Grenada's commitment to CARICOM and WIAS, it denounced the more conservative members as 'handmaidens of imperialism, serving not their people but masters in Washington and Wall Street' (*The New Jewel*, 9 August 1979). In its 1973 *Manifesto*, the NJM had argued that CARICOM could only become a 'meaningful reality' if it promoted 'the integration of the economies of the islands under the ownership and control of the people of these islands'. Further, it had stressed, all its achievements had simply 'made it easier for foreign companies to exploit us'. It was, therefore, a confident Maurice Bishop who went to the Sixth Summit of the Non-Aligned Movement in Havana in September 1979. Only a few months previously, the Sandinistas in Nicaragua had wrested power away from the Somoza dictatorship: 'imperialism', he said, 'is not invincible'. A 'new Caribbean' was being forged. 'Jamaica, Guyana, a new Grenada, Dominica, St. Lucia—governments attempting to build new societies with the people's support . . . We also see a new Latin American emerging—Cuba in 1959, Nicaragua now . . .' (Bishop, 1982c, p. 97). In fact, he spoke too soon. Far from being a harbinger of change, the Grenadian revolution showed itself to be a highly specific event arising out of Gairyism. Elsewhere in the region, the West Indian condition recovered its composure. Elections in St. Vincent in December 1979 and Antigua in April 1980 reconfirmed rightwing governments in office; those in St. Kitts-Nevis brought victory to a rightwing coalition for the first time. Seraphine's Dominican Labour Party regime collapsed in July 1980 amid widespread allegations of corruption and incompetence, to be replaced by a conservative administration led by the formidable Eugenia Charles. St. Lucia's radical government became immobilized by a bitter leadership struggle between George Odlum and what he regarded as 'caretaker leaders'. Relations with Guyana never wholly recovered after the PRG bluntly accused Burnham of complicity in the assassination of Walter Rodney, and its sharp criticism of his persecution of the radical Working People's Alliance of which Rodney had been co-leader with Clive Thomas and others. Most serious, however, was Manley's electoral defeat in October 1980 at the hands of

Edward Seaga. A staunch supporter of the PRG, he of all the elder statesmen of the Commonwealth Caribbean was a close confidante of Bishop. Overnight, Jamaica turned from being an active participant in the Non-Aligned Movement and an ally of Grenada to becoming the closest friend in the Commonwealth Caribbean of the United States. There was only a small consolation prize. A military coup in Suriname in February 1980 had brought to power a group of non-commissioned officers led by Sergeant, later Colonel, Bouterse. Although their socialist philosophy was imprecise and subject to sometimes violent vacillations, the new regime was both friendly to the PRG and, nominally at least, progressive.

Although the immediate apprehension of Grenada's neighbours proved unwarranted, they found a ready weapon in the PRG's stubborn refusal to hold elections. Secondary to this affront to constitutional values was concern over the increasing number of political detainees and the virtual emasculation of the detainee appeal tribunal; the closure of *The Torchlight* newspaper; the ban, for all intents and purposes, on all political parties and forms of political expression outside of the NJM; and tight control over the media, particularly Radio Free Grenada. Relations with Barbados over these issues became particularly poor. When Adams publicly admonished Bishop and his colleagues for their failure to hold elections, coupling it with a warning that without them, the CDB might be unable to attract loan funds from elsewhere (a suggestion which brought an embarrassing denial from the Bank) (*Advocate News*, 1 November 1980), Bishop angrily noted that Ronald Reagan had that night won the United States' presidential election. To Adams' comment that 'it is time . . . Grenada understands the spirit of CARICOM is in the direction of elections' and 'if Bishop cannot understand that he will put himself in the old cellar of vagaboncy that Eric Gairy occupied; if he continues to promote a government about which there is any possibility of saying that it is repressive, then Bishop does not deserve support', Bishop replied with a vehemence unprecedented in the West Indies.

In a country where political murders remain unsolved, and where murders and rape of poor people are on a constant rise, Uncle Tom Adams still feels that he hasn't got enough problems in his backyard that he can find time to wash his mouth in Grenada's business. Like an expectant dog barking for his supper, he rushes in to please his new master like all good yardfowls by attacking Grenada . . . We consider Adams' statement to be a provocative act . . . [*Caribbean Insight*, December 1980, p. 1.]

The bitterness that it expressed led to harassment of PRG ministers as they passed through the Barbados international airport, causing all official travel to be diverted via Trinidad. Not that Trinidad favoured their regime: its government made clear that its programme of economic assistance based upon large oil revenues did not apply to Grenada. 'So long as there is no properly elected government in St. George's, there is no possibility of co-operation ... All we are saying is—don't come to us for loans or assistance until you have cleared up this situation'. (*Caribbean Contact*, June 1980). In fact, the nadir had been reached at that point. The PRG recognized that it was virtually friendless in the Commonwealth Caribbean just as its neighbours realized that the perceived threat to their stability was receding. Painfully slowly, the principle of 'ideological pluralism' was accepted but not embraced within CARICOM, although considerable reservations remained. It was left to the United States, followed by a compliant Britain, to maintain and, as time proceeded, to intensify the pressure against the revolution.

Pressure from the Northern Colossus

Since 1973 the British had closely observed the NJM. Analysing its state-ments, they correctly concluded that its Marxist–Leninist sympathies were paramount. Much information was passed to Washington and as the British gradually withdrew, the interest of the State Department and the Central Intelligence Agency (CIA) increased. Not surprisingly, both agencies had large dossiers on the party when news of the insurrection seeped through. As events showed, little time was lost in using them. It was unfortunate for the People's Revolutionary Government that the insurrection occured at a time when the Carter administration was not only becoming more concerned about Caribbean and Central American affairs than hitherto, but was also stressing the security and military aspects of its relationship with the region rather than economic development. There had been since 1959 oscillations in American policy, swinging from a high to a low profile and from a stress on economic interests to those of security, not necessarily simultaneously. In the period to 1965, which marked the invasion of the Dominican Republic by the United States under the guise of the OAS to depose a left-wing but popularly elected government, Latin America as a whole was accorded high priority. Economic development and security assistance programmes under the 'Alliance for Progress' banner went hand in hand, to counter insurgency and create an environment conducive to business. From then until Carter's accession to office in 1976, the area was relatively neglected, responses being made to specific crises, as the State Department and the White House grappled with problems in Asia.

Carter, by contrast, was determined to give the area greater attention and to travel in a direction away from supporting dictators who grossly abused human rights in the name of anti-communism. In a series of initiatives, he began his administration by promoting human rights and collaborative and enlightened economic development projects; he also accepted State Department advice that Central American problems were different from those of the non-Hispanic Caribbean, a distinction which American policy began to reflect. It resulted in a political rather than a military response to the problem of change in the Caribbean sector; a senior adviser, Philip Habib, set out five principles which would govern America's relations (*Caribbean Contact*, January 1980):

(1) significant support for economic development;
(2) firm commitment to democratic practices and human rights;
(3) clear acceptance of ideological pluralism;
(4) unequivocal respect for national sovereignty;
(5) strong encouragement of regional cooperation and of an active Caribbean role in world affairs.

This was backed up by tours of the Caribbean by the liberal Ambassador-at-large, Andrew Young, and Mrs Rosalynn Carter. Aid was increased to the point that it was three times greater in 1979 than in 1976. An annual conference devoted to Caribbean issues was established in Miami to which government and business leaders were invited. Not surprisingly, Carter enjoyed considerable popularity.

But it became increasingly difficult to separate the Caribbean from Central America. The link, in Washington's eyes, was Cuba, which was suspected of expressing more than solidarity with the Nicaraguan and El Salvadorean guerrillas. Little evidence of military assistance was offered but the right-wing military leaders of Central America, unaccustomed to United States' disapproval, found ready ears in Congress, the Pentagon and the State Department for their angry complaints. Further, the commitment of Cuban troops to first Angola in November 1975, and then Ethiopia in December 1977, ended the period of rapprochement that had been developing between the two countries. Slowly, hostility against Cuba increased until, by 1979, it had been restored to the levels of the early 1960s. It had become 'a rotten apple in the middle of the Caribbean'. It centred upon the 'discovery' of a 'combat brigade' of Soviet troops on the island which needed 'to be neutralized' by a new Caribbean Joint Task Force based in Key West, Florida, and a very considerable increase in military activity in the area. No regard was paid to Castro's denial of the charge or of his protests against increased aerial surveillance. In May 1980, a massive naval exercise—Operation Solid Shield—

was staged, which included a landing of over 2,000 marines at the American base at Guantánamo, at the far south-eastern tip of Cuba. A total of 20,000 men, forty-two naval vessels and 350 aircraft were involved.

Carter's about-turn on Cuba and his downgrading of human rights as an international political issue can be partly attributed to a deep disquiet in Washington that the world's most powerful country was being 'pushed around'. One hundred-and-nine Americans from the United States Embassy in Tehran were being held hostage by Iranian revolutionaries and the course of events in Nicaragua had slipped beyond American control with the final victory of the Sandinista forces in July 1979. To his mounting number of critics, Carter had changed his mind far too late and had failed to influence the forces of change which were strongly asserting themselves in the Caribbean Basin. The Administration therefore decided to pressurize the PRG from its emergence to mould it in such a way that it represented no threat to its preferred order. Its tactics, and those of the succeeding administration of Ronald Reagan, were to become classic examples of destabilization.

At first, there was a 'wait-and-see' attitude. It followed CARICOM's lead and recognized the PRG. Its aid programme to the Eastern Caribbean had been expanded, one thrust being potential assistance towards the establishment of a regional Coast Guard following mercenary activity in Dominica. The Carter Administration decided that if Grenada were included as a recipient of this increased aid, 'the wrong signal about democracy' would be sent. It accordingly decided to withhold the extra assistance from the rebel island until Bishop's pledge on elections was realized (Pastor, 1984, p. 6). Ambassador Frank Ortiz was despatched from his Barbados base on 23 March to make contact, to describe the aid programme (of which Bishop seemed unaware) and to offer an increased number of Peace Corps Volunteers. Bishop and the Grenadian delegation were suspicious, if not occasionally hostile (interviews with American diplomatic personnel, June 1979), and Ortiz's diplomatic talents were not in evidence. Grenada's trade deficit of EC$19 million was noted, imports worth EC$32 million outshipping exports of EC$13 million. Ortiz warned that tourism, which the PRG hoped to encourage to lessen the gap, would be discouraged by alleged threats of 'mercenary armies by phantom armies' and the sight of armed and aggressive youthful troops. He reminded his hosts that the Manley administration was suffering from a severe down-turn in tourism, omitting to say that his government was actively playing a role by planting anti-Jamaican stories in the media and by sabotaging the economy through denial tactics at international financing meetings where the United States had a virtual veto. Fully aware of the arrival of the regime's pro-Cuban sympathies, he ended by passing over a statement, part of which Bishop made public.

Although my government recognizes your concern over allegations of a possible counter-coup, it also believes that it would not be in Grenada's best interest to seek assistance from a country such as Cuba to forestall such an attack. We would view with displeasure any tendency on the part of Grenada to develop closer ties with Cuba. [Marcus & Taber, 1983, p. 27.]

He also responded to a request for aid made by Bishop a day after the insurrection to the United States' Consul-General, who Bishop reported had been convinced of the economic ravages of Gairyism and 'impressed by the bloodless character and self-evident humanity of our prompt assurances . . . that the safety, lives and property of American and other foreign residents were guaranteed'. He offered US$5,000. It drew a stinging rebuke from Bishop.

Sisters and brothers, what can $5,000 do? . . . We are a small country . . . a poor country, with a population of largely African descent . . . we are part of the exploited Third World . . . but [a] proud people who are fighting for democracy, dignity and self-respect based on real and independent economic development . . . No country has the right to tell us what to do or how to run our country or who to be friendly with . . . We are not in anybody's backyard, and we are definitely not for sale. [Bishop, 1982c, p. 13.]

Ortiz's diplomatic clumsiness deeply offended the PRG but it reflected official policy. When his successor, Sally Shelton, voiced concerns about the growing Cuban military presence, she was asked to delay presenting her credentials for seven weeks, a move which led the United States eventually to refuse the accreditation of its ambassador to Grenada, in effect virtually breaking diplomatic relations. Washington also found a ready ally in the newly elected and right-wing Thatcher administration in Britain. After a visit to London by Habib, Britain ceased all aid save the remaining instalments of the 1974 independence gift, and specifically refused the export of two armoured cars in January 1980, ordered by the PRG. As the PRG's links with socialist states deepened, marked above all else by extensive Cuban aid to construct the new international airport at Point Salines, a fog of mutual incomprehensibility enveloped relations with the United States, from which neither could escape.

Cuba, the Soviet Union and the Middle Powers

The acceptance of Cuban arms and military advisers—which by mid-1979 the PRG did not conceal—placed Grenada fairly and squarely into the developing post-*détente* new Cold War between the Superpowers, whatever the PRG's perceptions of its policy as expressing 'positive non-alignment'. Fidel Castro welcomed the insurrection without reservation and pledged all possible support. The Soviet Union also welcomed it but refused any commitment until such time as the situation could be clarified and the NJM's non-capitalist direction made clearer.

The reaction of Mexico and Venezuela was juxtaposed between the two extremes of Washington and Havana. They neither condemned nor praised, restricting their concern to statements deploring the categorization of Grenada as a Cold War pawn. Both offered economic assistance, mainly with cheap oil, but none of a scale to be influential. A problem was that they considered themselves rivals for influence in the post-imperial era in the region and neither wanted to offend new friends they were wooing. But equally they did not like Cuba's thrust to the south, not so much for ideological reasons but that Cuba was also seen as a hemispheric competitor. Canada remained neutral and quietly maintained all its aid programmes. As for France, a delicate path had to be stepped. The presidential elections were on the horizon and Giscard d'Estaing was acutely conscious of the pro-PRG Socialist–Communist challenge. But the Grenadian revolution, if openly endorsed, would clearly encourage nationalists in Guadeloupe and Martinique to increase their demands for independence. For diverse reasons, therefore, none offered to be an 'honest broker' between the sparring partners. If they had and had been successful, the eventual tragic outcome might have been avoided.

The capture of some 25,000 documents by the Central Intelligence Agency after the October 1983 invasion gave analysts an unprecedented opportunity to examine and dissect the problems of a vanguard Marxist–Leninist party attempting a noncapitalist direction of development towards socialism in the West Indian context. There were four major insights. First, it was clear that the pre-insurrectionist habit of belatedly institutionalizing the party and formalizing procedures in piecemeal fashion continued virtually to the end of the revolution. Second was the realization that once most of the essentials of the basic structure were in place, intra-party communications paradoxically decreased in inverse proportion to the number of meetings held. In short, bureaucracy and over-extensive discussion in the search for a 'consensus' appeared more important than action. Despite massive paperwork and hours, even days, of debates, there was little monitoring of decisions when they were eventually made and few clear lines of responsibility were developed. The structure, it must be concluded, was never properly operationalized to further the revolution. Neither had the party a constitution.

The third insight provided by the captured documents is that despite the construction of a Leninist party apparatus, a critical part of which were the mass organizations, confidence that a vanguard of dedicated cadres could chart new directions for society and the economy was never justified. Far from developing 'an irresistible surge to socialism' by the masses, the NJM and the government clearly failed to retain the high degree of public support unambiguously accorded it after the insurrection. Mobilization campaigns became less effective and, over time, the branch network weakened. A communication gap between the party and the masses grew and widened; increased security measures designed to protect the leadership, especially after a bomb outrage in June 1980 when its members narrowly escaped death, served only to widen the gulf. The People's Revolutionary Army became ubiquitous as external threats grew; and the arrogance of some of their number rapidly became an irritant. More haemorrhaging of support followed an intensified application of 'revolutionary manners', or counter-revolutionary justice. Preventive detention without trial and the strict control of the media did not satisfy a people long used to expressing opinions. The party's reaction was to be more reactive than innovative. It recognized the problems but its strategy was dictated by the theory of noncapitalist development in so far as it could be applied to West Indian conditions. Leninist principles in party organization had to be intensified; discipline, commitment and tight chairmanship would bridge the gap; socialist policies had to be introduced and pushed ahead.

The fourth was not so much revelation as confirmation. The People's Revolutionary Government had full control of state power but not over the economy. Its revolutionary rhetoric and ideals could not be matched by deeds; rather, it pursued reformist policies within the established capitalist and dependency framework, whatever protestations it made to the contrary (Jacobs & Jacobs, 1980, p. 81). The various party organs never tackled what were legitimately called 'the explosive issues': the role of the church and the question of land distribution and ownership. There were only two policies which could be labelled 'revolutionary' in the West Indian context: the non-negotiable alliances with Cuba and other socialist states and the concept of participatory democracy as part of the general rubric of 'People's Power'.

A remarkable frankness characterized discussions of these weaknesses, albeit behind closed doors. In September 1982 Bishop, in his famous speech to party members, the *Line of March for the Party*, admitted that the Grenada Revolution was not socialist but national–democratic and anti–imperialist. It was national because it arose from a struggle of national liberation against Gairyism and imperialism, and aimed to give or restore rights and freedoms to the majority of the people. But it was not socialist because of the 'low level of the productive forces' and the small numbers comprising the working class. Therefore the first stage was socialist orientation, to be followed in time by socialist construction. A policy of socialist orientation led by a bourgeois leadership was defended. It had 'a working–class ideology and therefore an understanding of what was required to ensure that the working class will eventually take power'. That condition was essential, as 'no bourgeois can build socialism'. Fortunately, the leadership was 'way, way ahead ideo-logically of our people in general and also of our national bourgeoisie' and had a 'much deeper class consciousness'. The working class could only achieve power through a party shaped by their understanding.

If [the Revolution] is led by the petty bourgeoisie, the only basis on which it can build socialism is if the petty bourgeois leadership in the course of class struggle is transformed into a revolutionary Marxist–Leninist Party that then guides and directs the process. Without that transformation, it would be impossible ... Only the working class can build socialism. It is only under the leadership of the working class, led by a Marxist–Leninist vanguard party that the process can be completed and we can go on to socialist construction. [Bishop, 1982b, p. 4.]

Until that time was reached, it was more correct to stress that the revolution represented 'the entire working people with the anti-Gairy working people initially being in the operational vanguard of that dictatorship'.

Dictatorship of the Party

From the outset, the NJM had no doubt that it dominated all levels of processes of government. All of the members of the Political Bureau were part of the PRG, six being in the seven-person Cabinet. When the Cabinet was increased to ten in early 1980, nine were party members. The 'ruling council' of the government was only fourteen at first. Other than the immediate leadership, most were from 'the petty bourgeoisie, the upper petty-bourgeoisie and the national bourgeoisie'. This was deliberate, recalled Bishop in the *Line of March*, 'so that imperialism won't get too excited and would say "well they have some nice fellas in that thing; everything alright", and as a result wouldn't think about sending in troops'. But following a party meeting ten days after the insurrection, nine members were drafted in. The PRG of twenty-three was then gazetted as People's Law no. 12 on 29 March.

Apart from the need to show a respectable face to the world and retain power, the alliance with the middle stratum was of fundamental importance. Ideologically, it clearly fitted the noncapitalist thesis but there were many pragmatic reasons. The bourgeoisie was by far the largest class formation in the country. Socialism could not be built unless this vacillating class were won over. Failure to do so would mean victory for imperialism. Fortunately, their class consciousness was very low and 'they don't fully know what we are really doing . . . they are still hoping that what we are building is not socialism but as one of them puts it, "socialist capitalism or capitalist socialism"—whatever that means'. But there were also few effective managers outside the private sector and the NJM had virtually no international contacts in the world of commerce. Conversely, it was argued in the *Line of March* that it was in the best interests of the bourgeoisie to co-operate as 'they have contradictions with imperialism'. Letters of credit and loans had become very difficult to get because of the world capitalist crisis so 'the capitalists are vexed with imperialism'. The revolution also promised efficiency, economic reconstruction and increased trade, all potentially profitable, as indeed they were. Their patriotism also had to be harnessed, although party members were warned that many were equally unpatriotic and had to be exposed as such. Whatever the reasons, however, it meant that the NJM neither exercised, nor claimed, total power. It was not in a monopoly position but was hegemonial. It had, in other words, total control.

Although three of this stratum were to leave the PRG over the next three years—one, ex-PRG Attorney-General Lloyd Noel, being detained—their inclusion was a feature until the end of the regime. Two, Lyden Ramdhanny and Norris Bain, were especially dominant. Both became ministers. But both steadfastly refused offers of party membership in later years due to disagreement about certain aspects of policy, especially preventive detention, and a refusal to accept the discipline of a tightly controlled elitist party. Time and time again, however, the leadership stressed the critical hegemonial aspect of the alliance. Although the point of view of the patriotic national bourgeoisie had to be heard, they were 'not part of our dictatorship'. Said Bishop,

We bring them in for what we want to bring them in for. They are not part of our dictatorship because when they try to hold public meetings and we don't want that, the masses shut down the meeting. When we want to hold Zonal Councils and we don't want them there, we keep them out. When they want to put out newspaper and we don't want that, we close it down. When they want freedom of expression to attack the government or to link up with the CIA, we crush them and jail them ... In fact, if the truth was known, they have been repressed by the dictatorship ... All rights and freedoms are now for the majority who are no longer oppressed or repressed by a tiny minority ... That is what dictatorship or rule means. And that is how every state operates. [Ibid., p. 6.]

The Party Structure

All party organizations based upon a Leninist model are founded upon the principle of democratic centralism, and the NJM was no exception. The principle rests upon the necessity for all decisions to be taken democratically, all participants having equal status and agreeing to abide by majority decisions. The centralist aspect is that all lower organisms of the party are bound by the decisions taken by the highest. In most Leninist parties, this level would be a Congress of elected representatives of the members but in Grenada it was the entire membership, at least in the early days. As party membership grew, so did the need for a Central Committee which would act as the 'highest organism' in between sessions of the Congress or party meetings.

The structure that evolved after the insurrection owed much to the Cuban experience, to which many NJM members were exposed while training or on vacation in that country. One characteristic was certainly shared: that of a dominant personality at the head. Bishop's personality was magnetic. The party knew full well of the public need, especially in Grenada, for such a person, and he fitted the bill beyond all expectations. His ability to articulate clearly the objectives of the revolution through his capacity for analysis and simple language was extraordinary. He above all others inspired support at home and abroad. Although a Marxist, he was never regarded as such by most Grenadians and he retained his massive popularity to the end. The party and Bishop were acutely aware of the perils of personality politics. Behind closed doors, he was a chairman who strove for consensus. Furthermore, the structure of the party was 'scientifically developed' to promote and contain this collective decision-making as well as to routinize business and to execute policy in a structured manner.

There was also the Soviet experience to draw upon. Several members undertook political education courses at the Party School of the Communist Party of the Soviet Union. But Strachan readily acknowledged the party's indebtedness to Cuba in particular.

We believe that our course of development will be more or less the same as the Cuban revolution. There may be one or two minor differences, but nothing dramatic ... If we have taken a decision to socially transform our society, and we adopt the correct approach according to the laws of historical development, we [will] more or less have to go through the same process, with slight differences because of the unevenness, since some countries are more developed than the next. But, basically, the approach will be the same, if we are moving to socialism. [Bishop, 1982a, pp. 15–16.]

The most important development in the party after the insurrection was the establishment of the Central Committee (CC) in September 1979. The Political Bureau became one of its subcommittees, albeit the most important. All senior CC members were also members of the Bureau, which henceforth became responsible for monitoring the execution of CC decisions and drawing up the CC agenda. It also, of course, continued to provide theoretical and ideological direction. It met weekly under Bishop's chairmanship (or under Coard or Whiteman if he was absent), whereas the CC was convened monthly. However, between October 1982 and September 1983 the CC met at quarterly intervals, although for up to five days at a time to discuss and review policy over a longer time scale. But, on Coard's insistence, it reverted thereafter to monthly meetings. Although originally elected by the membership, subsequent additions and deletions were on its own initiative. Its deliberations were rarely divulged to the membership and, to that extent, it was unaccountable.

Other CC sub-committees were created during 1981 and 1982; the Discipline Committee, the Economic Committee, the Workers' Committee, the International Department and the Propaganda Department. There were occasional joint meetings, for instance, between the Political Bureau and the

Economic Committee. When these latter two bodies met as one they were known as the Political and Economic Committee. *Ad hoc* working groups, for example the Investment Committee, were created when required, the whole adding up to a bewildering bureaucracy where overlapping of responsibilities was more the norm than the exception. One example was the Workers' Committee. In practice, its work was limited to the affairs of urban workers, but as most of its members were active in trade unions representing this particular segment of the working class, 'the distinction became very blurred' (interview with Fitzroy Bain, June 1983). The Organizing Committee also became a CC sub-committee, its duties redrafted to oversee party organization. To aid it, a Party Secretariat was established in April 1981 but the premises and facilities were poor. As regards security and defence, a top secret committee was instituted in late 1981, replacing informal arrangements which had existed from just before the insurrection. The Security and Defence Committee's membership was never publicized, nor its deliberations made known. All records were carefully monitored but destroyed during the invasion because of their sensitivity. The Committee met fortnightly under Bishop's chairmanship, and included Lt.-Col. Ewart Layne, Chief-of-Staff Einstein Louison (or his active replacement during his training periods in Cuba and the Soviet Union) and the Chief of Counter-Intelligence, Major Keith Roberts (interview with Basil Gahagan, June 1984). General Hudson Austin, one-time prison warder, was also a member, besides being Minister both of Defence and of Construction in the Cabinet. Party control of the army was absolute and reinforced by an unwritten rule that all PRA officers had to be party members and, where possible, to participate in the committee structure. Bishop, as Comrade Political Leader, was Commander-in-Chief.

Stresses and Strains

By 1981, falling business confidence had become a problem. While world recession and falls in the export prices of Grenada's commodities were partly to blame, there was a widespread conviction by the private sector that it was under siege. There was also deep dissatisfaction at the lack of constitutional restoration, let alone advance. This was shared by the wider population. Bishop was well aware of it and quashed suggestions from the Political Bureau during 1981 and 1982 for accelerated socialization and communalization of the economy. He was particularly scathing about Coard's plan to nationalize nearly all businesses: it was 'totally inappropriate' and 'in variance to Grenada's circumstances' (interview with Bobby Clarke , March 1984).

Attention became centred upon the party structure and operation to discover reasons for the yawning gap between revolutionary intent and policy, and that of falling support. The fault was traced to poor leadership and low commitment by CC members. In April 1981, the Central Committee resolved to apply 'Leninist measures'. This imposing appelation was, however, pretentious since they only amounted to the minimum of administrative support normally expected of any committee structure. Recording secretaries were to be appointed to every committee but this was not made fully effective for over a year. Record keeping was poor; even the minutes of the CC and the Political Bureau were intermittent until mid-1982. Rarely were agendas circulated beforehand, let alone supporting papers, and if minutes were taken, their quality often left much to be desired. But these reforms, the CC insisted, had to be accompanied by 'self-criticism' as an 'essential ingredient in the class struggle' (Central Committee meeting, 15–16 April 1981). Leadership had to be improved but Bishop was not personally criticized; that was to come later.

Workloads gradually increased in time with bureaucratic demands and the accelerating number of development and other projects. Mid-1981 saw the hospitalization of some activists due to exhaustion. The CC responded by drafting 'schedules of rest' and a resolve to review the situation. This was done over some thirty hours during December 1981 and depressing results were reported. Communications between party levels had declined, especially to and from the branches. Further reviews in April and June 1982 confirmed the trend and the CC was forced to admit that its committees were indeed too bureaucratic and 'giving no guidance' to the masses. 'Control mechanisms', it noted, 'are not working' (Minutes of Extraordinary Meeting of The Central Committee of the NJM, 12–15 October 1982). And as for policy, 'the CC was not . . . seeking to tackle the most explosive issues of the Church and the Land'. It was decided to identify needs and to prioritize action. As a preliminary, the present character and stage of the revolution was analysed and it was followed by a close examination of the functioning of the party and the scope for improvement and development. The deliberations were summarized in the *Line of March*. No mention of the tensions within the CC was made, but considerable emphasis was put on the class alliance to reassure the zealous that revolutionary and socialist policies would eventually come and to chastize those who regarded the bourgeoisie with contempt. 'For as long as the alliance is there', insisted Bishop, 'it calls for a certain kind of political maturity at the level of our behaviour in dealing with those with whom we are building an alliance' (Bishop, 1982b, p. 6). To reinforce the point, it was stated that it was the task of members to ensure the leading role of the working class backed up by *some form* of the dictatorship of the proletariat. Bishop justified the emphasis: 'I said "some form" . . . because obviously at this stage we cannot have the dictatorship of the proletariat or the working class, but the form we have at this first stage is the dictatorship of the working people', which crossed class lines.

Five tasks were prioritized. The first was the need for socialism classes, 'sinking the ideas of Marxism–Leninism among the working people'. Only this would preserve and develop the revolution, given the scale of inherited values and ideas. Second was the need to organize and mobilize the working class through trade unions, mass organizations and the organs of participatory democracy. Third came the strengthening of the Leninist character of the party by bringing in 'the best elements of the working people and in particular the working class'. The penultimate was to build the economy on socialist lines together with the deepening of links with the socialist world, especially the Soviet Union, 'the land of Lenin'. Last was the need to strengthen the Militia and, within it, the party. There had been criticism that many 'non-party comrades' were leading the Militia: this had to be rectified. Strict observance of these priorities was called for. The reason was disarmingly clear. 'Because, comrades, as you know, another historic weakness of ours has been to set priorities one day and then the very next day to break the priorities that we have set; so we really need this time to take a very strong and firm position on this question.'

This mere hint of organizational and procedural difficulty was a clear understatement. The long heart-searching discussions preceding the speech had failed to impress the critics within the Central Committee. Matters came to a head barely a month later, when, in mid-October 1982, Coard announced his resignation from the CC. He recognized both his and the CC's failings and the growing discordance between theory and practice and between revolutionary socialism and reformism. He had decided upon this 'non-negotiable' course, he maintained, at the review meeting the previous April, as he was 'the only hatchetman and critique'. 'Everybody', he sighed, 'was depending upon him for everything especially in the area of the economy'. He despaired at the poor conduct of meetings and the 'low level of political awareness' of many of its members. More importantly, he was highly critical of the NJM's ideological direction and policies in the country at large. The arguments and struggles were 'emotional conflict situations' that 'sapped his energies' (Extraordinary Meeting of the Central Committee, NJM, 14–16 September 1983, pp. 43–4). But he made clear to CC members that he wanted them to realize that his dynamism led many to take a back seat: 'this stunted their political development'.

This was no exaggeration. The smallness of the Committee—membership never exceeded eighteen and was normally fourteen—and the poor educational standard of some, made dominance by powerful personalities, such as his own and Bishop's, inevitable. They had, moreover, sharply contrasting management styles. Whereas Bishop was essentially pragmatic in his approach to policy formulation and inclined to make use of *ad hoc* structures and discussions, Coard was far more authoritarian in nature, preferring decision-making in a highly structured environment. They largely complemented each other; while they certainly competed one against the other, it was largely beneficial. But Bishop saw him as a potential rival and Coard knew it. As Chairman of the Organizing Committee, he complained of the ineffectiveness of its parent, the Central Committee. It was failing in its duty to guide members' work and progress and to pass work to other committees. He was reluctant, he said, to take 'corrective action' or 'it would result in personality clashes with the Chairman of the Central Committee'. All this, of course, was highly confidential and kept from the public. Later, once it became known, it was seized upon as a clear indication that Coard, known to be a superb tactician and highly ambitious, was engaged in a disingenuous power struggle with Bishop. According to this view, his resignation was to enable him slowly and quietly to gather supporters around himself and his views through the unofficial OREL group. He did not want to be associated with the sharpening contradictions between intent and practice; he would be able to re-join the Committee by acclamation as a political saviour, bringing firm Leninist leadership and revolutionary socialist policies to the revolution when collapse seemed very likely. The very habit and expectation of personalism helped promote this view. But not only is there no evidence to support such a conspiracy theory but also it would have required an extraordinary degree of prescience. Certainly none of the participants at the time appeared to perceive such motives.

They were, however, shocked into action. After a prolonged debate, in which Strachan and Phyllis Coard (who remained a member) supported Coard's arguments, the Central Committee concluded that the party 'stood at a crossroads'.

The first route would be the petty bourgeois route. This would only lead to temporary relief, but would surely lead to the deterioration of the Party into a social-democratic Party and hence the degeneration of the Revolution. This road would be an easy one to follow given the objectively based backwardness and petty bourgeois nature of the society. The second route is the Communist route—the route of Leninist standards and functioning, the road of democratic centralism, of selectivity, of criticism, of self-criticism and of collective leadership. [Extraordinary Meeting of the Central Committee, NJM, October 1982, p. 3.]

The CC clearly reaffirmed that the second was the Party's route. The first step was a purge of those members who, by a complex system of measurement, were declared unsuitable. Kendrick Radix scored the lowest and was obliged to resign from both the CC and the Political Bureau. He exhibited 'deep seated individualism' and a 'petty bourgeois opportunist attitude to criticism'. United Nations Ambassador Caldwell Taylor had to leave the Central Committee because of 'mysticism'; others, such as Unison Whiteman, were reprimanded or put on probation. Bishop scored highly, as did Phyllis Coard. There had been demotions before. One of the earliest was Lloyd Noel who was dismissed from the Political Bureau in January 1977 for lack of revolutionary zeal. He retained party membership but was subsequently dismissed as Attorney-General in 1980 for disagreeing with aspects of detention policy. He was then stripped of membership and detained in 1981 following participation in a newspaper, *The Grenadian Voice*, which challenged the PRG's press monopoly. Of the three others demoted before the October 1983 crisis, the most notable was Vincent Noel. His chairmanship of the Workers' Committee was considered to be poor and his arrogant response to criticism unacceptable. Temporary suspension was suffered by Major (later Lt. Col.) Layne and Major Cornwall in 1980 following very rough treatment that they had meted out to some detainees. Their party membership was also suspended and they had to tour all the PRA camps to say why. Their humiliating penance done, their organizing ability was once again recognized by their full participation in the party and the CC.

These momentous decisions had been preceded by a heart-searching analysis. Three 'bases of the crisis' were identified. The first was the 'Material Basis'. Grenada's society was 'backward and underdeveloped' with a 'large petty bourgeois influence', which reflected itself in the CC's practical work. It was complemented by the 'Political and Ideological Basis', manifested in the failure of CC members to study Marxism–Leninism, which was directly responsible for 'the non-Leninist manner of functioning, slackness, timidity and "ducking" from making principled positions'. Lastly, the 'Organizational Basis' went to the heart of it. It was seen in the 'poor functioning' of many party organizations, the 'inadequate functioning of many members and the lack of reporting and monitoring of decisions'.

Practical action soon followed. It was clear that overwork had reached 'epidemic proportions'. Personal workplans were to be introduced for all CC members, but this never transpired as nobody was apparently given direct responsibility to introduce them. In any case, CC members were not alone with the problem. It had been decided in late 1979 to introduce the membership structure of the Communist Party of the Soviet Union. Three categories were formally established: Full, Candidate and Applicant. In reality, there was also a fourth category: Potential Applicant. This was to ensure through a tight screening process that 'opportunists, careerists and self-seekers' who saw membership 'like a badge and passport to fame and prestige' were weeded out. Potential Applicants had to show four qualities: a 'genuinely revolutionary democratic outlook, engagement in disciplined political work in a particular area, honesty and non-opportunism and non-exploitation of labour if they owned private property'. They were invited to join classes where their commitment to the NJM and to the tenets of Marxism–Leninism was tested. Their elevation to Applicant was a major step as applicancy status was normally only for a year. If the probationer clearly showed acceptance of 'the science' and willingness to make sacrifices necessary to be a member, then promotion to 'Candidate' followed. There were four requirements for membership: regular collective ideological study organized by the party; consistent political work under the guidance of a party organ; consistent payment of dues (fixed at 5 per cent of gross salary) and an understanding and acceptance of party principles and willingness to accept party discipline. The hurdles to be passed for Full membership were commensurate with the status. There were six formidable criteria. Heading the list was ideological development, followed by correct leadership and a professional approach to political work expressive of Leninist organizational standards. Others were an ability to supervise and guide the work of junior comrades; removal of petty bourgeois faults and the development of a character worthy of emulation; the development of 'very good' relations with the masses and other party comrades; and the development of technical and professional skills needed to fulfil the tasks alloted by the party.

Despite the length of time and amount of effort involved, some members wanted a fifth category, that of Prospective Potential Applicant. But this was resisted. None the less, Bishop stressed in the *Line of March* that membership numbers should be kept low and the quality raised. The hurdles were necessary 'to ensure that when a certain issue causes class struggle to be seriously heightened, then chosen comrades would not cut and run.'

The truth is that it is not really a case of the party leadership laying down harsh conditions; it is real life and the demand of the struggle that make it necessary . . . and to ensure that comrades who are full or . . . candidate members are truly the finest representatives of the working class and the most selected in struggle, in commitment and in total commitment for the working class and their interests . . . We believe that it must become more and more difficult for comrades to become full members and candidate members and it must become more difficult for new comrades to remain as members and candidate members; and those who are

unwilling to live up to the demands of this membership will have to be moved . . .
Being a Communist, comrades, means becoming a different kind of person. [Bishop,
1982b, p. 8.]

In reality, it was committee rather than political work with the masses
which appeared the most important. But advancement was very difficult by
mid-1983 and even Applicants found that the year's probation was extended
for no reason. Between March and September, only five Candidates became
Full members, all senior PRA officers who had undergone advanced political
training in socialist countries. One Candidate recalled an average of nine
'rather pointless' meetings per week, all outside working hours; another
found that he had to choose between divorce and the party, but became
mentally ill in the process, perhaps fortuitously in the circumstances. The
number of women who successfully passed the tests was disproportionately
few.

The numbers were indeed small. By October 1983, those in the Full category totalled only seventy-two, including seven based overseas (confidential
membership file, supplied anonymously). There were ninety-four Candidates and approximately 180 Applicants, giving a total of some 350. Another
estimate totalled 500 but appeared to include Potential Applicants (Hart,
1984, p. xxiv). A year earlier, the numbers were eighty, eighty-three and 193
respectively (ibid., preface, p. 1): clearly some weeding out had taken place or
some Full or Candidate members had let their membership lapse. Although
strictly speaking no overseas branches were permitted, party members in
Havana and Moscow—diplomatic personnel, students and others on training
courses—met regularly and conducted business as if there were a branch in
each capital. Occasional meetings were also held by party members in Budapest on the same basis. By contrast, there was a large NJM Support Group in
London (which survived the revolution's collapse) with many expatriate
Grenadians participating, by no means all socialists. Other support was given
by the Caribbean Labour Solidarity group. There were similar support
groups in Toronto and New York although party members passing through
the United States would, when possible, meet in the Washington house of
Dessima Williams, PRG Ambassador to the OAS. The various left-wing West
Indian groups in New York occasionally offered support but they were often
regarded with some suspicion as being dominated by Trotskyists and anti-
Soviets. Regionally, the Workers' Party of Jamaica and the Working Peoples'
Alliance in Guyana were highly regarded and visiting members were invited
to their meetings.

After Coard's resignation, Louison attempted to establish himself as the
Central Committee's ideologue by chairing its Study Group. But he was

never really accepted as such; not only did study meetings continue under Coard's direction but Louison's organizational abilities were more highly regarded than his expertise in Marxist theory. It helped to lead him to resent Coard and eventually to disown him. Another result of the meeting was the establishment of the Discipline Committee to oversee members' work and recommend promotion. Under Strachan's chairmanship (he was also Minister of National Mobilization), a Code of Conduct and Discipline heavily influenced by the Cuban model was drawn up and approved by the Central Committee in December 1982. Procedural rules of all meetings were thereby tightened, personal workplans again drawn up (although completed for very few) and progress files established. A personal assistant was appointed for all CC members and an area of 'mass work or political work' assigned to each to supervise. All had to undergo a crash course in Marxist–Leninism in which works by J. V. Stalin enjoyed a prominent place. Non–CC party members were to be given more information, particularly as 'to the strategy and tactics of CC resolutions', as part of a 'conscious effort . . . to develop leadership outside of the CC'. Finally, it took note of Coard's criticism of the Political Bureau. Besides resolving to formulate agendas and record minutes, it was reorganized to permit it to fulfil its alloted role more forcefully and credibly.

Despite these corrections, embarrassments mounted as even relatively minor administrative decisions had to run the gauntlet of the committee structure. Civil servants, very apprehensive about possible adverse political consequences of initiatives, became passive. The Ambassador to Cuba, Leon 'Bogo' Cornwall, was faced with arriving students and others without notification, and at one point suffered an electricity and telephone cut-off when nobody in St. George's arranged payment of outstanding bills (correspondence from Cornwall to Layne and Austin). On some occasions, the deep-water pier was unoccupied while highly exasperated captains of cruise and cargo ships anchored off shore, their telexes unanswered. Plans for a Soviet-style House of Culture were lost for nearly a year and angry architects threatened legal action.

Neither was the party structure complete, according to the adopted Soviet-style model. Conspicuously absent was a party Congress, due to take place every five years. Although there were discussions as to the inaugural date, nothing was arranged. One major difficulty was the absence of a party constitution. A draft was begun in 1978 but was overtaken by the events of the following year. Nothing else was done until late 1982. It was planned to finalize the draft by the close of 1983 or early 1984, for adoption at a special meeting of members. It would then have had to be formally ratified by the Congress, which would also have approved nominations for the Central Committee. Besides 'fraternal delegations', delegates from party branches, mass organizations and the armed forces were to attend. Their major task, aside from the constitutional, was to have been the discussion of all major policy and the review of achievements. It was also planned that a five-year economic plan, to be drawn up with the aid of Czechoslovak experts, would be presented for discussion and approval (interview with George Louison, February 1984).

The Search for Orthodoxy

Despite tardiness in institution building, the party leadership was anxious to construct a superstructure as close as possible to that established as 'orthodox' by their Cuban and Soviet mentors. There is no evidence to suggest that advisers from these and countries of similar philosophy had pressurized NJM leaders; indeed, the opposite is true. A member of an East German technical assistance team privately opined that it was 'ludicrous' that 'what was suitable for a persecuted party in exile (i.e., the Bolsheviks in Switzerland before 1917) was equally applicable in an open society like Grenada's' (private interview, June 1982). The Soviet government refused to arrange a meeting between Bishop and President Andropov during what was Bishop's final visit to Moscow in April 1983, being more aware than the zealous Grenadians that such an apparent endorsement of the PRG would lead to a strong American reaction. But the NJM would have none of this: it had to show that it was a genuine pro-Soviet Marxist–Leninist party. Those working or studying in socialist countries were charged with this task, but there were many disappointments.

Coard's ex-colleague at the University of the West Indies, Richard Jacobs, was especially anxious to project such an image. A convinced communist and often intolerant of those who did not share his conviction, he helped to strengthen the Cuban alliance as Ambassador in Havana. But the task was harder when he was relocated as Ambassador in Moscow. Although his former racist tendencies died away on contact with the Russians, he complained bitterly in a series of reports to Bishop and Foreign Minister Whiteman at the low level of Soviet officials detailed to cover Grenada. The NJM was not always taken seriously as a Marxist–Leninist party—its membership of the Socialist International was suspect and unconvincingly explained away—and as an English-speaking country, Grenada was grouped with the United States and Canada by both the Soviet Communist Party's International Department and the Soviet Ministry of Foreign Affairs! Only 'strenuous and prolonged lobbying' eventually placed Grenada in the Latin American sections of both organizations.

Grenada is regarded as being on the path of socialist orientation. There is a general acceptance among Soviet authorities that we are at the national–democratic, anti-imperialist stage of capitalist orientation . . . in terms of their priorities, the countries of socialist orientation come right after the socialist community . . . The comrades in the International Section . . . operate on the basis that the NJM is a 'communist party' [but] one is not too sure of the authoritativeness of this statement . . . The core of the matter, however, is that they regard Grenada as a small distant country and they are only prepared to make commitments to the extent of their capacity to fulfill, and if necessary, defend their commitment [Letter, 'Relations with the CPSU' 1983, p. 3.]

Jacobs' advice to the PRG was twofold: to make the Moscow Embassy serve as the representative of all progressive groups except for those in Jamaica and Guyana in the English- and Dutch-speaking Caribbean.

Grenada's distance from the USSR, and its small size, means . . . we figure in a very minute way in the USSR's global relationships. For Grenada to assume a position of increasingly greater importance, we have to be seen as influencing at least regional events . . . and be the sponsor of revolutionary activity and progressive developments in this region at least. At the same time we have to develop and maintain normal state to state relations with our neighbours and concretely operationalize our good-neighbourlyness policy [Letter, 'Grenada's Relations with the USSR', 1983, p. 5.]

Jacobs also warned of Soviet distrust of self-proclaimed Communist parties which, after enjoying Soviet support, became 'agents of imperialism' such as in Egypt and Somalia. The NJM, he said, had to show stability and predict-ability of behaviour in terms of policy and positions, illustrate a clear and consistent socialist orientation and be clearly willing to develop relations. He himself took every opportunity to remind his hosts of Grenada's consistency in supporting the Soviet position on Afghanistan and all other international issues. He stressed the need for the party Congress to which a high-level Soviet delegation would be invited, thus endorsing the NJM's position. Sadly, however, he reported on a meeting with Cuban Vice-President Carlos Rodriguez in Moscow: it had taken fifteen long years for close Cuban–Soviet relations to develop. 'I would say', he wrote, 'that I have been converted to the concept of TIME.' For the foreseeable future, he had 'reluctantly' to accept Grenada's position as on the level of Kampuchea and Mozambique, and other exiled Third World Marxist groups domiciled in Moscow.

The general sense of anxiety to fit the orthodox mould at home and abroad ultimately became a witch-hunt, searching for those responsible for the painfully slow progress towards noncapitalism. Reasons for deepening economic and financial crises had to found and extra courage drummed up to withstand the unrelenting and stifling opposition of the United States. The sincerity of the NJM comrades was not in doubt; what was in doubt was their ability to operationalize the ideological road that they had shaped for themselves. Initial enthusiasm had not been hard to encourage. The difficulty lay in maintaining the momentum as the problems, both practical and theoretical, of 'People's Power' were revealed.

People's Power

Part and parcel of the party structure were the various manifestations of what was collectively termed 'People's Power'. Its institutions owed much to the original ideas of the Movement for the Assemblies of the People (MAP). The broad philosophy was two-fold. In the first place it was rooted to MAP idealism. The objective was to construct a political and constitutional system suitable for Grenadian conditions which would develop national identity, patriotism and pride. The Westminster system bequeathed by colonialism served only to encourage adversorial divisions and disunity, pit class against class and, more importantly, worker against worker. The *Manifesto* was clear: 'it fails to involve the people except for a few seconds once in every five years when they make an 'X' on a ballot paper' (New Jewel Movement, 1973, p. 9). Further, the Westminster system constituted a Tweedledum and Tweedledee situation with 'two parties which were two sides of the same coin' simply replacing each other (Searle, 1979, p. 174). Bishop's apparent promises of early elections were forgotten, if indeed any were seriously made. All demands by external critics who insisted on them for legitimacy's sake were firmly rebuffed. But constant denial served only to reinforce accusations of dictatorial intent. There could, however, be no retreat as it assumed the proportions of a 'principled position'. Clearly, the world would have to wait until the PRG was ready. In any case, said one PRG minister, 'the masses have far more important things to do, like providing enough food and shelter for everyone to be distracted and divided by elections' (George Louison, quoted in the *Daily Gleaner*, 28 May 1981). Bishop went further.

We want to say to Reagan here and now that the kind of democracy that he speaks of and the kind of democracy that he practises—we in Grenada are not in the least interested in that kind of democracy. A democracy that fires 10 million workers . . . which cuts social benefits to the poorest people . . . which closes down hospitals and schools . . . which removes housing subsidies (Bishop, 1982a, pp. 25–26).

The other rationale was deeper. The traditional system conditioned the people to accept dependence, which was thereby disguised by a cloak of constitutional legitimacy. The impress of history, the young radicals argued, had created a belief that there was no alternative framework. Therefore, the umbilical cord with the past had to be broken by involving the masses individually and collectively with the decision-making process and in the development of their country. It became abundantly clear as PRG rule progressed that People's Power was, in reality, to mobilize support for the revolution. But this was inevitable: a democratic-centralist structure could not exist if genuine decision-making was undertaken outside the party, or at least away from the Central Committee.

There were four sets of institutions: the mass organizations (including the Militia), the village-based structure of participatory democracy, industrial democracy and a new people's constitution. None were complete by the time of the invasion—indeed, work on the constitution had barely begun.

The Mass Organizations

The Leninist model clearly dictates the need to link the party and the masses primarily through mass organizations. They became the principal means of popular mobilization and political education in Grenada, and reviews of their development and well-being were accorded high priority. All bar the trade unions were regarded as part of the party, being effectively controlled by Central Committee members.

That with the highest profile related to youth. Founder member George Louison had played a cardinal role in its mobilization. Formerly co-ordinator of the youth work of the Caribbean Council of Churches in Grenada, he had fashioned the Grenada Assembly of Youth (GAY) in January 1971 out of the National Youth Council, once patronized by Gairy. Catering in the main for the unskilled and poorly educated, GAY was complemented by the establishment of a Union of Secondary Students (USS). This emerged from the series of strikes by students in 1970, protesting at attempts by Gairy to extend state control to certain church schools to enable him to dismiss teachers unsympathetic to his views. Lyden Ramdhanny, scion of a well-established East Indian merchant family, was the student leader. He was helped considerably by Unison Whiteman, then a teacher at the main Catholic college. The presidency of GAY passed to Basil Gahagan in 1974. He was instrumental in merging it with another, smaller group, the National Youth Organization, which had emerged during the independence crisis. Its name was adopted and, like GAY, was closely allied to the party, underscoring the close identification of youth with the revolution. This was reinforced by the murder by 'police aides' of a NYO member, Alastair Strachan, during a demonstration in June

1977. Calls to emulate his 'sacrifice' became common in later mobilization campaigns. A formal institutional link with the party was established by the formation of the NJM Youth Committee in June 1978. However, this only really existed on paper as its members were those of the NYO executive. Some of the executives of the USS and, to a lesser extent, of the Catholic Youth Congress, were also members of the executive, although these bodies were never part of the party machinery. After the insurrection, the USS gradually became defunct, being replaced by, to all intents and purposes, the National Students' Council. This was much closer to the party (interview with Lyden Ramdhanny, June 1984).

The work of the NYO prior to March 1979 was important in that significant sections of youth were mobilized. Members helped organize transport and supply stewards for rallies; sporting competitions in particular helped to keep the party's name in the forefront. Its newspaper *FIGHT!* was widely read. After the insurrection, sporting and cultural activities were broadened and, after a more formalized structure was introduced in early 1980, became more closely allied to political work. Its Employment Committee attempted to broaden work opportunities but with limited success: many unemployed youths preferred the armed forces rather than productive work. Strenuous attempts were made to encourage agricultural skills but a lack of motivation for farming meant slow progress. When in February 1980 a group of Rastafarians led by a former supporter of the revolution perceived the new regime as representing freedom to seize land and grow marijuana for export, the NYO was quick to denounce their anti-social behaviour as 'ultra-leftism' and supported their indefinite detention.

By late 1981, membership had reached some 9,000 in about 100 branches, but not many were active. A massive membership drive, aimed at a target of 15,000 by March 1982, and thence by stages to 30,000, was launched but completely failed. By late 1982, it had dropped by 35 per cent to 6,000, and to below 4,000 in 1983 (interview with Basil Gahagan, June 1984). The reasons for failure were familiar: over-rapid expansion without adequate leadership, poor administration and a low level of political education and direction. A request was therefore made to the Cuban Union of Young Communists (UYC) for assistance in political mobilization and training, and in propaganda work. Many NYO members sent to the UYC school had been 'poorly selected' with 'no thought in Marxist–Leninist trend'. Additionally, the NYO International Relations Department was reorganized to project the organization as the leading progressive force in the region, and to propagandize more effectively. Further aid was granted by the Socialist Union of Youth in Czechoslovakia in mid-1982, after a full acknowledgement was given of the Soviet Union 'as the bulwark for peace in the world' and recognition given to the need 'to combat anti-sovietism on a reactionary policy of imperialism' (National Youth, Organization, June 1982). Aid was also sought from the Soviet youth organization, Komsomol.

A further outburst of despair was apparent in a party report assessing the feasibility of introducing the Cuban model of a National Service and Labour Army to complement the NYO. For production and defence respectively, they were compulsory for all Cuban youth not in the armed forces. They were judged very difficult to achieve in Grenada, whose society 'is rebellious to any form of strict discipline and organization' and 'has no military tradition'. Worse, Grenadians had a 'visa mentality', insisting on freedom to travel. To make compulsory service work, this would have to be severely controlled (Central Committee Report, Progress Report of Commission No. 5, 1982, p. 3). Therefore, only a Labour Army was recommended in the first instance, on a voluntary basis, until 'skilful propaganda' prepared the masses and youth 'for further implementation'.

The other major mass movement was the National Women's Organization (NWO). But whereas the NYO had a mass membership from the start with minimal entry qualifications, the NWO adopted a restricted nomination system for prospective members when it was formed in December 1977 under Phyllis Coard's leadership. It only became a mass organization in December 1980 when, at its First General Meeting, it made effective a decision in favour of mass membership taken the previous May (National Women's Organization, February 1983, pp. 4–5).

The NWO was a clear recognition of the important role of women in politics and the support of many for the NJM. Its pre-insurrection duties were wideranging: secretly distributing party literature, undertaking household surveys to find the most deserving cases for help, and lessons in child health and upbringing, were but a few. By the insurrection, there were six groups comprising 120 women, all applicants suspected of pro-Gairy sympathies being firmly excluded. The transition to mass membership soon saw 1,500 enrolled in 47 groups and, after an intensive recruitment campaign, it peaked at 6,500 in 155 groups at the close of 1982 (Hart, 1984, p. xv, claims 7,000 members in 170 local branches). An activist's claim of 12,000 (Payne, Sutton & Thorndike, 1984, p. 30) was wishful thinking, particularly as there were probably less than a thousand who were in any way active at the time of the revolution's collapse. After the insurrection, the NWO broadened its work, both practical—for example, in sewing, nutrition, childcare and first-aid—and political. Sport and cultural events were organized and involvement in community development and defence encouraged. It distributed nearly

4,000 kilos per month of free dried milk, as well as cooking oil, to the most needy and helped provide much-needed material and other support for rural primary schools (National Women's Organization, November 1981). The enormous work involved, however, was to take its toll.

Both organizations were active in gathering support for voluntary projects, especially road repair, community centre construction and house rebuilding. The latter utilized materials supplied by the National House Repair Programme. Most Sundays, up to 85 per cent of villages saw some degree of such work which was clearly popular and well organized. The peak of this activity appeared to be late 1982 and it declined thereafter. One activity, however, retained its popularity to the end, that of the national literacy programme under the auspices of the much praised Centre for Popular Education (CPE). The NWO was successful in persuading women to participate, as well as their menfolk on occasion. The NYO played a similar role, persuading young adults with poor functional literacy to take advantage of the 'second chance'. The CPE workbooks received much acclaim from educationalists overseas and were held up as an example of modern literacy methods. They were naturally used for mobilization purposes as well through carefully selected words, examples and concepts, and were mostly printed in Cuba. For these reasons, the CPE was one of the first programmes to be abandoned after the invasion.

Of the other mass organizations, the National Students' Council found great difficulty in operating and developing because of the NYO. Gradually, an unofficial division of labour emerged: the NYO would, as before, concentrate on mobilization and political work, sports and music events being important, while the Council became more of a consultative body, engaging in occasional discussions with head teachers and education ministry officials. The Productive Farmers' Union met a similar fate but for different reasons. It was useful in distributing new seeds and establishing productivity groups (which, however, were very temporary in nature), but attempts at political education wilted in the face of firm peasant resistance. The least successful mass organization was the Young Pioneers. Parents preferred traditional church-based associations, and the Scouts and Guides organizations, for their children. In reality, the only participants were children of NJM members and their uniforms, the ubiquitous red neck-tie modelled on the Soviet organization, were seen only on rare occasions.

Of a different character was the Militia. It was broadly successful in organizing popular participation in national defence and imparted the sense of crisis of a nation under siege. In doing so, it undoubtedly helped to bolster support for the PRG. The Militia was seen as essential and named the second of 'three pillars of the revolution', the first being People's Power generally, and economic reconstruction the third. At an international solidarity rally, Coard made clear its central role.

A Revolution which has the support of the people but which cannot defend itself very soon would be no revolution at all . . . Having the people but not having the material means for the people to defend themselves is a lesson we have to learn from [Allende's] Chile, Jamaica and other countries. But having the material means and not having the people are what Pinochet and Duvalier are all about. Therefore comrades, the people and the material means to defend the people are indispensable and interconnected in the processes of the Revolution. That is why the question of arming of all our people, the involvement of all our people in the People's Militia, is of such fundamental importance [Coard, in People's Revolutionary Government, 1982b, pp. 27–8.]

Military training took place at local platoon level on Wednesday afternoons but, in spite of official pressure, attendance was persistently erratic. Young people of school age were discouraged by parents, teachers and church alike, but it appealed to some of the young unemployed. Manoeuvres were held annually, lasting three days, amidst great publicity, giving the impression of a nation under arms. While this was untrue, of all the countries in the region bar Cuba, by 1983 Grenada had the highest proportion of its population able to use firearms. Over a four-year period (1980–3), an estimated 3,500 received instruction. But for many, it was of a very superficial nature. None the less, this vigilance against what Strachan at the same rally called the 'provocation of imperialism' reached a peak in March 1983 when American naval exercises very close to Grenada led to a full alert. Strachan felt fully justified in insisting that:

This voluntary people's militia, where our people are picking up guns every week to defend the benefits brought to them by people's revolutionary democracy shows their ultimate commitment to our process. For this same process, comrades such as we are . . . here in Grenada, is the greatest threat to the bogus, artificial and hypocritical lie of democracy that imperialism suspends over the world to cover up the revulsion and shame of its blood-soaked crimes. [S. Strachan, in ibid., 1982, p. 92.]

But organization was lacking, despite officer-training sessions by Cuban civil defence experts. Constant sentry duty was of little interest and, over time, enthusiasm had ebbed. When the test eventually came, militia resistance was virtually non-existent although a different story might have been told if Bishop had been alive at the time of the invasion.

Popular Participation

Popular participation in the revolution was, to the outside world, most apparent through the concept of participatory democracy. It was based upon the seven Parish Councils (including Carriacou). Before March 1979, there were NJM branches in every parish. After the insurrection, the PRG revived the long-defunct councils and instructed the branches to work closely with them. At first, participation was restricted to members and known sympathizers but soon they were open to all. Each Council was chaired by a Central Committee member or nominee. Parish Council meetings enabled local people to discuss policy with, and question, the PRG leadership, civil servants and heads of state enterprises and so permitted their views to be known on various issues. Such was their popularity that by late 1980, it was decided to organize Zonal Councils at village level. Each Zonal Council reported to its Parish Council, which channelled opinions to the national level via the NJM party branch. In practice, due to the relatively small numbers involved in the organization of the structure, the same people often filled leadership posts at zonal, parish and party branch levels. Parish Councils had residual work allocated to them and were to be discussion forums for workers and women. But this wastefully duplicated the work of local trade union and NWO branches and it never worked in practice. Thirty-six Zonal Councils eventually emerged but like the Parish Councils none had any legal standing.

Co-ordination with the mass organizations, and the Militia and trade union branches, was through Village Coordinating Bureaus (VCBs). In time, these, rather than the Parish Councils, became through custom the main link with the party and therefore the government. Occasionally, delegates from Parish and Zonal Councils, VCBs and the mass organizations came together in a National Conference of Delegates. Called to debate a particular issue, such as that of the budget and the PRG's annual financial assessment of all the sectors and activities that made up the national economy, a conference was normally only for one day since all the prior discussions on the draft was supposed to have taken place. To the *Free West Indian*, such 'ongoing participation by the people' ensured a deep grasp of what 'imperialism is in concrete terms'. Mobilization on that scale, it proclaimed confidently, was designed to prepare the masses 'for the broad objectives of building socialism' (*Free West Indian*, 13 March 1981). As a contemporary commentary enthusiastically put it,

Today in Grenada, Parliament has moved out of town into the communities. Government has escaped ... and spread into community centres, school buildings, street corners, marketplaces, factories, farms and workplaces around the country. Political power has been taken out of the hands of a few privileged people and turned over to thousands of men, women and youth ... in every nook and cranny of Grenada, Carriacou and Petit Martinique. [People's Revolutionary Government, 1981a, p. 30.]

In reality, the situation was nothing of the kind. The fulcrum of power clearly and unambiguously lay with the Central Committee. Without doubt, suggestions could be made and passed up the chain by the councils and local branches of the mass organizations, but from early 1981 there was less opportunity to question ministers and other members of the political elite. Once the NJM Central Committee and the PRG had drawn up proposals, the council's duty was to explain, not discuss. It was clear that party policy was at best only marginally influenced by these institutions whose primary purpose was to mobilize support for local and national development projects and for the government generally, to provide political education at village level, disseminate information and generally defend the revolution. There could have been no alternative in the democratic–centralist system. Not surprisingly, public participation fell away, especially in the north and east, and in Carriacou. Coard recognized the problem and successfully urged the Central Committee in September 1983, after he had rejoined it, to revise and reform the structure to reverse the decline in popular grassroots support. But it proved to be too late.

Industrial Democracy

Understandably, the development of this aspect of People's Power was hampered by the lack of industry or commercial establishments of any size. The general philosophy was none the less clear. In Coard's words, the PRG was 'a worker's government which has exactly the same wishes and goals as all militant and progressive trade unionists' (Coard, quoted in People's Revolutionary Government, 1982d, p. 30). Therefore, all anti-worker legislation was repealed and the Trade Unions [Recognition] Act proclaimed in May 1979 as People's Law No. 29 of that year. Its principal architect was Vincent Noel, whose struggle to force Barclays Bank to recognize the Bank and General Workers Union in February 1979 had helped set the scene for the insurrection. The critical provision was section 3 (1). It laid down that if a union claimed that a majority of workers in a bargaining unit wanted it as their bargaining agent, the Ministry of Labour was obliged to organize a poll. If positive, and subject to appeal, the decision of the poll was final as far as the employer was concerned (Smith, 1979, p. 39). Not surprisingly, trade union membership rose from 30 to 80 per cent of the workforce by October 1979. A particular success was the Agriculture and General Workers Union led by Fitzroy Bain. This was reinforced by a clear commitment to workers' rights, particularly in the private sector. Alleged unfair dismissal always struck sympathetic government cords but action was never taken to depress general business confidence unduly. The issue of the W. E. Julien Coca-Cola bottling plant was a case in point. The company dismissed two workers but they successfully argued for reinstatement before the Labour Commissioner with the aid of the Commercial and Industrial Workers' Union. The reply was a lockout but the workers responded by taking over the plant and resuming production. Under government instruction the police did nothing. Rather, the government opened an account to which subsequent profits were paid and this was handed over to the owner, when after nearly two years, he agreed to reinstate the workers. The principle was clear: unless employers respected workers' rights, their rights would not be protected by the state (Hart, 1984, p. xviii). A later lockout, by the Bata shoe company, resulted in a clear announcement that if operations did not recommence by a stated date, the company would be regarded as having abandoned its business in Grenada and appropriate action would be taken. The message was clear and the union claim (for a profit-sharing agreement) was granted.

By 1981 this pro-worker philosophy was augmented by proposals for institutionalized Industrial Democracy. Following the Cuban example, Production Committees with joint management and union representation were to be established in every workplace. Responsible for drafting, discussing and operationalizing work plans and monitoring management to prevent 'abuse of power', they were to be paralleled by Disciplinary, Education and Emulation Committees. The last, Coard said, would set production and productivity targets, 'devize and organize brotherly and sisterly competition' and reward the efforts of exemplary workers (People's Revolutionary Government, 1982d, p. 30). Although very few were in any form of operation by October 1983, the framework was there. Other than motivation, the major practical difficulty was the small size of many workplaces. Often family operated, these were not amenable to such organization. Discussions had taken place within the Ministry of National Mobilization on the possibility of establishing networks of committees over workplaces involved in similar work, but were temporarily shelved. Where some semblance to the plan existed—largely in government departments and the public sector—the work was mostly confined to work plans (which proved useful for managers who could then legitimately criticize those who did not fulfil what had been agreed) and to compulsory education periods where Marxist and progressive texts and ideas would be studied and discussed. There was, predictably, resistance to such political education and more so when it became compulsory for civil servants in mid-1983. Within a few weeks, an angry Strachan was forced to issue a stern warning that those who disregarded it risked dismissal (*Caribbean Insight*, September 1983, p. 6). Others organized by trade unions were equally unpopular. 'The emphasis on the ideological development of the workers has not shown any improvement,' complained one CC member, and 'a lot of people fall asleep'.

Despite the co-operation of some trade unions in this and other spheres, such as volunteering labour to work with NYO and NWO activists on community development projects, none considered themselves to be allied to the party. Although the leaders of five of the eight unions were party members, they had as a common aim the vigorous pursuit of union interests. None was so active as the Public Workers' Union (PWU), led by Basil Harford from early 1981. He, however, was not in the NJM. The PWU reacted strongly not only to the poor pay levels relative to the private sector (up to 125 per cent) (Public Workers' Union, 1981) but also to the number of expatriate Grenadians recruited by the PRG, and non-nationals ('internationalist workers'), who were placed in senior levels with tax-free salaries. Although politically wholly acceptable to the government, the professional standards of some were questioned by the union. But this issue was non-negotiable; that, however, of pay was. Negotiations for improvements began in December 1980, based upon recommendations by the Salaries Commission which Gairy had been forced to establish in the 1973 independence crisis, the year of the last increase. Coard, as Minister of Finance, countered the claim of 57.5 per cent over two years by insisting that in 'the revolutionary situation, it was the joint task of government, workers and unions' to reach an equitable solution (People's Revolutionary Government, 1980, p. 4). He warned of redundancies which could be avoided only if the unions helped to find the money. More would mean 'the re-distribution of revenue from the farmers and agro-industries'. The PWU, with the Grenada Union of Teachers and the Technical and Allied Workers' Union, declared that they were 'not hostile to the government' and 'not pursuing a political act', although they realized 'the political implications'. The impasse led to industrial action in March 1981. Coard reacted angrily. 'I am astonished', he declared, 'at the sheer selfishness and avarice [of] 'privileged civil servants and state employees in comfortable jobs.' (Free West Indian, 8 March 1981). This event also highlighted the problem of party-union relations. The TAWU President, James Wardally, was a party member of long standing. He was summoned to the Disciplinary Committee, where he was told by Strachan to choose 'between higher and lower priorities', who made it clear which was the superior. Wardally insisted, as did other trade unionists afterwards, that the party and the union were different and separate and that any attempt to redress workers' just demands by 'simply putting a party man in their midst' was doomed to failure. His loyalty was to those who elected him but his personal loyalty to the NJM remained firm (interview with James Wardally, December 1984). That he was subsequently nominated as future Ambassador to the GDR despite leading other strikes against state-owned enterprises indicated that the argument was accepted, however reluctantly.

The crisis was certainly serious as the government carried out its threat of dismissals. Eventually a settlement was reached and most of the dismissals rescinded. But it left a climate of mistrust and disharmony between the party and civil servants in particular which did little to encourage administrative efficiency and enthusiasm.

The Constitution

The persistent refusal of the PRG to conduct elections was attributed to the need for a new constitution to provide a revolutionary framework for them. It was not until June 1983 that a five-person Constitutional Commission was appointed to draft the formal institutionalization of the revolution. It was charged, amongst other things, to ensure

The widest possible participation by the people in the Country's decision-making process and the day-by-day administration of affairs of the State and of matters affecting their work and residential communities. The concept of popular democracy should be reflected in the provisions of the Constitution whereby the structures therein contained shall be designed to facilitate continuous popular involvement. Something more meaningful is required than the illusions of popular control by the right merely to enter a polling booth once or twice every four or five years. [*Free West Indian*, 18 June 1983.]

The Commissioners had two years, and once adopted by referendum, elections were to be organized although no date was set. In their few meetings (the first Public Hearing was scheduled for October 25, the day of the invasion), they analysed constitutions of a variety of countries, including that of the state of California (interview with Richard Hart, December 1983). It may be surmised that the ideal was a one-party state wherein all strata would be represented, including the elites, which would fulfil three conditions: popular democratic endorsement and participation, the vanguard nature of the New Jewel Movement and democratic centralism. Whether it would have been achieved in the West Indian environment is a question that can now never be answered.

7 Populism and Marxism: Analysis of Achievement

The People's Revolutionary Government's struggle against dependency underpinned and informed its policies of economic development, education and social advance.

Grenada's economic fate, and therefore ultimately of its people, was perceived to be in the hands of rich and powerful capitalist states which effectively controlled the prices of Grenada's imports and agricultural exports. The relationship accounted for Grenada's underdevelopment and amounted to imperialist exploitation. Bishop made it very clear that:

We contend, comrades, that the real problem is not the question of smallness *per se*, but [that] of imperialism. The real problem that small countries like ours face is that on a day-by-day basis we come up against an international system that is organized and geared towards ensuring the continuing exploitation, domination and rape of our economies, our countries and our peoples. That, to us, is the fundamental problem. [Bishop, 1982c, p. 190.]

There were four identifiable manifestations of dependency, and policies to tackle them had been gradually shaped since 1973. The first was psychological dependency. The persistence of deep-rooted prejudices and values nurtured by the long exposure to colonialism clearly conditioned the people to think alternative political systems and modes of thought were to be distrusted. Through the institutions of People's Power, education and the techniques of mass mobilization, Grenadians would no longer accept dependency as inevitable and would forge their own political destiny. The second, directed dependency, represented the actions of powerful capitalist states, whether done consciously or not, to direct and make effective their control over the levers of Grenada's fragile economy. This was to be challenged by a foreign policy stressing non-alignment, independence and an insistence upon Grenada's sovereign right to deal with whomsoever it pleased. It was recognized that it was impossible to control export prices and the cost of imported manufactures, fertilizers and food. Also, the scope for redirecting the economy away from export crop production was limited given the clear constraints of small size and population. But an independent foreign policy, the PRG confidently believed, would help diversify sources of imports and aid and locate new markets.

Only within this general context of support for a 'new international economic order' could the effects of the third and most important manifestation, that of structural dependency, be alleviated. Increased food production, industrial development and diversification of exports and infrastructural investment were essential. Easier to implement were policies directed at the reform of functional dependency. Greatly increased welfare expenditure was planned in education, health, housing and social services to expurgate the legacy of deprivation suffered by the masses.

It was argued that these policy thrusts were in accordance with the non-capitalist thesis of socialist orientation. But it was recognized that petty capitalism was deeply rooted at virtually all levels of society; the working class was small; there was no widespread land hunger to satisfy and no particularly rapacious capitalists to act against. This much was clear to any outside observer, who could also be forgiven for characterizing the PRG's economic and social policies and achievements as more populist than socialist in style and content. There were few apparent systematic ideological directives and ultimately they amounted largely to programmes aimed at reform, moral uplift and the amelioration of destitution. The constant juxtaposition of 'the will' of the masses and concepts of 'justice' and morality, and the theoretical direct link between the masses and government were clear examples. Similarly, populism could be seen in accusations of conspiracy and manipulation by first, the Gairyites, and thereafter by assorted 'counters' against the popular will; the immediate development of a direct and emotionally charged relationship between the masses and their leader; and the establishment of a corruption-free technocratic elite in government, whose aim was to serve the people efficiently. The welfare programmes were widespread and popular. But structural reform of the economy was minimal although the effect of the new international airport would have doubtless been felt in the long term. Very little diversification in trade and tourism was achieved, and socialist largesse was, bar that absorbed in the airport project, outweighed by what Grenada was denied by its traditional sources. In short, the 'Improbable Revolution' was rarely to be seen except in the chanceries of hostile countries.

The objective socio–economic reality of Grenada was clearly to blame for these limited achievements. Bishop's *Line of March* speech made this clear: what he was not to know in September 1982 was that the regime would only have limited time. Speaking of proposed successive five-year plans, which would take Grenada to the end of the century, he outlined the tasks of 'the economic essence of the national democratic path'. Primary was the building of the state sector to be predominant in the society, together with the assumption of total control of all financial institutions, foreign trade and 'some aspects of internal trade', and of all public utilities. The achievements of the highly successful Marketing and National Importing Board (MNIB) were singled out as indicating the way forward. As for the future, one operation was earmarked for attention, that of Cable and Wireless, a multinational company formerly owned by the British government and responsible for all Grenada's external telecommunications. This would be nationalized once the Soviet Union had built a satellite dish. The infrastructure would continue to be built and the manufacturing and industrial sectors widened as much and as quickly as possible. Tourism was to be encouraged, 'not to say that we like tourism, that is because we have no choice'. He warned party members, however, that these developments would also 'lay the basis for capitalism' and 'if we are not careful capitalism rather than socialism will be the end product'. The young Soviet Union had experienced the same dilemma but had resolved it.

Simultaneously we will be nurturing the shoots of capitalism and the shoots of socialism and the question is which one becomes predominant and how you can control and ensure that socialism comes out and not capitalism. We have the same problem as the young Soviet Union faced but a million times more difficult, because our state sector is much smaller and does not have the potential in this immediate period for providing the profits to build the economy and the country. And of course, we have a much smaller and less ideologically developed working class. On top of that we have this massive petty bourgeoisie; you have this low level of development of class consciousness; you have this total backwardness and primitiveness in the economy. In other words comrades, we have a tightrope that we have to monitor very carefully as we walk it—*every single day*. [Bishop, 1982b, p. 8.]

Clearly, the prioritised tasks determined in the *Line of March* had to be operationalized to overcome this problem.

Redirection, Reorganization and Reconstruction

In practice, these tasks and policy thrusts were directed at three broad objectives. The first, the redirection of the economy towards the public sector—'which would lead the development process'—should have been the primary. However, it was clearly secondary in terms of achievement for all the reasons Bishop outlined. More important, in practice, therefore, was the reorganization of economic activity towards new and more efficient production and marketing. The trinity was complete with perhaps what was the most far reaching legacy of the PRG, the reconstruction of the economy after years of neglect. The promotion of agriculture was central and positive results were readily observable. Under this heading can also be put what was the single most important achievement, the building and near-completion of the international airport. But this was such a major step forward and was so intimately (and tragically) linked to the PRG's foreign policy that it clearly deserves a special category of its own.

The NJM agreed some time before the insurrection that a mixed economy was most suited for Grenada's state of development, at least for the foreseeable future. The *Line of March* made this clear. Although the alliance with the patriotic bourgeoisie was essential, the total private-sector free enterprise system—'your Seaga of Jamaica or your Puerto Rico model of development'—was totally ruled out. Also eliminated was its opposite, the total state-sector approach. The mixed economy, however, had to be state rather than private sector dominated (ibid., p. 2). None the less, public enterprises had to be competitive and the economics of the marketplace would prevail except where the public interest dictated otherwise. Such competition would avoid inefficient government monopolies which were said to plague many socialist countries (interview with Maurice Bishop, May 1979). There was already a substantial public sector inherited from Gairy, mostly in agriculture, and further nationalization was limited. The properties owned by Gairy were immediately seized, to emerge as the Grenada Resorts Corporation. Some belonging to Knight were also sequestrated. Management shortcomings prompted the takeover of the Electricity Corporation, renamed Grenlec, and the Grenada Telephone Company, Grentel. Two Canadian banks sold out: the Imperial Bank of Commerce was reborn in 1979 as the National Commercial Bank while the Royal Bank became the Grenada Bank of Commerce in 1983. The Canadian owners of the Holiday Inn were pressured to sell after a disastrous fire. It was reopened as the Grenada Beach Hotel, just in time to be taken over by the American forces as their main base.

The PRG therefore concentrated more upon providing efficient planning machinery in its economic redirection policy. Selective import and price controls were imposed and certain basic commodities purchased centrally, bypassing the merchants. The MNIB played a critical role. Such a body had been advocated in the 1973 *Manifesto* although with much wider ranging powers than what was eventually legislated. For instance, it advocated a monopoly over *all* imports. Drugs and hospital supplies, fertilizers, powdered milk and cooking oil were purchased from Cuba, the United States and Britain and the European Community. Bitumen from Trinidad and Cuban cement were purchased at cost price and in substantial amounts. But handsome retail profits were made from the public as prices equalled those that had been charged by the private sector. Only the government, as a consumer, benefitted. Profit margins of up to 40 per cent were common due to the low purchase price, compared to many private-sector items which were subjected to strict price control with margins of 5 to 10 per cent. This did not encourage the private sector and a general feeling of despondency spread. By 1981, the private sector was in absolute decline (People's Revolutionary Government, 1982c, p. 64) and, noted the 1982 report of the Chamber of Commerce, its annual investment had fallen by over 25 per cent.

The government reacted. The thirty-eight public-sector enterprises were, in the main, losing substantial sums of money. 'Productive state enterprises', declared Coard in his 1982 budget address, 'are supposed to make money for the people, not take money from the people.' (People's Revolutionary Government, 1983b, p. 53). The reasons were legion: lack of capital, low level of expertise, poor marketing, maintenance and management, limited human resources and the like. But the losses caused by these technical, financial, managerial and personnel constraints had to be made up by the private sector until such time as they could be cut. Occasional fulminations continued to be uttered in private against the readily identifiable and 'particularly parasitical' comprador capitalists who, 'in the full-time service of international capitalism' on which they depended for trade and profit, 'produce nothing' and for the most part 'engage in no form of manufacturing or industrial activity at all' (Bishop, 1982b, p. 2). But a consultation process was begun, a prominent feature being a national conference with the private sector after the budget presentation by the delegates from the mass organizations. Tax and other concessions were announced, together with a new Investment Code Incentives Law (People's Law No. 13 of 1983) aimed at both domestic and foreign potential investors. Certain sectors of the economy were reserved for Grenadian entrepreneurs after extensive discussions with the Chamber of Commerce.

Together with other incentives previously announced, these resulted in an increase in private sector activity in 1982 and a 10.4 per cent rise in company tax revenue. The government was confident that the Code would not lead important sectors of the economy to fall under the influence of multinational companies; Grenada's small size and low profit potentiality would see to that. In fact, the private sector found much to its benefit. The end of Gairyism with its corruption and victimization of those recalcitrant capitalists who refused to contribute large sums to him and the GULP, stimulated business and normalized conditions for capital accumulation. Without doubt, many in the private sphere disliked the emphasis on the public sector and aspects of People's Power. But none could deny the fact of economic growth and the benefit from the generation of extra spending power, contracts and trade. To a substantial extent, therefore, the private sector had the best of both worlds: Gairy had gone and collectively it shared economic power with the government. None the less, morale remained poor. The lack of constitutional restoration, let alone advance, bred insecurity. The Westminster model might have been justifiably discredited under Gairy but it represented far more than a parliamentary system. It stood for freedom of speech, association and publication, and an independent judiciary. Neither the private sector nor the people at large accepted the argument that they were 'bourgeois' and, as such, unacceptable in the struggle for socialism.

A major priority from 1981 was the strong encouragement of a manufacturing base. In this sphere, redirection and reorganization objectives came together as state investment was heavily involved. That part of the private sector involved in manufacturing undoubtedly benefited. Processed food was high on the list. The raw material and labour force was at hand, and markets available. A successful private company in this area of activity was supplemented by Grenada Agro-Industries, which specialized in sauces and tinned nectars. Founded in 1980, management and other problems meant that production was less than half of target after three years. Its largely Eastern European machinery was destroyed in the invasion. A similar fate met the 'Sandino' building materials plant, built with Cuban assistance. Other industries encouraged were largely privately owned, making furniture and processing alcoholic beverages, soft drinks, poultry feed and coconut oil. Those which were notably successful related to flour and wheat products, and textiles, which registered profit rises of 7.8 per cent and 10.6 per cent respectively from 1981 to 1982, or nearly EC$2 million and EC$6.6 million. The old-established state-owned Grenada Sugar Company virtually broke even as did the Coffee Processing Plant. The profits would have been substantial if more coffee had been grown since a large regional market existed. But the Forestry Development Corporation, Grenada Farms Corporation (GFC) and, above all, the National Fisheries Company, performed poorly. Equipped with Cuban boats, the fish company only reached 16 per cent of its 1982 production target. Ultimately, an embarrassed PRG had to accede by mid-1983 to Cuban demands that its personnel be pulled out (Minutes of the Political Bureau, 10 August 1983, p. 5).

Two other innovations deserve mention. Grencraft, the marketing arm of the Grenada National Institute of Handicraft, was from its establishment in late 1981 a resounding success. Much cottage industry work was created and besides sales to tourists in Grenada, exports to Trinidad grew although hampered by insufficient production. The other was the National Transport Service (NTS). In an island where transport was monopolized by private minibus owners, services were only provided where and when profitable. The NTS ran timetabled services over eighteen hours and, although they lacked the popularity of the brightly lit private buses with their noisy music, they were a considerable success.

Finance for these and other projects came from the Grenada Development Bank, established after independence and financed by external aid funds and credits, and the banking system. The GDB loaned over EC$1.5 million in 1982–3 to 238 private-sector projects, and twice that to the public sector. But the financial uncertainty of much of the public sector for the ordinary banks meant that heavy reliance had to be put upon the two nationalized banks to maintain liquidity.

The one sector where the private sector suffered a serious decline was that which it dominated: the tourist business. In common with sister parties in other islands, the NJM was ambivalent in its attitude to the trade. The negative features of tourism were plain to see; to Bishop, it was 'beset with all the worst features of imperialism' such as foreign ownership and control, racism and the development of enclaves within the economy where no linkages existed with other sectors and which benefited very few. The visitors, furthermore, brought with them 'all the worst aspects of their culture', including drug abuse, prostitution and gambling. Many young Grenadians took their cue from this: instances of tourists being questioned by zealous youths as to their possible CIA connections became an embarrassment, and organizers of cruises sometimes experienced sullen reception to their requests for berth space. But tourism had to be encouraged in the struggle to diversify and to bridge the payments gap on visible trade. A 'New Tourism' philosophy was therefore announced. Henceforth, particular emphasis was to be put on local ownership, food and handicrafts, and the breaking of 'the relationship between tourism, class and colour'. Non-white visitors were to be 'courteously encouraged'. Above all, Bishop announced, tourism was 'an instrument of world peace and understanding' and visitors and hosts alike had much to learn from each other (Bishop, 1982c, pp. 71–2).

This worthy objective was later married with promotion. Increased tourism was, after all, the major justification for the new international airport. Tourist arrivals had been falling steadily and the North American recession was only partly to blame. Adverse publicity in the North American press put about by the United States International Communications Agency did widespread harm (Bishop, 1982a, p. 258). Also, devaluation and high hotel and other prices had led to the desertion by 1980 of West German and British tour firms to the cheaper pastures of St. Lucia. In their place came increasing numbers of West Indians. Although welcome, they spent little money. In a visitor survey conducted by the Barbados-based Caribbean Tourism Research and Development Centre in December 1982 during the high season,

American visitors were still the largest contingent (27 per cent), followed by Canadians (19 per cent) and British and Continental Europeans (15 per cent each). The proportion of West Indians was nearly 20 per cent (Caribbean Tourism Research and Development Centre, 1983, p. 2). The last increased dramatically in the cheaper summer season to give an annual average of 42 per cent. The arrival statistics were amended in 1983 to include visiting Grenadians resident overseas. They amounted to 9,121 in that year. Taken together with other West Indians, they totalled a high 61.5 per cent. To cap it all, the government imposed a tax on hotel improvements of 85 per cent of value, excepting on those that it owned.

Table 1: Tourist Arrivals (excluding cruise ship passengers)

Country of Origin	1978	1979	1980	1981	1982	1983	% of 1983 total
United States	9,191	9,081	6,767	5,124	5,031	5,277	16.3
Canada	2,977	2,926	1,991	1,910	1,524	1,520	4.7
Europe/UK	6,998	11,371	6,774	5,618	5,166	4,095	12.6
Venezuela	498	287	472	438	362	183	0.6
Caribbean	8,773	7,981	7,655	8,509	9,725	10,828	33.3
Other	3,899	657	5,813	3,473	1,462	10,556	32.5
Total	32,336	32,303	29,418	25,072	23,270	32,459	100.0

Source: Caribbean Tourism Research and Development Centre, *Statistical Report*, 1984, p. 67.

The PRG's reasoning was that ultimately tourism was, and remained, clearly secondary to agriculture, and that scarce resources had to be diverted to farmers. It followed that agriculture was at the centre of reconstruction policy. Much time was to be spent in debating its future in a socialist economy. The first task was to improve land productivity and surveys quickly discovered that an astonishing one-third of cultivable land was idle, mostly in estates whose owners had emigrated. It was resolved that, through the Land Utilization Act proclaimed six months after the insurrection, unless absentee or other owners with idle land produced acceptable plans for agricultural development, it would be compulsorily taken over on ten-year leases. Thousands of acres were released in this way to the Land Reform Commission. They were either allocated to the GFC if adjacent to any of its twenty-three units, or to unemployed youths who wanted to be small farmers. Over four years, about 2,000 took up the offer. Their productivity levels were poor but those of the GFC were appalling. In the GFC, the average value of labour productivity was two or three times less than the average wage.

New feeder roads and a reformed marketing system, however, made a considerable impact on food output. The percentage of food in the import bill fell from 30.6 per cent to 27.5 per cent between 1979 and 1982. It would have fallen further but for the highly successful diversification programme. The fruit and vegetable trade with Port of Spain meant that by 1982, Trinidad and Tobago was second only to Britain as Grenada's most important export market, taking 31 per cent of exports by value. Britain took 36 per cent, mostly bananas shipped by Geest Industries Ltd (People's Revolutionary Government, 1983b, p. 29). The Netherlands was third at 15 per cent, being the major cocoa market. The development of fruit and vegetable production and the agro-industries meant that whereas in 1979 93 per cent of exports were 'traditional'—bananas, cocoa and nutmeg—by 1982 this had fallen to 63.4 per cent.

But there were major setbacks. Hurricanes and floods in August 1979 and January 1980 destroyed 40 per cent of banana production, 27 per cent of the nutmeg trees and 19 per cent of the cocoa crop, together worth US$27 million. Road damage was widespread. Since the traditional tree crops, except bananas, take time to mature, the effect was longstanding as Table 2 shows. Another problem was falling prices, due in part to the depreciation of the pound against the dollar in 1982. This hit the nutmeg farmers hard as it coincided with an increase in production. Arrangements were made for the Soviet Union to purchase much of the accumulated stockpile as part of a wide-ranging trade and cultural agreement, but it was not ratified in time. The United States later bought it.

The critical role of agriculture in the economy, made starkly evident by its problems, led the Central Committee to consider its collectivization. Between October 1982 and February 1983, intensive discussions took place both in the Committee and the Political Bureau.

The main conclusion was that 'the development and modernization of agriculture holds the key to winning the peasantry to socialism and the transformation of the countryside along socialist lines'. Further, it was necessary to construct a firm alliance between the working class and the peasantry. Three consecutive priorities to attain these aims were itemized. The first was to make the GFC the 'leading vehicle' for the socialist transformation of agriculture. It had to be restructured, assume control of 6,000 acres of idle land and establish thirty-six farm units in eight semi-autonomous regions. Second, the peasantry was to be 'won gradually to socialism' by tax and other incentives, investment in rural infrastructure, the strengthening of existing

Table 2: Grenada—Exports of Major Agricultural Commodities

Commodity	1975	1976	1977	1978	1979	1980	1981	1982
BANANAS								
Volume ('000 lbs)	29,700	33,800	30,900	31,500	31,220	27,470	22,410	21,620
Value (EC$'000)	6,600	7,900	8,586	9,288	10,449	11,097	9,646	8,814
Price per lb. (¢)	0.22	0.23	0.28	0.29	0.33	0.40	0.44	0.42
COCOA								
Volume ('000 lbs)	5,100	5,900	4,600	5,300	5,260	4,110	5,900	4,680
Value (EC$'000)	7,100	8,883	8,883	19,575	27,027	16,200	15,340	12,168
Price per lb. (¢)	1.39	1.50	1.93	3.69	5.14	3.94	3.12	2.57
NUTMEG AND MACE								
Volume ('000 lbs)	3,800	7,000	7,100	5,000	5,810	3,910	4,710	5,220
Value (EC$'000)	9,900	15,984	17,577	12,293	14,553	10,361	9,984	13,572
Price per lb. (¢)	2.60	2.28	2.48	2.48	2.50	2.65	2.82	2.50

Source: Department of Agriculture, Grenada, *Statistics*, 1975–82.

'machinery pools' and other services and, above all, through reinforcing the role of the Productive Farmers' Union 'to further build the mass organization of the farmers as the organ for carrying out the tasks of the Party among the peasantry'.

The last priority was to be joint venture companies 'with large estate owners who are willing to produce, remain in production but [who] may be faced with economic crisis or bankruptcy'. Such ventures, it was urged, might also be extended to 'appropriate capitalists' not presently in agriculture but who might be willing to invest in that area. The state would accept a minority interest holding 'given the managerial inputs the capitalist can make in production at this time' (Central Committee Report, 'Resolution on Agriculture', January 1983).

The agriculture resolution document was marked 'confidential' in the knowledge that, although the measures proposed were, in the circumstances, practical and sensible and which in no way threatened the peasantry with forced collectivization and other drastic measures, it was a highly sensitive issue given the social composition and values of Grenadian society. Similar secrecy surrounded a Central Committee resolution in June 1983 to establish a Ministry for State Enterprises. The banking sector was earmarked for nationalization, and expanded public ownership was to be accompanied and sustained by trade with the socialist community. This had followed on from an earlier report, completed in the previous March, by another working party charged with examining the feasibility of a State Trading Organization. A principal feature of this institution would have been the encouragement and supervision of such trade. No action was taken on its recommendations as it was expected that the new ministry would assume responsibility. It made clear that in its view, Grenada's deepening balance of payments' deficit was due to 'entanglement in the world imperialist system' and that alleviation could only be found by the re-alignment of foreign trade and greater state control and direction of productive enterprises. Import controls had to be extended and new markets urgently found. State intervention in export control was specifically recommended and several options presented. One was the nationalization of the marketing boards and the creation of a State Trading Corporation on the Cuban model, or their incorporation into the MNIB. Another option was that the state should limit its activity to control of exports to socialist markets; an even more watered-down option was that only annual export levels to these markets be set.

The option chosen was the most comprehensive: a state monopoly export corporation covering all products and markets. It was well appreciated that there would be strong opposition from the merchants and warning was given

of possible sabotage and counter-revolutionary acts. 'Concrete steps to positively alter the balance of forces' were essential, the report intoned, especially
through 'political work'. But as regards the workers in newly controlled
industries, a note of cynicism crept in. 'When it comes to the bottom line,
what is most important to the ordinary worker is continued unemployment.
When forced to choose between continued employment with the State and
unemployment, workers are not likely to opt for unemployment'. (Central
Committee Report, 'State Trading Corporation for Effecting Grenada Trade
with the Socialist Countries', June 1983, p. 6). Opposition from capitalist
shipping lines was expected and so new shipping agreements with socialist
states might be necessary. In fact, some had already been signed by the Shipping Division of the MNIB with those of Cuba, the Soviet Union and the
German Democratic Republic (GDR). But potential problems were outweighed by the advantages. The state could control all foreign exchange and
be able to use it wisely for the benefit of all. Above all, new and favourable
markets and new services would raise farmers' incomes and so 'undoubtedly
raise the prestige of the revolution'. But it failed to mention that the PRG was
forced to turn down an offer by the GDR to purchase bananas as the price was
less than half that negotiated with the European Community under the
Lomé Convention arrangements (interview with Lyden Ramdhanny, June
1984).

The Growth Debate

Considerable publicity was given by the PRG to its achievements but after the
invasion, doubts were expressed as to their veracity. While some detractors
were clearly politically inspired, others were acknowledged experts in international institutions whose judgment was respected. Allegations that statistics
and financial returns had been deliberately forged became legion although
no hard evidence was ever found except a brief reference to a suggestion by
Bishop that something on those lines *might* have to be done to meet the strict
International Monetary Fund (IMF) accounting rules. 'We [should] use the
Suriname and Cuban experience in keeping two sets of records in the banks
for this purpose', he advised his colleagues in mid-1983. He was echoed by an
'internationalist' adviser. 'It becomes necessary', he said, 'to keep different
books so as to make any necessary adjustments' (Minutes of the Political/
Economic Bureau, 3 August 1983, p. 6).

The extent of the financial crisis caused by the cost of the overlarge
number of projects, dominated by the international airport, and the
American-orchestrated financial embargo on the PRG, was clearly shown

when, after the collapse of the revolution, the United States State Department and the post-PRG Interim Administration discovered the treasury to be nearly denuded of ready cash. The PRG had been forced to go to the IMF in early 1983 due to a critical cash-flow crisis. The denial of expected aid for the airport project had caused an unofficial order to be given by Coard to skim up to 15 per cent from every budget. Very strict expenditure limits were put on all ministries, with monthly allocations that could not be exceeded. Subscriptions and payments to regional and international organizations were deferred (interviews, June 1984). The IMF was comparatively easy in its conditions, in sharp contrast to its harsh treatment of other Commonwealth Caribbean countries, notably Guyana and Jamaica. A total of US$36.7 million was agreed, but only US$9.7 million could be spent up to June 1984. US$14.2 million had to be repaid immediately to liquidate previous loans negotiated by Gairy while the remainder, US$12.8 million, had to be allocated to the private banks to improve their critical level of liquidity and so increase investment lending to the private sector. The banks' parlous position arose from the imposition in early 1983 of very tight credit restrictions. All were forced to make special deposits of 20 per cent of liquid assets with the government, which were used for the airport. The PRG protested at these 'excessive' conditions. Radix, Minister for Industrial Development, argued that the credit might never be taken up by the private sector; further, that if a private company was to take advantage of the IMF facility and then go bankrupt, the government would have to stand the loss (Minutes of the Political Bureau, 10 August 1983, pp. 2–4). But there was no alternative.

The IMF's easy terms, which included an expectation of an improvement in the foreign exchange position through increased export receipts and tourist arrivals, were partly due to the professionalism of the PRG's treasury staff in presenting Grenada's case and partly to the achievements of the regime. Taking inflation into account—which, at an average of 7 per cent, was the lowest in the West Indies—real living standards rose by 3 per cent during the period of PRG rule, reflecting a dramatic change in the growth rate, which the government claimed had climbed from minus 3.2 per cent in 1978 to 5.5 per cent in 1982. In terms of income *per capita*, the rise was from US$450 in 1978 to US$870 in 1983. In the final financial year of PRG rule, tax revenue was nearly 10 per cent higher than estimated (EC$67.6 million to EC$74.1 million). All this meant, Coard was proud to say, that only 3.7 per cent of export earnings, or 3 per cent of production, had to be allocated to debt servicing, giving Grenada one of the lowest debt ratios in the world (People's Revolutionary Government, 1983b, p. 16). He attributed this not only to NJM leadership but also to the capital expenditure programme. It totalled nearly EC$237 million over three years, nearly all of which was fin-anced by soft loans and grants from the European Community, the UN Development Programme, OPEC and several countries, notably Mexico, Venezuela and France.

This massive amount of investment achieved in only four years stands on its own as a remarkable achievement, and it completely overshadows the tiny amounts spent on capital projects during all of Gairy's 25-year dictatorship . . . [It] reflects the growing confidence which other Governments and International Organizations now have in our people and Revolution, and in the ability of the Government to govern the economy. [Ibid., pp. 16–17.]

It certainly impressed the World Bank. In its report of August 1982, it singled out the careful husbandry of public finance for special praise. 'The present targets of the Government for 1982–85', it concluded, 'are encouraging'. It fore-cast improvement in 1985 and 1986, 'the share of exports in Gross Domestic Product [rising] gradually from 38 per cent in 1982 to about 47 per cent' four years on (World Bank, 1982, p. vi, p. 8). But it assumed that the PRG's plans would be only 'largely' fulfilled, if world prices stabilized and foreign invest-ment could be attracted. The United States was scornful, pointing out that its calculations appeared to show recurrent expenditure rapidly overtaking receipts, that the trade gap was widening and that foreign investment was dry-ing up. Although precipitate, it was certainly true later. By mid-1983, recurrent expenditure was one-third higher than recurrent revenue. As for trade, the 1982 import bill was EC$150.9 million, offset by only EC$50 million worth of exports, the value of which had fallen by 5 per cent from 1981.

Ignoring these allegations, the PRG stressed its job creation record. Unemployment, it was claimed, had fallen from a massive 49 per cent in early 1979 to 14 per cent in 1982; further, it was an estimated 10 per cent in late 1983. Youths and women particularly benefited from this. Coard firmly dispelled any doubts. 'Where are the youths who used to be seen in our well-known liming-spots, on walls and street corners all over the country during working hours? They are working on the Eastern Main Road in St. David's; they are building farm roads . . . putting up new Telephone Company build-ings . . . rebuilding the Careenage in St. George's'. [People's Revolutionary Government, 1983b, p. 6.]

But he omitted to say that a substantial number of unemployed youths, some 1,500, had been gradually recruited into the armed forces, and that the number was rising. He also failed to report the 30 April 1981 census results which had showed thousands of Grenadians to be 'missing'. The 1970 enumeration had registered 92,775 persons. Birth and death statistics led to an estimate of 110,137 in 1979. But only 89,088 were counted two years later. Admittedly, three categories were not counted: members of the PRA, those Rastafarians living in inaccessible places and Cuban and Soviet nationals (Government of Grenada, 1984b). But it was estimated that the first two categories only totalled 1,800 at that time. The fall can mainly be attributed to accelerated emigration during the last years of the Gairy era, particularly by younger people. This was borne out by the relatively low percentage under thirty-five years, 52 per cent. But the outflow certainly continued after the insurrection, for political as well as economic reasons. The figures were not published until May 1984.

After the revolution's collapse, the statistics were re-examined. The interim administration put out contradictory growth figures. In a February 1984 submission to an aid donor's meeting in Washington, DC, the rates of growth for 1975-7 and 1978-82 were calculated to have been 3.8 per cent and 0.2 per cent respectively (Government of Grenada, 1984a, p. 10). Later, in a budget commentary, an average annual growth of 3 per cent over 1979-82 was said to have been achieved, followed by minus 2 per cent in 1983 (*Latin American Regional Report: Caribbean*, 1984, p. 7).

Social Advance

There was far less dispute over the scale and success of the PRG's social development programmes (Payne, Sutton & Thorndike, 1984, ch. 2). Over 22 per cent and 14 per cent of the 1982-3 budget were allocated to education and health respectively, the highest proportions anywhere in the Commonwealth Caribbean. The meagre 6 per cent for defence, however, clearly showed the PRG's reliance on external military aid. Many Grenadians took advantage of new scholarships offered by socialist countries, and others could again enrol at the University of the West Indies once outstanding debts from the Gairy years were paid.

Education received the highest priority. Schools were rebuilt and a wide-ranging National In-Service Teacher Education Programme (NISTEP) was introduced to upgrade low standards, especially at primary level. Introduced in October 1980, it centred on tutors and 'teacher-partners'. Experienced teachers worked in groups with some 500 of their untrained colleagues for up to two days a week. There were many coordination problems due to Grenada's chronic shortage of middle-level management skills and the lack of resources. There were also complaints that some tutors were too academic in their approach, thus reflecting their own training. But NISTEP was judged a success: one radical departure that it sponsored was the recognition given to the importance of 'creole', as opposed to 'proper' English, children being taught in both versions.

When their teachers were absent on the NISTEP programme, pupils participated in the complementary Community Day School Programme (CDSP). Its two aims were inter-related: first to develop community-school relationships, the second to introduce a work-study approach. Together, they emphasized the importance of practical education in agriculture, health, nutrition and crafts, utilizing the skills of the local community who were expected to volunteer. By such means, pride in manual skills was to be promoted as well as new values and behaviour patterns (Clean, 1981, p. 10). The experience of similar models in other countries was extensively drawn upon, particularly Cuba and the People's Republic of China. But once again, administrative shortcomings took their toll. Coupled with indifference in many areas, particularly where there was little experience of community involvement, it led to disillusionment. Also, where it worked, it tended to perpetuate the 'two-track' problem. Because secondary education was—and continued to be under the PRG—open only to those who passed the entrance examinations, slower pupils in many primary schools tended to be allocated to gardening, woodwork and home economics lessons, leaving the academic subjects for their brighter colleagues. Under the CDSP, those schools—nearly all rural—which had the most untrained teachers became, in effect, 'half-work, half-study' schools and serious deficiencies in literacy and numeracy began to appear to the concern of the government. However, by 1981 those at secondary school enjoyed free education.

More successful was the Centre for Popular Education (CPE). The help of the mass organizations led it to promote a rapid expansion in adult literacy beyond the minimum functional stage. It also had a clear political aim: to instil new values, attitudes and habits. Said Bishop:

It is . . . going to have tremendous relevance to the success of building a deeper and greater sense of national unity, and of raising the national consciousness . . . it will be much easier for them not to be misled . . . it will be much easier for them to understand *Imperialism*. It will be much easier for them to understand what we mean when we talk of *de-stabilization*, what we mean when we say that the Revolution is for the people, and that the people *are* the Revolution. [Bishop & Searle, 1981, p. 39.]

In short, 'work and study are part of the same dynamic, the same process, the same dialectic'.

The official objectives of the CPE made this clear. There were four:

(a) To assist in the conscientization of our people.
(b) To consolidate the presence of the people in the revolutionary process through the development of a critical awareness.
(c) To consolidate the right of the people to be informed participants in the development through the eradication of illiteracy, the understanding of the nature of poverty and exploitation; and the acquisition of skills to build a new revolutionary society.
(d) To assist in the re-definition of education and the formulation of a dialogical and revolutionary pedagogy. (People's Revolutionary Government, 1979, p. 1).

The CPE's role in reconstruction, it stated, was critical since the problems of under-development could only be solved by the people understanding 'the causes and nature of these problems' and by 'relating popular education with the transformation of reality on a national scale'. It is not surprising that, given the limited time that was to be available, the programmes were never fully realized. But productivity rises and better vocational training for more people were credited to it. When its objectives were put into a readily under-stood form, they attracted a lot of interest. As a letter of invitation to workers to attend a CPE seminar put it,

Why is our country poor? Are there no social classes in Grenada, and if there are classes, to which social class do the workers belong? Will there always be rich and poor? Why must we as workers try to produce more? When were our trade unions formed and for what reasons? Have there always been trade unions? And, finally, how does our economy work? And much, much more. [Searle, 1983a, p. 83.]

By early 1983, political education had spread to schools. Syllabuses were drawn up, down to primary level, and plans made to curtail the time allocated to religious studies. But there was little impact. A shortage of manpower combined with a noticeable lack of enthusiasm by many teachers and those charged with the task assured that. Headmasters and teachers in secondary schools considered unsympathetic, however, were sometimes removed to less sensitive posts.

In the area of health, the emphasis was upon the preventative rather than the curative. This was realistic given the resources available. It went hand-in-hand with administrative reorganization, an end to corruption, the recruit-ment of Cuban medical personnel—especially dentists, as there had been no government dental service for years—and the return to Grenada of several trained nationals who, in the Gairy era, had left in search of greater oppor-tunities elsewhere. To attract local doctors into the new system of public health and community-based health centres—normally at Parish Council and village levels—private practice was permitted. The condition was that doctors scheduled their public service clinics at the health centres and at St. George's hospital, and their private practice at their private offices, a distinction not always respected in the past. Health and associated workers outside the wards concentrated upon health education, nutrition and family planning, especially for young people. Mobile teams in rural areas became a regular feature.

There was also assistance from the St. George's University, a United States offshore medical school established for American students who were unsuccessful in their attempts to enrol in mainland medical schools. The University encouraged its specialist clinical staff to advise their Grenadian counterparts and the students themselves spent some of their periods of training in both St. George's and in nearby St. Vincent.

A notable feature of the revolution was the strong support given to it by women. The NJM had from the beginning stressed the need to improve their position in Grenadian society and to recognize their critical role in family life. The 1981 census noted there were 9,495 households with female heads, only 2,011 of whom were married. The Women's Desk in the Ministry of Education and Social Services eventually became a quite separate ministry. It provided a strong lead in promoting greater job opportunities, removing forms of discrimination and establishing pre-school and day centres. Low-income young mothers with illegitimate children were a special priority. Not only were they given a second chance through the CPE, but also cash benefits were advanced to help them with the cost of school uniforms and other expenses. A very popular and overdue innovation was maternity leave, introduced in October 1980. Applicable to all, it was of special benefit to the large number of poorly paid domestic servants. Less successful, however, was the attempted implementation of a policy declaration on equal pay made in the aftermath of the insurrection. In agriculture, different types of work were traditionally undertaken by men and women and the proposal met considerable resistance. Much time was spent by the Women's Desk determining through consultation with women which types of work were of equal value (Joseph, 1981, p. 9). The NWO was also involved, as it was in all other aspects of women's development, although it naturally tended to concentrate more on political education and mobilization.

The NWO with the NYO also contributed to the successful National House Repair Programme through volunteer labour. The natural disasters of 1979 and 1980 made the work all the more urgent and, during the four years of the revolution, over 2,000 houses were repaired. A more universal benefit was the National Insurance scheme loosely copied from the long-established

British example. Introduced in late 1982, it had not developed fully by the time of the invasion. The prospect of unemployment and sickness pay in a Third World economy was indeed bravely innovative.

The impact of the revolution on culture is harder to assess since calypso—a traditional and widespread form of expression known for its rhythm, often outrageous sexual licence, explicitness and savage satire—had for long been a political statement set to music. It was not confined to Grenada but was, and remains, a powerful cultural force elsewhere in the region and in its birthplace, Trinidad.

The revolution undoubtedly ushered in far more overtly political messages by such calypsonians as 'The Flying Turkey', 'Explainer', 'Lord Melody' and 'The Mighty Survivor'. As the Turkey (Cecil Belfon) exclaimed, 'People want to hear you come out in defence of the Revolution, people want to hear you come out and rage hostility upon imperialism, rage hostility upon Reagan and American interventionist attitudes' (Searle, 1983b, p. 58). Survivor (George Peters), who also led the police band, emphasized calypso 'as a messenger of the people, getting the information of the day, putting it into song and giving it back'. Another based a calypso on Walter Rodney's observation that 'the greatest miracle is the survival of the Caribbean man—because he was in a system designed to kill' (Holmes, 1982, p. 14). The revolutionary experience also clearly influenced calypsonians on other islands. 'The Mighty Gabby' (Tony Carter) of Barbados became a star overnight with his satirical treatment of the militarization of the Caribbean by the United States prior to its spear-heading the invasion, and he fell foul of Prime Minister Adams. 'Boots' was played all over the region.

> Can we afford to feed that army?
> While so many children go naked and hungry?
> No, no, no, no.
> Can we afford to remain passive
> While that soldier army grow so massive?
> No, no, no, no.
> Well don't tell me, tell Tommy
> He giving them four square meals
> Some of them so fat, they could hardly
>   run
> And they shooting bulls eyes with
>   automatic gun. [Manning, 1984, p. 14.]

Other forms of expression were encouraged, especially poetry. The Minister of Health, Chris 'Kojo' de Riggs, was one of the foremost in the field.

In 1982, the PRG signed a wideranging cultural agreement with Cuba covering film, drama, music and books. It had been decided beforehand that, in common with other socialist countries, a House of Culture was to be established. Cuba contracted to aid the project (People's Revolutionary Government, 1982a). Designs were commissioned from Trinidad but work never commenced, being cut short by the revolution's collapse.

Revolutionary Manners

These numerous economic and social achievements were marred in the eyes of many, both inside and outside Grenada, by the application of 'heavy manners' against those deemed to be against the regime. A term imported from Jamaica, denoting Michael Manley's threat to those who stood in the way of progress, it was translated into preventive detention without trial, strict censorship and a general harassment of opponents. During the period of PRG rule, over 3,000 people were questioned and about a tenth of these were imprisoned, the majority only for a matter of days. But over one hundred political prisoners were in Richmond Hill prison at the time of their release on 26 October 1983, six having been incarcerated since the insurrection. The highest number, 183, was recorded on 1 January 1982 (Report of Langston Sibblies, Deputy Director of Prosecutions, 26 January 1982). During that year, ninety-one were released and another thirty-one detained. Two died in detention, leaving 121 (Memorandum from Victor Husbands to Bishop, 14 December 1982). Twenty-three were released in January 1983 and another ten the following June, but eleven were arrested. People's Law No. 29 of 1981 imposed restriction orders on many of those released, restricting travel and area of residence; 106 were under such orders at the close of 1982 and 65 at the time of the invasion. Its provisions applied to the few foreigners detained as well: a Vincentian was to be deported but only after a year. He was released only on condition that he did not leave Grenada in that time. He had made allegations of torture and his restriction 'might serve to counter any desire on his part to publicize the treatment he received on the Fort' (People's Revolutionary Government, 1983a).

The fort referred to was Fort Rupert. There is no doubt that forms of torture were perpetrated there. One ex-detainee said that it was not systematic and only concerned a few, particularly Rastafarians, and was 'largely the result of poor discipline and the fear many of the PRA and Militia guards had for their superiors who were over-enthusiastic political sadists'. The 'rigorous' regime was mostly confined to beatings and, on three known instances, making detainees run and jump by firing bullets into the floor behind them. Unfortunately it led on one occasion to a bullet going through the legs of a detainee and removing the end of his penis (Marshall, 1984, pp. 14–15). After the invasion, this incident gave rise to allegations that castration was a normal feature of prison life. At all other times, detainees were kept in a special block at Richmond Hill prison with very small cells—eight feet by four—but with some free association before night lock-up.

Some political prisoners were put on trial on criminal charges. When their sentence was completed, several deemed to be 'security risks' were served with detention orders. More fortunate were those who suffered only a short spell of house arrest, temporary confiscation of property and general harassment, such as the journalist Alister Hughes. Once close to Bishop and very supportive of the insurrection, he represented those who sincerely believed that the NJM would restore traditional civil liberties. George Brizan was also harassed but, being very cautious in his public utterings, escaped the party's wrath. All detention orders were signed by Bishop in his capacity as Minister for Internal Affairs. He could be vindictive and ruthless even to party members who for one reason or another crossed him. He made his point clear to the Central Committee in September 1982: 'Consider how people get detained in this country. We don't go and call for "no" votes. You get detained when I sign an order after discussing it with the National Security Committee of the party, or with a higher party body. Once I sign it—like it or don't like it—it's up the hill for them' (Bishop, 1982b, p. 6).

Irregular reports were made on detainees with recommendations for release by the Detainee Affairs' Committee chaired by Secretary Victor Husbands, 'Special Investigator'. The block releases in early 1982 were primarily due to gross overcrowding but there were many for whom it was admitted 'there is absolutely no evidence of an incriminating nature available and it is therefore advisable not to lay charges against them'. This especially applied to suspected 'petty criminals and troublemakers' who were regularly arrested prior to major rallies and festivals, particularly if foreign dignatories were expected. There were, however, many cases in this category who languished in cells for years without a hearing as it normally took eighteen months to investigate individual cases. When finally they were released, it was justified on the grounds that, although there was no evidence against them, 'the fact that detention in some cases exceeds three years is tantamount to prison sentences under conviction' had evidence been available. Pleas by relatives were ignored and no compensation offered to victims of false identification, of which there were at least two. There was one consolation for the PRG, however. Gairy's police aides—labelled 'Bad Johns'—arrested after the insurrection, were reformed through re-education. 'It is now difficult, save for their physique, to recognize those men with their past having gone such a tremendous change of attitudes and behaviour' (Memorandum from Victor Husbands to Bishop, 20 December 1982).

Justification for the detention policy varied over time. Arrests after the insurrection of the Mongoose Gang and Gairy's ministers were applauded. There was also a well-founded belief that Gairy would organize a mercenary-led counter-attack; this remained a threat throughout as the numbers of anti-PRG *émigrés* grew in Trinidad and North America. By late 1979 there were strong rumours of plots against the government which culminated in the bomb outrage at the Queen's Park rally in June 1980. The fate of the three schoolgirl victims fanned the flames of justifiable public anger. The Budhall brothers were held to be primarily responsible and were sentenced to be hanged: but no execution took place. Thereafter, the United States came to be regarded as the greatest threat. Any opposition to the regime became more and more to be perceived as attempts at destabilization by the CIA, 'the fountainhead of lies and imperialist intrigue' (Searle, 1983a, p. 79). Fears began to verge on the paranoidal by 1982 and internal security was stepped up. From May of that year all areas were analysed by PRA intelligence agents, who gradually compiled a comprehensive list of supporters, suspected 'counters' and potentially 'very dangerous' people.

Although the German Democratic Republic had advised on intelligence and surveillance, a request was made to the Soviet Union to provide training for four counter-espionage and one foreign-intelligence agent (letter to Andropov from Hudson Austin, 17 February 1982). A 1981 report called for 'the monitoring of all Big Business/Upper Class Types who are HOSTILE to the Revolution'; Rastafarians and Muslims; and 'suspects who have developed links with foreigners or local counter-types who have emitted signals in the past'. All gatherings were to be monitored 'regardless of how innocent they appear' (People's Revolutionary Army, 1981). The medical school was a surveillance target and its international telephone calls and telexes were recorded. By February 1983, a report urged that this monitoring be extended to tourist hotels and church leaders (People's Revolutionary Army, 1983). Much of this followed the advice of the GDR experts. They were clearly respected: all references to 'The Specialist' were made in suitably reverential terms. But no concrete action was taken against what the leadership per-sistently identified as the most important threat to the revolution, the churches. A top secret report warned that 'if serious measures are not taken . . . we can find ourselves with a Polish situation'. After much heart-searching, it recommended an intensification of political and science education, circumscription of religious education in schools and the removal of deeply religious teachers (Memorandum from Major Roberts to Bishop, 12 July 1983, p. 4). Earlier, the Cuban Communist Party had made available an expert on religion to advise on tactics to be adopted to control it. Bishop could only suggest that everybody should read his report, press for cinemas to open during church times and for the state to 'start a progressive church' on lines suggested by him. But, to the end, religious broadcasts on Radio Free Grenada remained a prominent feature.

The radio service was, none the less, strictly controlled. Bishop was nominally responsible for it but Phyllis Coard was the real power behind the scenes. The press took longer to control but when it was, local news was largely limited to sport, news of rallies and details of speeches made by ministers and supporters at home and overseas. For instance, all reports of bad feeling between Cuban internationalist workers and Grenadians, which occasionally erupted into violence, were classified top secret and never reported in the *Free West Indian*.

Censorship began with the suspension of *The Torchlight*, owned by the publishers of the Trinidad *Express*. Consistently anti-PRG and anti-Cuban, the final straw was its publication of details of all security installations and photographs of Bishop's personal bodyguards. By 1980, the sale of West Indian newspapers, such as *The Nation* (Barbados) and the *Trinidad Guardian* was forbidden. Ironically, British newspapers could be purchased as well as *Newsweek* and *Time*. Later in 1981, an attempt by Leslie Pierre to publish another newspaper independent of the NJM, *The Grenadian Voice*, was aborted after one issue. The 'Group of 26' who sponsored it—which included Alister Hughes—were labelled 'the foot soldiers and parasites of imperialism'. In short, they were

a handful of elements . . .manipulated by funded by external enemies, including the CIA . . . who have been unable to influence the public by their vicious rumours and propaganda to rise up against the government. We are confident of the support of the great majority of Grenadians. The political criminals who are anxious to destabilize this revolution will not be allowed to succeed. [*Caribbean Contact*, November 1980.]

While no evidence was given to support this charge, there were many who believed it since the paper appeared to have enough capital to distribute thousands of free copies to Grenadian communities overseas. Both Noel and Pierre were detained indefinitely and the PRG rushed out a People's Law (18 of 1981) to make 'temporary provisions' concerning publications 'until the formulation of a National Media Code'. All newspapers or pamphlets reporting 'political matter' were banned except for those published by the government, and all acts by the security forces against the 'Group of 26' 'shall be deemed to have been lawfully done'. By such means, Grenada was 'cleansed' of 'hypocrites' whose actions had clearly destroyed any notion that a 'free' press did not exist (*The New Jewel*, 20 July 1981).

'Revolutionary Manners' were, therefore, far-reaching and effective. But the illiberality that it represented was indefensible and could not be reconciled with the populist nature of the regime; it was its weakest point. It led Grenadians to equate socialism with repression. Popular morale necessary to resist destabilization was undermined. The PRG was a regime that clearly felt itself to be under siege from a hostile world which only firmness and 'principled positions' could combat.

The struggle against directed dependency, and economic dependency generally, was aimed directly at the capitalist world. The People's Revolutionary Government's pronouncements and actions in the pursuit of a 'non-aligned' foreign policy had a dual objective: the destruction of the economic umbilical cord that had bound Grenada to traditional metropolitan markets for so long and the gain of allies in its search for security. But, as events were to prove, the umbilical cord could not be cut as Grenada's new-found friends could not, or would not, substitute themselves as trading partners. Arms shipments, as they flowed in, served only to increase tension and, ironically, steadily reduced security. To believe that Grenada was not in anybody's backyard was an exhilarating experience—but it was an illusion.

Principles of Foreign Policy

The NJM had since its formulation made clear its commitment to the struggle for a new international economic order and to the principle of anti-imperialism. Consistent with this was a total commitment to the principles of the Non-Aligned Movement (NAM), clearly recognized by Grenada's election to its Coordinating Bureau at the Havana summit in September 1979. As Bishop told the movement in his maiden speech, its 'fundamental principles have had a most dramatic impact upon the development of our own revolution in Grenada' (Bishop, 1982c, p. 47). He was to sum these up later as the rights of sovereignty.

That small as we are, and poor as we are, as a people and as a country we insist on the fundamental principles of legal equality, mutual respect for sovereignty, non-interference in our internal affairs and the right to build our own process free from outside interference, free from bullying, free from the use or threat of force. [Bishop, 1982c, p. 118.]

It followed that clearly identifiable 'principled positions' devolved from this. First and foremost was the need for regional security against American interventionism, not only for progressive forces but for all the governments and peoples of the Caribbean Basin. This would be secured by the designation of the Caribbean Sea as a zone of peace. This was followed by demands for the right of self-determination for all peoples in the region, particularly in the non-independent territories such as Puerto Rico; the acceptance of the principle of ideological pluralism and an end to propaganda and 'economic and violent' destabilization as so recently witnessed in Jamaica; an end to the arming and financing of counter-revolutionaries and 'anti-progressive' regimes; respect for the sovereignty, legal equality and territorial integrity of all countries in the region; and freedom to join whatever international organizations or regional or sub-regional alliances or groups were deemed to be in the best interest of the Grenadian people (for an elaboration of these principles, see Whiteman in People's Revolutionary Government, 1982b, pp. 105–24).

The most clearly expressed manifestations of these principles was the alliance with Cuba, solidarity with national liberation movements in Central America and Southern Africa in particular and support for the Palestine Liberation Organization. Its solidarity was reciprocated: the First International Conference in Solidarity with Grenada in November 1981 included forty-one foreign delegations from socialist states and organizations. 'You have reminded us', Bishop said, 'of the meaning of true solidarity . . . of the meaning of expressing in a real and tangible way support for a process that is taking shape.' (Bishop, in People's Revolutionary Government, 1982b, p. 125). A second, planned for 1985, was to top fifty. But Grenadian foreign policy also included very considerable efforts to cultivate relations with the United States—which were rebuffed—and with the European Community (EC). A good working relationship was established between Bishop and Claude Cheysson, then EC Commissioner for Development. To the PRG, such eclecticism was logical. Like any Third World state it needed to acquire development assistance and find new markets in a world of diminishing opportunities. The difference lay in its determination to develop ties with ideological partners. In that, it was very successful. Scholarships, lines of credit, aid and machinery arrived from Cuba, the Soviet Union, Hungary and the German Democratic Republic. Other assistance came from equally non-traditional sources such as Bulgaria, North Korea, Syria, Iraq and Libya. This aid was more than simply symbolic: it indicated the PRG's confidence.

But Grenada's neighbours and the United States saw it differently. It was not to be long before confidence gave way to a sense of defensive siege. As criticisms mounted, the PRG counter-attacked. Its extraordinary sensitivity became self-fulfilling. Criticism was imperialist-inspired; its reaction evidence of a mounting communist canker. The Eastern Caribbean islands believed that they had legitimate concerns and were not anxious to reinstate Gairy. They did not at first realize the ideological foundation of the NJM—not surprisingly, as neither did the great majority of Grenadians—and full support was given to the offer by Barbados to assist in holding free elections.

The rude rebuff to an act done in good faith served only to alienate. Their leaders and press pinpointed the repressive aspects of PRG policy. PRG scorn meant that potential friends said little about the escalating techniques of destabilization which the United States was gradually bringing to bear against it. Grenada's representatives in regional meetings began to be cold-shouldered. As one analyst noted sorrowfully,

Insistence on the correctness of a position may be psychologically rewarding to a country's leadership but does not necessarily rebound to the advantage of a country. But the David Syndrome of responding forcefully to every challenge and error by external Goliaths is a reality of Grenadian policy. It is a position that makes no concessions to the concern of others, friend or foe, and yet demands recognition of one's own concerns. [Gill, 1981, p. 3.]

Realization of growing isolation led to this change of direction during 1981. It helped lead to the formal acceptance of the principle of 'ideological pluralism' by Grenada's CARICOM colleagues at the CARICOM Summit held in Ocho Rios in November 1982. Regional tolerance of the PRG was thereafter reinforced at the next Summit in Port of Spain the following July. Here, Bishop struck up a good working relationship with Prime Minister Chambers, apparently agreeing to hasten the electoral timetable (*Caribbean Insight*, August 1983, p. 1).

Grenada and the United States

The Goliath of the United States was in no mood for tolerance. A symbiotic relationship developed between American hostility and the various arms agreements signed by Grenada. The original one with Cuba of mid-March 1979 was followed by another in 1981. Two were signed with the Soviet Union in October 1980 and July 1982 respectively, and another with North Korea in April 1983. The Cuban-Soviet deliveries were worth US¢25.8 million, although most of the small arms were second-hand reconditioned. North Korea was generous with US$12 million worth. Common to the treaties with all three suppliers was the clause which bound both parties to 'take all measures . . . to assure the secrecy of the military assistance'; that with Cuba (article 12) was especially strict, stressing the need to keep secret 'the permanency of the military personnel in both states and the character of [their] activities (People's Revolutionary Government, 1981c). Although the fact of arms shipments could not be hidden, the amounts were not known and neither was the stipulation in all five agreements that transfers to third parties could not be made except with the permission of the supplier. Additional to the arms was agreement over the stationing of Cuban military advisers and the placement of several PRA personnel in Cuban and Soviet military training establishments. The first two advisers arrived in April 1979; by October 1983 there were some thirty. A long-term agreement pledged twenty-seven permanent and twelve to thirteen temporary experts (ibid., Annex no. 1).

This assistance enabled the People's Revolutionary Army to swell from 1,100 (1980) to nearly 2,000 in 1983, consisting of one regular and five reservist battalions, plus support units. It was planned to expand the PRA rapidly from 1983. The Soviet Union was requested to assist the creation of another three regular and nine reservist battalions by 1985, making a total of over 11,000, or about 15 per cent of the adult population (Request for Military Assistance, July 1982). Not unexpectedly, the original Cuban arms were Soviet-made and the later agreements made direct with Moscow made clear the Soviet Union's main role as military supplier. But for some time only Cuba had an embassy in St. George's. It opened in late 1979—the first permanent diplomatic mission in Grenada since independence—together with an office of the Cuban news agency, *Prensa Latina*. It was not until September 1982 that a Soviet embassy was established. Headed by Ambassador Gennedy Sazhenev, a seasoned Latin American expert and quickly named by the American media as a former KGB colonel, its eventual total of thirty personnel (including technical assistance staff) plus dependants lived and worked in a secure compound and were rarely seen.

The first reaction of the United States was one of denial. It refused the credentials of Grenada's designate Ambassador, Dessima Williams, as she was 'too young' but could not prevent her accreditation to the Organization of American States (OAS). But it was able to delay OAS assistance to Grenadian farmers after the 1980 floods. Together with Britain, it banned all official aid for later disaster relief although assistance was offered to banana growers on the other Windward Islands who were associated with those of Grenada through the Windward Islands Banana Producers Association (WINBAN). WINBAN refused to accept the United States Agency for International Development (AID) aid on principle. Later, AID assistance to the Commonwealth Caribbean disbursed through the Caribbean Development Bank was also subject to the same condition. This time, such were the needs of the recipients that the CDB's protests had to be ignored and the veto respected. Britain justified its position by referring to 'the unattractive record of the Grenada government over civil liberties and democratic rights' (*Caribbean Insight*, July 1979). It was unfortunate that, coincidentally, it restored full relations and aid to the Pinochet regime in Chile. In reality, it was, as a British Foreign Office Minister indiscreetly remarked, because 'Grenada is in the process of establishing a kind of society of which the British Government disapproves, irrespective of whether the people of Grenada want it or not' (*Caribbean Contact*, March 1981).

Denial was incorporated in early 1980 into wider forms of destabilization. Bishop had forecast it several months earlier:

The first part of the plan was aimed at creating dissatisfaction and unrest among our people and wrecking our tourist industry and economy. A second level of the Pyramid involved the use of violence and arson in the country. And if neither of these two methods of destabilizing the country worked, the plan was to move to the stage of assassinating the leadership of the country. [Bishop, 1982c, p. 22.]

In fact, the sequence was correct. There had already been arson outbreaks and press distortion. In November 1979 the 'De Ravenière Plot' was unearthed, a grandiose and totally unrealistic scheme by mercenary-led *émigrés* and dissidents to invade the island. Arms caches, explosives, radio equipment and written plans were put on show and many suspects rounded up. There followed the bomb outrage of 19 June 1980. It failed to kill the leadership as planned and the finger was firmly pointed at the CIA. No firm proof was offered but circumstantial evidence linked those who planted it (and another a week later) with active overseas opponents who enjoyed American support. The allegation was officially denied by the United States but evidence of past malpractice in the region by the Agency led many to believe that there was a grain of truth in the allegation. Four months later, there was an outbreak of shooting and bombing which ushered in the Terrorism (Prevention) Law—People's Law no. 46 of 1980—largely modelled on British legislation designed for Ulster. Within weeks, five young men were killed in a terrorist attack.

There was to be no respite. President Reagan's accession to the White House marked the renaissance of the 'domino' theory, its discredited history in America's Asian conflicts set aside. The Caribbean Basin was a 'sea of splashing dominoes' which, as they fell one by one as victims of an evil Havana–Moscow conspiracy, edged ever nearer to the last domino itself, the United States. The thesis of United States Ambassador to the United Nations, Jeane Kirkpatrick, was endorsed by Reagan. Most Third World countries, she charged, fell basically into two categories: Marxist–totalitarian dictatorships and right-wing autocracies. Right-wing autocrats were less repressive, more susceptible to reform and more compatible with American interests, and consequently rightists deserved American support. Certainly the United States should not collaborate 'in deposing an erstwhile friend and ally and installing a Government hostile to American interests'—which she charged the Carter administration with having done in Iran and Nicaragua. Change, she added, rarely represented improvement in the Third World. Certainly, socialism did not necessarily bring justice, and revolutionaries who promised democracy often ended up by aligning their countries with the Soviet Union and imposing 'extremist' rule

(Kirkpatrick, 1979, pp. 3–10). Autocracies, therefore, were to be supported particularly if 'vital' American national interests were involved, but totalitarian regimes deserved no corner. Indeed, the unfolding nightmare of a communized Caribbean demanded military action. Liberals in the State Department were purged in favour of hard-liners involved with a 'cleansing' mission, nearly all veterans of covert action in South-east Asia. Central America suddenly became the front line, El Salvador in particular. A massive rise in military aid and the despatch of 'advisers' was followed by a policy of hostility to the Sandinista *junta* in Nicaragua. Denial was quickly succeeded by economic sabotage and then overt military action through the funding and organization of the 'contras', anti-Sandinista forces mainly operating from Honduras. The rationale was the belief that 'the insurgency in El Salvador has been progressively transformed into a textbook case of indirect armed aggression by Communist power', using a Cuban conduit and a willing Nicaraguan accomplice. (Pearce, 1981, p. 240). Not surprisingly, therefore, new diplomatic and economic sanctions were applied against Cuba. Anti-Castro propaganda was considerably expanded with the establishment of Radio Martí in the Florida Keys, while massive military manoeuvres based upon the Guantánamo base became a regular feature.

On the day of Reagan's election and again on his inauguration, the PRG despatched letters of congratulation, making clear that it hoped for friendly relations between the two countries. The first was only formally acknowledged, the second not at all. A third was sent in August 1981. Again unanswered, it was publicized by the PRG with the warning that 'If you should allow this letter also to go unanswered . . . then we shall have to conclude that your government does not desire even normal or minimum relations . . . in which event we would be obliged to consider further measures necessary to consolidate and to defend the social, economic and political transformation process'. [*Caribbean Contact*, April 1982.]

The lack of response was not surprising since it was part and parcel of the strategy of destabilization by propaganda. Editorial comment and news coverage in both regional and North American media became almost uniformly hostile. In May 1981 the United States International Communication Agency publicly hosted a conference of Caribbean editors where offers of assistance were made in return for collaboration in isolating Grenada through damaging publicity. The result was spectacular. On 20 September 1981, identical front-page editorials appeared in five major regional newspapers. They made pointed reference to the closure of *The Grenadian Voice* and the arrest of the 'Group of 26' the previous June, and called for 'freedom for the people of Grenada'. Bishop, who denounced this 'extraordinary level of co-ordinated vulgarity', reiterated his government's belief that a clear link had existed between the *Voice* and the CIA. As the editorial pressure increased, so the tourist trade fell. The sheer scale of the operation could not be ignored. At an address to Caribbean journalists in April 1982, Bishop was moved to detail it. Over a nineteen-month period from June 1980 to December 1981, he said, a survey of major regional newspapers showed that there were, on average, three articles on Grenada per day: 60 per cent was editorial, 40 per cent 'straight news'.

About 60 per cent of these articles were negative towards the Grenada Revolution, being either downright lies or subtle, or not so subtle, distortions. Furthermore, 95 per cent of the PRG's rebuttals to many of these scandalous and libellous articles were never published. It is clear that no other topic has attracted such vast coverage in . . . the Caribbean press over the last three years. [Searle, 1983a, p. 156.]

But future and more drastic plans by the CIA for destabilization involving possible assassinations, received a rebuff by a Congress concerned at the rapidly deteriorating image of the Agency and, by its actions, of America's name generally, after so much trouble and effort had been expended on rebuilding it after the excesses in Vietnam and Cambodia. The Senate Intelligence Committee in July 1981 ordered a stop to direct political action (*New York Times*, 25 July 1981). Thereafter, the scene shifted to the economic, and specifically to the denial of the necessary foreign exchange funding for the new international airport.

The Point Salines airport project was by far the most visible manifestation of the Grenada–Cuban alliance and what in retrospect was a truly outstanding Cuban aid programme. It clearly overshadowed the important medical, agricultural and general engineering and maintenance programmes. To the United States, it epitomized Grenada's alignment with the Soviet bloc; it fitted into Grenada's anti-American policy like a hand in a glove. Grenada was siding with Cuba and the Soviet Union on every international issue, notably Afghanistan, regularly inviting Puerto Rican *independentistas* to solidarity meetings, developing close relations with America's enemies, and its soldiers were openly flaunting their Soviet weapons. The Cuban Ambassador, Julien Rizo, was seen as a shadowy but highly influential figure, as indeed he was. Cuban involvement in the airport project—massive considering Cuba's economy—clearly had a military objective as the length of the runway was manifestly too long for Grenada's modest air traffic. In short, a Cuban–Soviet military base was in the offing.

The International Airport

In fact, the first plan for an airport at Point Salines, on the arid south-western tip, was made as early as 1926 by the British. But the physical problems involved, such as the filling in of salt ponds and the levelling of small hills, led to the much cheaper construction of a grass strip at Pearls, on the opposite side of the island, which opened in January 1943. Over time, the strip was tarmacked and extended to its limit of 5,250 feet (1,600 metres), hemmed in by hills on three sides and the sea on the fourth. Night flying was impossible due to the topography and its site forced pilots to make a visual, rather than an instrument, approach, always assuming weather conditions permitted. Prevailing winds had made the construction of a 'crosswind' runway impossible, athough flat land was available. Thus Pearls was destined to handle only Avro 748 turbo-prop aircraft carrying up to firty-eight passengers, its aged buildings described as 'a squalid leftover from colonial days which looks for all the world like a Victorian railway station transported to the tropics' (*Daily Telegraph*, 26 October 1983). In addition to the expense of having to stay overnight in Barbados, tourists had the discomfort of a sixteen-mile journey over a poor road with innumerable hairpin bends before St. George's was reached. It is not hard to see why regional tourist authorities characterized Grenada as being 'highly desirable' but 'touristically disadvantaged'.

Clearly, tourism could not be developed unless something was done. The first serious survey of the Point Salines site and its salt ponds was undertaken in 1955. The British consultants, Scott, Wilson, Kirkpatrick and Partners, recommended the construction of an airport. Another recommendation followed in 1960 by the former West Indies Federation. Yet another was publicized in 1967 by a 'Tripartite Economic Commission' established by Britain, Canada and the United States, the basis of which was a report by the Canadian team who found the economic case proved. Finally, the original consultants were once again commissioned in 1969 and they reported favourably. When, therefore, the World Bank recommended in 1976 yet another examination, Grenada's patience was understandably beginning to wear thin. As an exasperated Coard was later to put it, 'There are thousands of people who earn their livelihood in writing economic and technical feasibility studies continuously over and over into the future. It is an industry all by itself . . . I plan personally to write a study about the politics of construction of international airports in the Caribbean, and Grenada's will be a case study in imperialism'.

In its 1973 *Manifesto*, the NJM made clear its opposition to Gairy's plan to build the airport. It would divert resources away from basic needs and, in any case, if it was constructed under Gairy's government, corruption would dominate the project, ultimately paid for by the working classes. But once in power, the PRG realized that it was essential for the future. 'In many countries the critical factor at a particular historical moment is to identify the major bottleneck, the major fetter to further rapid economic development and growth,' said Coard at a major co-financing conference at the EC Commision in Brussels, adding that the airport was to Grenada what the railroads had been to the United States (People's Revolutionary Government, 1981b, p. 41). The existing studies were re-examined and, in September 1979, Cuba agreed to supply US$40 million' worth of labour and machinery. It was announced publicly by Bishop on 18 November 1979 and the first of the 250 construction workers arrived the following January; 1,500 tons of steel, 4,000 tons of cement and 1.5 million gallons of fuel were pledged in the first instance (*Caribbean Contact*, December 1979). The terrain and climate was such that many of the Soviet machines succumbed and had to be replaced at considerable expense by mainly Japanese plant.

However, the total cost was US$71 million, incorporating air-traffic control equipment, lighting and ancillary works. Other aid was therefore required. The cost, allowing for inflation, was considerably higher than previous estimates since airline operators had moved to wide-bodied aircraft and a minimum 9,000 foot (2,750 metres) runway was therefore required. The plan was later extended to 9,800 feet (3,000 metres) to permit operation by a fully-loaded Boeing 747, with substantial unpaved sections of safety areas at each end. Contracts were placed with two Florida companies, Layne Dredging of Miami to fill in the salt ponds, and Norwich Engineering of Fort Lauderdale to design the fuel storage complex. Plessey, from Britain, was contracted to supply the radar and air-traffic control apparatus and associated electrical work to specifications produced in Havana. A Finnish company was also involved in terminal building work. A cash-flow analysis was made for potential aid-givers, using only 'the most incredibly conservative and limited calculations', to show that the airport would generate enough income to enable a surplus to be made after five years and to repay loans thereafter. It assumed that Grenada's share in total Caribbean tourism would move from 0.4 per cent (1981) to 1 per cent in 1990 and offered a low (5 per cent growth in tourism) and high (8 per cent) scenario. The former would need 437 extra hotel rooms; the latter 661. But, although it was admitted in 1981 that 'the very magnitude' of even the lower figure 'over the next ten years is at least as much or more than the investment in the airport itself', Coard pointed out there already existed a 40 per cent excess capacity, that 'concrete proposals' had been received by prospective hoteliers, and that the existing infrastructure on that part of the island, near as it was to St. George's and the Grand Anse resort area, would need little improvement.

The size of the project, coupled with effective American and British opposition in reducing the aid available, created a grave financial burden. The

EC only gave a disappointing US$2.2 million, and a further US$4 million promised by Libya and Iraq did not, for the most part, materialize, due presumably to bureaucratic inefficiency. France, Mexico and Canada refused aid directly for the airport but, by assisting other projects, enabled the PRG to transfer some of its capital budget to Point Salines. The 1983 budget greatly understated actual expenditure on the airport by the PRG. Only EC$15.6 million was earmarked although EC$50.6 million had to be found in that financial year. But approximately EC$39 million was spent by the government (information from interviews, Grenada Treasury, March 1984). Cuba increased its commitment and as opening day—scheduled for 13 March 1984—grew nearer, increased the labour force to some 600 to ensure that the terminal building, apron and the five-mile approach road was completed on time. By October 1983, the value of Cuban assistance for the airport reached the impressive sum of US$60 million.

The strain was such that even the Soviet Union was approached. The PRG by now realized the potential political repercussions as EC$15 million was requested in strict secrecy. Moscow deferred consideration for not only did it rarely grant aid in valuable convertible currency but if it were to do so, it risked needless provocation that would only increase the regime's growing vulnerability.

Sabre-rattling

The United States capitalized on the PRG's problems by intensifying pressure. As Cuban and Soviet aid grew, the nascent fears of Grenada's neighbours were carefully nurtured. They shared Washington's concern about the size of the armed forces, the presence of Cuban and other Soviet-bloc military advisers and the swelling of the two PRA bases at Calivigny and Egmont, a few miles east of the Point Salines' airport site. But they differed over the consequences. The Organization of Eastern Caribbean States plus Barbados and Trinidad-Tobago dismissed as fanciful American claims that the alleged Cuban–Soviet bases on Grenada would be used to invade them. Rather, they feared that the island would be a jumping-off point for subversion by small vanguard groups all over the Caribbean. The scenario was a simple one. They would operate with the benefit of the massive 75 kilowatt transmitter built by the Soviet Union at Beausejour in Grenada (later downgraded to 50 kilowatts after widespread protests) which was to replace the existing 1 kilowatt operation of Radio Free Grenada. Their subversive activities, financed by Cuban aid channelled through Grenada, would not be hindered or contested by local defence forces because such forces scarcely existed. Once a foothold had been achieved, they could then request and receive the help of Grenadian forces without fear of local opposition. As evidence of this, regional politicians pointed to the various solidarity meetings hosted by the PRG at which local Marxist and other progressive groups played a vocal role, joining those from Central America and Cuba, and Soviet bloc 'fraternal' delegates. An armed transit station designed to further Cuban and Soviet aims was, they thought, in prospect.

The United States readily concurred but added a more strategic dimension. The case was first outlined by Thomas Enders in December 1981 to the Senate Foreign Relations Committee. The 'Cuban–Soviet base' at Point Salines threatened the Venezuelan and Trinidadian oil fields and the oil shipping route through the deepwater channel between Grenada and Tobago. 'All types of Soviet aircraft' would be able to use it 'to land and refuel', particularly on the Cuba–Angola route. Indeed, such was the importance attached to the airport by the State Department that the possibility of Soviet MiG-23 and MiG-25 aircraft being based there was cited as a major reason for the Senate to ratify the sale of F-16 aircraft to Venezuela (Enders, 1981). In vain did the PRG plead that Barbados and Guyana had originally been used as staging posts for Cuban troop carriers to Africa and that the runway length was comparable to those of Antigua, St. Lucia and Trinidad—all originally built by the Americans—and smaller by over 1,000 feet as compared to airports at Guadeloupe, Aruba and Barbados. Invitations to visit the site and to see that there were no military facilities, such as underground bombproof hangers for fighters and well-protected fuel facilities, were ignored. The runway was completely exposed with the British-equipped control tower on a hill. Plessey confirmed the non-military character of its work. The British government had extended export credit guarantees to the company, hardly the act of a pro-Reagan government if it did not believe that tourism was the airport's real purpose.

The apogee was reached on 23 March 1983 when Reagan announced the new Strategic Defense Initiative. It centred upon space weaponry and so was quickly dubbed the 'Star Wars' speech. The television presentation included aerial pictures of Point Salines with the runway and Cuban workcamps (at that time housing some 400) pinpointed. He decried those who denigrated the importance he attached to Grenada just because it was small and exported nutmegs. 'People who make these arguments', he declared, 'haven't taken a good look at a map lately . . . it is not nutmeg that is at stake in the Caribbean and Central America, it is the United States' national security.' The American chargé d'affaires in Barbados followed this up three days later. The threat came from the 'Calivigny–Egmont–Point Salines complex' which, 'as a separate entity' from the rest of Grenada, 'could be thought of as a stationary aircraft carrier' (*Latin American Regional Report: Caribbean*, 13 May 1983).

This allegation was made in the midst of military manoeuvres. They had become a regular feature from 1980 and their sheer scale was a provocation in itself. Those of 1983 were within sight of Calivigny, being only six miles off-shore. The August 1981 manoeuvres—codenamed 'Ocean Venture '81'—off Puerto Rico included over 120,000 troops, 250 warships and 1,000 aircraft. This involved more ships than were used in the Allied landing on Normandy in 1944 (*Miami Herald*, 25 August 1981). Within it was a clearly provocative exercise, 'Amber and the Amberines'. Amber is near Point Salines but for the exercise, Vieques was invaded by United States Rangers. Their objective was to capture the mountainous island, organize American-style elections for a people denied them and install a 'friendly' government. The allusions were unsubtle. 'Amber' was supported by 'Orange' (Cuba), which in turn was supported by 'Red' (the Soviet Union). Rear Admiral McKenzie praised the air mobility of the forces, declared Grenada, Nicaragua and Cuba as 'practi-cally one country engaged in exporting terrorist activities' and stated that the objective of the exercise was to 'reinforce in the eyes and minds of those watching our military commitment around the world—to give an example of one facet of the US capability to respond in the Caribbean basin' (*Caribbean Contact*, September 1981).

The wide publicity accorded to Grenada's protests led to less overtly political exercises. But they were none the less threatening. Indeed, the presence of seventy-seven American and allied warships off Grenada in March 1983, which used Barbados as a major base, caused Bishop to cut short his participation in the Non-Aligned Summit in India and to put all Grenada's armed forces on full alert. A year earlier, at a conference of Carib-bean journalists in April 1983, he made Grenada's position scornfully clear.

Like an overgrown child at his bathtime, President Reagan is about to drop into what he believes is his bathtub, his fleet of toy battleships and aircraft carriers filled to the brim with plastic planes and clockwork marines. Such huge military manœuvres, so perilously close to our shores . . . only demonstrate one more time the proximity of war and the blasé, imperial and Monroe doctrine-like attitude of the United States to our region and waters. [Searle, 1983a, p. 158.]

Less dramatically, the denial policy continued. During 1981, several Caribbean leaders led by Seaga formulated a 'Mini-Marshall Plan' for the Caribbean, whereby several donors would co-operate in providing funds for a widespread economic reconstruction and development plan. The United

States responded favourably but as it began to name its conditions, the other potential donors, notably Canada and Mexico, dropped out. Seaga was not unhappy, for Washington's ideas fitted his 'new right' philosophy: that security assistance to combat alleged Cuban subversion and exploitation of economic distress was at least as important as aid to alleviate the distress itself. Eventually, the Caribbean Basin Initiative (CBI) finally emerged in August 1983. Billed as a 'trade-and-aid package', its original plans to liberalize entry of Caribbean Basin goods into the American market had been considerably diluted by Congress while the direction of the aid clearly showed concern for political and military considerations. El Salvador and Jamaica were to get most; Honduras and the Eastern Caribbean islands the least; and for Grenada and Nicaragua, nothing at all. Grenada's response was predictable. Bishop denigrated the plan to a PRG rally.

This plan is meant only to deal with narrow military, security and strategic considerations of the USA and is not genuinely concerned with the economic and social development of the people of this region ... the CBI plan reflects the chauvinism and ugly Americanism of Reagan, in the vulgar way in which he has completely ignored and discarded the views of Caribbean countries, as to what kind of plan they wished to see. The concern of his plan is with his warmongering 'national security' interests ... his Basin plan has turned out to be the con game of the century. [Bishop, 1982a, pp. 275–6.]

But many of the arrows were finding their target. Swallowing its pride, the PRG decided to attempt to once again try to reach a settlement.

An Aborted Rapprochement

Just as the airport concentrated American fears, so it was the prime reason for a *rapprochement*. The airport would be economically viable if the North American market was secured. There was also a slow realization by the Central Committee that anti-American sloganizing was counter-productive. It therefore agreed with Bishop's suggestion after the March alert that a moratorium would be appropriate. Whatever its public fulminations about the CBI, it hoped that the American attitude would soften and that it would, after all, include Grenada. As the July 1983 First Plenary Session of the NJM concluded, 'the private sector must be encouraged to explore opportunities in the area of investments by the CBI. However, this area must be closely monitored by the Party to ensure that the capitalists are not provided with an effective new base for covert activity by the USA.' (Central Committee Report on First Plenary Session, 13–19 July 1983.)

At first, the omens appeared poor. In December 1982, Vice-President

George Bush declared to the Miami Caribbean Business Conference that Grenada was 'repressive', 'economically weak' and 'dependent' upon Cuba and the Soviet Union. Grenada's reply was quiet and very diplomatically worded, arguing that the PRG's economic and social achievements 'compare favourably with those of the American revolution, whose earliest years themselves constituted a glorious period in the history of the United States of America'. It rejected the charge of repression: 'Grenada has certainly been obliged to be alert and vigilant. Such vigilance cannot reasonably be interpreted as repression'. It ended by offering to send a 'high level emissary' to brief the Vice-President; and sent a copy of the World Bank Report (*Caribbean Insight*, February 1983, p. 5). It also intensified a process begun a few months earlier, that of patching up relations with its OECS and CARICOM neighbours. Foreign Minister Whiteman sent conciliatory messages and Grenada's overseas representatives and delegates to regional meetings were instructed to be as co-operative as possible. He himself calculated that by 1983, 80 per cent of his time was spent on relations with Commonwealth Caribbean states, which he perceived as a bastion against American aggression (Payne, Sutton & Thorndike, 1984, p. 114).

Grenada's reply to Bush was at first met by a stony silence, but a few weeks later Secretary of State George Schultz sent what seemed a lifeline to Bishop. Not only was it the first official communication since the warning, in the first few days after the insurrection, against involvement with Cuba, but it was conciliatory in tone. It was dispatched outside the diplomatic framework, via the Trinidad-born leader of the black caucus in Congress, Mervyn Dymally, and indicated that all American personnel at the Barbados Embassy were to be accredited to Grenada bar the Ambassador, Milan Bish. For his part, Congressman Dymally invited Bishop to Washington. He had the support of the influential Afro-American foreign affairs lobby group, Trans-Africa, and could not be ignored. These moves were all the more remarkable since they coincided with Reagan's most belligerent speeches attacking Grenada.

The visit was finally arranged for 31 May through 10 June 1983. Bishop requested a top-level meeting but was rebuffed: 'not the President, the Vice-President, a secretary or even a fortieth secretary'. He turned down as 'inappropriate' a meeting with the United States Ambassador to the OAS. However, once in Washington with representatives of the Grenadian private business and tourism sectors, strong Congressional and very favourable media pressure forced the American government to concede a thirty-minute meeting with National Security Council chief William Clark and Assistant Secretary of State Kenneth Dam, who deputized for Schultz. The announcement of the constitutional commission was welcomed and, although the meeting was mutually agreed to be strictly confidential, it is known that the possibility of reducing the Cuban presence and of revitalizing the private sector was discussed. Emphasis was also put by the American side on the need to arrest the deepening of relations with the Soviet Union. Away from Washington, Bishop's visit was a triumph for the 2,500 Grenadians and other West Indian nationals who packed New York's Hunter College auditorium. As a local West Indian magazine vividly reported, 'Standing before their very eyes was the Luke Skywalker of [Reagan's] March 23rd "Star Wars" speech. He had come to challenge Darth Vader and the Force was with him. The standing, screaming, stomping ovation must have lasted a full three minutes ... Mohammed had come to the Mountain'. (*Everybody's Magazine*, June/July 1983, p. 41.) He went on to media press conferences and other successful meetings, most arranged impromptu as the popular reaction to his visit gathered pace, in a series of cities extending as far west as Detroit.

On his return to Grenada, Bishop issued instructions that the moratorium on anti-American rhetoric was to continue. But there was doubt as to how much had actually been achieved at official level. The request for a United States diplomatic mission in St. George's was only 'to be considered' although it had been agreed that a Congressional delegation would visit Grenada the following autumn. Dam had, in effect, stone-walled on most of Bishop's proposals. At home, however, Bishop was suspected by some on the Central Committee of possibly going beyond what had been agreed. Strict guidelines had been laid down by the CC. It was not the fact that the Dam meeting was unscheduled that was the concern, rather that Bishop had attempted to conduct negotiations on a very sensitive level without prior reference and guidance. Bishop retorted that the punishing schedule and the distances involved had made this impossible. The doubters reluctantly agreed and went on to press successfully at the July Plenary to 'move rapidly to firm up relations with the Socialist World'.

It was such sentiments which barred any further *rapprochement*. Grenada was Cuba's ally and Cuba was the main target. But, other than preserving its revolution, what had Cuba done to deserve such odium and approbation?

Cuba and the Caribbean

Cuba's foreign policy was bound to offend the United States at every turn as it implicitly attempted to end its isolation in the western hemisphere. It had to neutralize external hostility and support national liberation movements sympathetic to its principles. In short, it searched for friends. As with its domestic policy, Cuba's foreign policy was conducted over the years with a blend of idealism and pragmatism, socialism and nationalism, the combination of which varied with time and circumstances. There were four broad phases of development.

The first two, the 1960s and 1970–5 respectively, contrasted vividly. The 1960s were characterized by an idealism on the offensive, with strong support being given to revolutionary movements, particularly in Latin America. In the Caribbean, the policy was singularly unsuccessful and served merely to convince the Latin members of the OAS that diplomatic and economic sanctions were the only answer; Cuba had been effectively excluded from the alliance in January 1962. In July 1964 these sanctions were imposed following a Venezuelan initiative, with only Mexico refusing to implement the decision.

By the close of the decade, continued failure coupled with the electoral success of Salvador Allende's Marxist party in Chile led to a complete change of tack. Castro was no doubt influenced by Allende: he publicly conceded during a visit to Chile in 1971 that there were alternatives to violent confrontation in the struggle to build socialism. A new pragmatic and passive period commenced with emphasis put upon economic development and the deepening of ties with a previously sceptical Soviet Union. These were cemented by a generous economic treaty in 1972 and a state visit by Brezhnev in January 1974. In 'progressive' states such as Panama and Jamaica, the radical left was advised not to attempt violent overthrow; likewise for 'liberal-democratic' regimes such as Mexico and, more pragmatically, states of political and economic importance to Cuba, notably Venezuela and the Dominican Republic (Levine, 1983, p. 11). The constraint, however, did not extend to pro-American, anti-communist regimes. Foreign aid programmes developed and by the close of the decade, some 50,000 technical assistance experts were working in thirty-seven countries. Trade was encouraged and Cuba's isolation began to lessen.

It was soon rewarded, in the first instance, by the newly emergent English-speaking states. Trinidad called for Cuba's readmittance into the OAS in 1970, but the decisive breakthrough was two years later when, led by Jamaica and Guyana, diplomatic relations were established with the independent members of CARICOM. The Latins then responded; on Peru's initiative, the OAS boycott was lifted in 1974, thus heralding the third period, one of initiative. Relations with Jamaica became particularly close, and Cuba found many in the West Indies who applauded its decision to fulfil countless Third World pledges and actually to fight imperialism and apartheid in Southern Africa. Admittedly, Barbados expressed reservations, seeing the Angola exercise as more an intervention in Angolan internal affairs, and there was powerfully expressed opposition within Jamaica at the extent of Cuba's involvement in the Jamaican economy if not the political system. But with Manley's re-election in 1976, the strengthening of progressive forces in the region generally and the spectacular collapse of the American position in Vietnam, Cuba could be forgiven for thinking that the 'correlation of forces' in world politics had decisively moved in favour of anti-imperialism and socialism. Events continued to be favourable: the United States was finally forced to concede the eventual transfer of sovereignty over the Panama Canal to Panama, and Cuba became a full member of the Latin American Economic System (SELA), established in 1975 to negotiate common trade policies and to provide a diplomatic front regarding economic relations with the United States. There then followed the NJM insurrection and the collapse of the Somoza dictatorship in Nicaragua within five months of each other in 1979. Cuba was no longer alone.

The pinnacle was finally reached in September 1979 when Castro was acclaimed chairman of the Non-Aligned Movement (NAM) at its summit in Havana. But within months, the fourth phase, that of decline, set in. The Soviet intervention in Afghanistan in December 1979, without warning to Cuba, spotlighted Cuba's betrothal to the Soviet Union. Alone with Grenada, it defied the NAM position which demanded the evacuation of all foreign troops from that unfortunate country and positively supported the Soviet Union, particularly in the United Nations. By now, Cuba was more economically dependent upon the socialist bloc than ever before. Soviet aid and trade subsidies ran to some US$3 billion per year, in addition to military assistance (Pastor, 1983, p. 200). This was virtually doubled by a further agreement in 1981 so that an astonishing approximate 30 per cent of GNP was allegedly attributable to such assistance (*Daily Gleaner*, 29 February 1982). Not surprisingly, 'proxy' theories began to abound, Cuba being characterized as the Soviet 'Trojan Horse' in Latin America, the Caribbean and Africa. But a more sober assessment would be that Cuban and Soviet interests 'converge', and that Cuban personnel are much more suited by experience and temperament than Soviet colleagues to work in those areas (Millett & Will, 1979, pp. 132–48).

Difficulties thereafter multiplied. Electoral swings to the right in several Caribbean states, notably Jamaica, were compounded by the determination of the Reagan administration to restore American hegemony. By late 1981, Colombia, Costa Rica and Jamaica had broken diplomatic relations. Relations with Venezuela came close to breaking point when charges against four Cuban *émigrés* in Caracas accused of blowing up a Cuban Airlines plane off Barbados in 1976 were dropped. Protests met with the cessation of oil shipments at concessionary prices. The death of General Torrijos of Panama cost another friend; and the well-publicized sight of thousands of disaffected, mainly working-class, Cubans fleeing the revolution in the so-called 'Mariel boat-lift' in mid-1980 did nothing for Cuba's image among the region's dispossessed. Further, as American military involvement in Central America was stepped up, Cuba could offer few promises to the increasingly beleagured Sandinistas and Salvadorean insurrectionists. Increasingly, therefore, Cuba was forced upon the support of, and for, only one friend—Grenada. It is in this context that the Cuban-Grenadian alliance must be judged: they both needed each other.

Grenada and Cuba

It was the PRG who first wooed Cuba, not the other way round. The initial shipment of arms and cement, the former in response to the counter-revolutionary threat which Grenada's traditional allies refused to recognize, and the vastly expanded aid programme thereafter, could not have been possible without the general empathy that the NJM leadership held for the Cuban leadership. Bishop made clear this enthusiasm time and time again. At the Havana summit, he urged fellow delegates to remember that:

Cuba laid the basis for Grenada, Nicaragua . . . The example and spirit of the Cuban revolution has therefore had international impact. But, perhaps, most important of all is the fact that it is now the best example of what socialism can do in a small country for health, education, employment, for ending poverty, prostitution and disease. It is now the best example in the world of what a small country under social-ism can achieve. That is what socialism is all about. [Bishop, 1982a, p. 94.]

He followed this up in a speech celebrating the first anniversary of the insurrection. 'The greatest debt of gratitude owed to the Cubans', he announced, 'is that if there had been no Cuban revolution in 1959 there could have been no Grenadian revolution in 1979' (Bishop, 1982a, p. 114). The hyper-bole apart, there did clearly exist a high degree of personal admiration for the achievements in the social and welfare field by the Cuban government. Over time, a deep personal friendship grew between Bishop and Castro.

Whether this personal element played a significant role in Cuba's escala-tion of assistance is debatable. What is certain is that Grenada represented not only an opportunity to show the world what Cuba could do but was also Cuba's ally. Besides giving full support to the Cuban and Soviet positions in international organizations and conferences, the PRG amply fulfilled that hope. If anything, it heaped more praise upon the Sandinistas and the Salvadorean guerrillas than did its mentor, at least publicly, although it clearly could not support the Nicaraguan revolution materially or militarily.

The chairman of the ruling junta, Daniel Ortega, was guest of honour at the first anniversary celebrations, and Bishop and Castro shared the platform at the equivalent occasion in Managua. Before the Second Congress of the Cuban Communist Party in February 1981, Bishop clearly pledged solidarity. 'We give our solemn pledge that wherever circumstances require we shall unhesitatingly fulfil our internationalist responsibilities. Imperialism must know and understand that if they touch Cuba, they touch Grenada, and if they touch Nicaragua they touch Grenada' (Gill, 1981, p. 4).

Grenada's willingness to receive Cuban aid and the readiness with which it was given was formalized in June 1979. Aid at that point was mostly concerned with the widespread medical aid programme and the granting of scholarships. By mid-1982, over 250 Grenadians were studying in Cuba. Cuban aid also encouraged improved agriculture, water supply and fishing, stemming from a widespread sixty-three point economic and technical agreement signed in June 1980. Public declarations of the alliance were the inauguration of direct flights by Cubana Airlines to Grenada in February 1981, and the cancellation of visa requirements for nationals travelling to and from the two countries. The following July saw a further agreement expanding the areas of co-operation and an agreement to sell sugar, rice and cement at subsidized prices. Cuba's anxiety to help its new partner was again shown by two further pacts in June and December 1982 respectively. In short, it is hard to see how the PRG could have survived without Cuban assistance. Therefore, its alliance with Havana was totally non-negotiable.

The strategic–military aspects of this relationship, coming as it did at the critical juncture of American foreign policy, sealed the fate of the Grenadian revolution. But there was no alternative to Cuba for the construction of the airport, and Cuba would not have been so generous if the PRG had not made its progressiveness and socialist preferences so crystal clear. Taking Grenada's foreign policy in its totality, the challenge to the United States was to be unsustainable, no matter the justification and the correctness of the struggle against dependency and hegemony. Grenada's provocation and Washington's relentless opposition led 'principled positions' to be more stubbornly pursued but, in the final analysis, undefendable. Solidarity was a moral advantage but could not be translated into military support. The only power able to consider assistance, Cuba, was in the event not willing. Besides the logistical problems, there was the overwhelming force of American military might. But, in any case, Castro turned his back on a derailed regime that had killed its leader in the search for ideological purity.

Part III
The Reckoning

9 Derailment

The New Jewel Movement had, on Bishop's own admission in his *Line of March* statement to party members on 13 September 1982, passed through five stages. It was, he said, entering into a sixth stage as he spoke. But his forecast was totally at variance with what was to happen. Further, he was not to know that there was to be a seventh, that of military dictatorship. In its development the party was to go full circle—from ultra-leftism to ultra-leftism.

The first stage was identified as beginning with the merger of JEWEL and the MAP in March 1973. The strategy, admittedly partially forced upon it by the independence crisis, was one of organizing strikes and demonstrations as methods of mass mobilization. But 'a deep class approach was not taken . . . and there was an over-reliance on spontaneity and the possibilities of crowd politics'. Ultra-leftist practices dominated since 'the major weakness . . . was the subjective factor, the fact that a Leninist approach to party building and to strategy and tactics were not adopted'. The second stage, to June 1977, was to Bishop a period of 'early childhood', characterized by 'a constant struggle withn the party to put Leninist principles into practice and in a concrete way'. The contesting of the 1976 election and policy on party alliance 'were evidence of a developing political and ideological maturity'. There followed a 'quantitative leap forward' between July 1977 and August 1978, when increased party work amongst the masses was complemented by incremental Leninist organization. But failure of its work amongst the rural workers—the bulk of the population—was admitted. Fortunately, the party 'moved into top gear' in the period from August 1978 to the insurrection in the following March. Thereafter, the fifth stage was one of 'mass activity', of supervision of the 'state apparatus' and 'in running the state generally'. But despite deepening links with the masses through the mass organizations, socialism classes and the institutions of 'People's Power', several of the new structures were not working well. Neither was the economy. The new stage was therefore a 'corrective' one, marked by an acceleration of the Leninist process. Henceforth, considerable emphasis was to be put upon party domination of the armed forces, especially the Militia, at all levels, the extension of public ownership and communalism, an intensification of political education and the application of Leninist discipline and seriousness.

The lengthy analysis was necessary for three reasons. The ideological was the continuing necessity to build the party as a vanguard, ushering in the eventual dictatorship of the working class. The party had to be built on Leninist principles 'because the working class does not have the ideological development or experience to build socialism on its own'. It was 'our primary responsibility to prepare and train the working class for what their historic mission will be later on down the road'. The second was strategic, namely the need to apply Marxist-Leninist scientific principles to determine and direct the convergence of the objective factors—the economy and the national democratic alliance with the middle stratum and petty bourgeoisie—and the subjective factor, the party. Only through such a convergence could Grenada proceed from the first stage of the noncapitalist path, that of socialist orientation, towards socialism. The third reason was, however, clearly tactical. Bishop was well aware of the tensions building up within the Central Committee over the alleged lack of ideological direction within the party and unsatisfactory policy direction and implementation. If he had hoped by his speech to deflect some of these criticisms away from himself, or even to defuse them, only limited success was achieved. It certainly did not prevent Coard's resignation a month later. He had, however, the satisfaction that the membership enthusiastically endorsed his strategy. In subsequent weeks, strenuous efforts were made to fulfil the tasks outlined by the *Line of March*. Only in one—the creation of an international climate of opinion favourable to the revolution—was there a measurable degree of success, substantially due to Bishop's magnetic personality. In the others, the intensification of socialist education and especially an awareness of the 'true nature' of the American threat, an increased commitment to the mass organizations, the strengthening of Leninism in the party, better planning for faster economic growth and the construction of a well-trained and motivated Militia (General Meeting of NJM Members, 14 September 1982, p. 6), there were to be serious shortcomings.

Sharpening Criticism

At first, all went well. The purge of 'unsuitable' Central Committee members was a cathartic relief. The December 1982 CC meeting decided to concentrate efforts on three priority areas, agriculture, industry and the Centre for Popular Education, the CPE. It was also agreed to restrict the number of rallies and solidarity meetings and to ease workloads in general. But only in agriculture was any thought given to future policy. The intensive discussions that culminated in the Central Committee resolution on agriculture of March 1983 ended there. The sensitivity of the issue precluded action. A similar fate met the more radical proposals for a Ministry of State Enterprises, which stressed the need to extend public ownership, and for a State Trading Organization. Overall, the working parties responsible for the reports adopted a pragmatic approach, in sharp contrast in tone and content to the rising demands of the radical zealots in the Committee. Their underlying dissatisfaction surfaced again in March 1983 when the CC received a report alleging, correctly, that 'the party was close to losing its links to the masses' and that this was retarding 'the important task of party building'. Although they were not to know of the deepening crisis within the party, visitors sympathetic to the aims of the revolution could not help noticing a sharp fall-off in political work. The Zonal Council activity had atrophied while church attendance remained as high as ever. To redress matters, the first ever Plenary Session of the NJM was called for 13–19 July 1983.

Full and committee members met together for a total of fifty-four hours. For the first time, the question of leadership clearly emerged. To the by now well-worn complaints about the 'continued failure of the Party to transform itself ideologically and organizationally' was added a lack of 'firm leadership on a Leninist path'. Much of the time, however, was spent on analysing specific problems. Concern was expressed at the 'spreading of anti-communism', particularly by the church. The mass organizations, the National In-Service Teacher Education Programme and the CPE were suffering from bureaucratic and leadership inefficiency. Village militia units had decreased in number, and those based in work places were discouraged. The economy was deteriorating sharply. There was a serious cash-flow problem because of the diversion of income to the airport project created by the difficulty in raising aid funds. The problem was compounded by a fall in banana export receipts, caused by the steady devaluation of the British pound sterling against the Unites States' dollar and hence the EC dollar. It was apparent not only in deteriorating roads and water and electricity services, but, more importantly, by a fall in morale amongst both party members and the population at large. 'The alliance with the bourgeoisie to create a national economy', one member stated, 'has become more complex and must be re-examined.' (Handwritten comment, CC Report on First Plenary Session, July 1983, p. 2.) By this time, public dissatisfaction was certainly showing. Rallies were poorly attended—two in St. George's had to be abandoned due to lack of support—and, in Sauteurs, party cadres were on one occasion chased down the street by irate villagers who dismissed their propaganda as 'communist'. The problem was acute in St. Andrew's parish, on the east coast. There was anger that virtually all new investment—by mid-1983, 90 per cent of which was from the state—was concentrated on the west coast at St. George's and Point Salines. There was particular apprehension that once Pearls airport closed, the imbalance would worsen. Although the primary agricultural area, St. Andrew's feeder roads went unrepaired as did other infrastructure.

After a wideranging review of the activities and problems of all the subcommittees—organization and secretariat, workers, international relations, farmers, teachers, youth, women and propaganda—a series of positive decisions was taken. All had a common focus: the need to restore the revolutionary momentum and deepen the ideological process. For members, 'ideological and character qualities' and 'organizational skills' had to be further developed and entry qualifications made even higher. For the general public, workers' education classes were to be extended to the private sector. To counter 'inconsistent attendance' and 'low involvement' by workers, material incentives were to be awarded to participants in the CPE programmes at each successfully completed level. The work of the CPE was to be 'massively stepped up' and its organization revamped, since it was acknowledged that 'the CPE among the workers was one of the weakest areas of the worker's work', a failure 'linked to the weakness of the CPE administration centre itself' (CC Report on First Plenary Session, July 1983, p. 11).

Political education for teachers was especially emphasized. Although 'progressive forces' now controlled the Grenada Teachers' Union, 'the majority of teachers remain backward politically'. Also, there was the problem of the 'unsatisfactory disposition of students to the Revolution', especially in the secondary schools. They continued to be affected 'by the growing influence of the Church'. Also, sports 'are still being conducted without firm political control and direction and has not taken on a mass character'. Therefore, unsuitable head teachers were to be removed, the NISTEP programme extended to secondary schools, and their students involved more in 'proletarianism' and community work. Political education at all levels, including the primary, was to be stepped up and religious instruction declared optional and restricted in hours.

Farmers were also to receive more ideological attention. There had been a 'total absence of propaganda' and the Political Bureau and the Central Committee were to supervise this work closely. The lack of action on the agriculture resolution was deplored. The national leadership was specifically blamed for problems in the National Women's Organization, although no criticism was levelled at Phyllis Coard. Many NWO members harboured 'petty bourgeois' ideas and were 'unaccustomed to working on their own'. This coded reference to inefficiency had 'to be seen in the context of the deep petty bourgeois nature of our party' which was a 'privileged clique'. Both the organization and propaganda work of the party 'were in deep crisis'. The state of the Militia was such that people would think that 'imperialism no longer existed'. As for St. Andrew's, a task force would be based there and 'counter-intelligence, army and police' instructed to tackle those responsible for the parish having become 'a major source of counter-revolution' and rife with 'a proliferation of petty rumours'. Also to be tackled was the continued cultivation of marijuana and, more vaguely, 'the hoarding of money' by the peasantry and rural petty bourgeoisie. Priority would be given to the east coast in the industrialization programme. George Louison was asked to organize the task force, partly due to his proven ability in rural mobilization but also because of his agricultural portfolio. He was reluctant to accept, preferring the chairmanship of a pivotal public-sector body that was expected to emerge from the working parties' reports on industry, trade and agriculture. Committee member and leading trade unionist John 'Chalky' Ventour questioned Louison's ability to handle a post of such strategic importance for the party and economy. This only served to increase Louison's resentment against those in the forefront of the rising criticism.

'Onemanism' and Joint Leadership

Bishop's leadership had not been specifically pin-pointed by the Central Committee in the July Plenary. On the contrary, his role in making his visit to the United States in June such a resounding success could not be ignored. The People's Revolutionary Government basked in the reflection of his international stature, to say nothing of his continued popularity with the Grenadian people. But this very pre-eminence led to resentment. It seemed that only he was the revolution, and that only he could represent and articulate its aims, policies and principles. Added to this was an unspoken concern felt by some that *rapprochement* with the United States risked ideological compromise and vacillation in the face of capitalist temptations. A similar ambiguity surrounded Bishop's successful participation in the two CARICOM summit meetings in Jamaica and Trinidad. Did he concede too much? The moratorium on anti-American rhetoric imposed in early 1983; the release of many detainees as a gesture of international goodwill; and the apparent promise to Dam in his unscheduled meeting to reduce the Cuban and Soviet presence once Point Salines airport was opened—all had to be carefully reviewed.

But it was Bishop who first began to perceive the tensions in personal terms. He remarked to several committee members immediately after Coard's resignation that 'a leadership struggle was well under way'. He was known to be super-sensitive when and if his personal prestige appeared threatened; he was, for instance, a bad loser at cards and sometimes abandoned a sports' game in a fit of temper if he was clearly losing. Coard had insisted that he would not articulate his serious criticisms of the way the work of the party was being conducted for fear of leading comrades to think that he was against the prime minister. Bishop summarily dismissed this as 'facile' and 'a smokescreen'. To his dismayed colleagues, his attitude showed 'ideological weakness and immaturity'. It was clear to one minister that 'although his humanitarian ideals were progressive, the practical aspects of Marxism–Leninism caused him considerable problems'. He was informed that there had to be 'collective liability' rather than personal accountability for 'the irresponsible acts done by the party and identified by Comrade Coard'. In short, although 'everybody was responsible for the lack of direction and the practice of "tailing bureaucrats" ', he became 'increasingly personally sensitive' (interview with Chris de Riggs, December 1984).

Tension began to build up at a CC Emergency Meeting called by Bishop on 26 August to consider a report from Leon 'Bogo' Cornwall, ambassador to Cuba. He had returned, he said, to find a very disturbing state of affairs. Speaking on behalf of 'senior party comrades', he expressed concern at the committee's peformance and the lack of action over resolutions agreed at the July Plenary. 'Tan' Bartholomew reported complaints by Cuban and GDR workers over housing and administrative arrangements which prevented them from doing a proper job. He also strongly criticized the 'neglect' of the Militia. Its low morale was being matched by that of the army. Right-wing elements controlled the police, and the police had little respect for the party. Hudson Austin confirmed widespread dissatisfaction and demoralization in the army which he attributed to poor pay and conditions. Liam James stressed that 'we are seeing the beginning of the disintegration of the party' and de Riggs made clear that 'the heart of the crisis is the Central Committee'. James also claimed that committee members were timid and feared being labelled revisionist. But, 'they must be ready to criticize'. An Emergency Meeting was arranged for mid-September. In his summing up, Bishop conceded that 'there is reasonable basis to share the concern that many key decisions of the party, if not the majority, have been made informally outside of higher organs'. He asked everybody to consult members and 'rap with key sections of the masses', study the history of the Communist Party of the Soviet Union and reflect upon the strengths and weaknesses of each individual com-

mittee member (Minutes of Emergency Meeting of NJM Central Committee, 26 August 1983, p. 5).

The stage was set for confrontation. Many thought that the September
meeting would follow the pattern of the others and generally review the
situation. But no prior agenda was circulated—an unprecedented act—and
two days before the meeting was due to begin, all CC members overseas were
ordered home. During the period from 26 August, the battlelines began to be
drawn between those who were in the forefront of criticism and those who
took a more pragmatic view. In the minority, the latter were not so strident in
their concern and did not see the same necessity for constant introspection
and ever-stricter Leninist discipline, while so many and obvious obstacles to
the building of socialism in the daily reality of Grenada and its society needed
to be tackled. The critics met privately to discuss the situation. Opinions
differ as to whether Coard was present after returning with his wife and
family from a month-long holiday as guests of the Soviet government. There
is no doubt, however, that he was kept fully informed and was consulted. In
the event, all were present for the three-day meeting, which was to prove
crucial, except Austin, *en route* from North Korea, and Ian St. Bernard, who
was ill. The critics seized the initiative from the start by dismissing Bishop's
agenda as 'it missed the point'. 'Chalky' Ventour's alternative was accepted. It
was to analyse the present state of the party and revolution; to assess the work
of the Central Committee; and to determine the way forward.

Convening as usual in Bishop's house at Mount Wheldale, Layne opened
the discussion by reiterating much of what had been said in earlier meetings.
Despondency and dissatisfaction among the public was high and 'the
revolution now faces the greatest danger since 1979'. The party's international
reputation 'is being affected'. The morale of party members was 'very dread'
and the committee was too formalistic and on a path of 'right opportunism'.
As Grenadian society was overwhelmingly petty bourgeois, it was all the
more necessary to create a vanguard Marxist-Leninist party to lead the way to
revolutionary change. Ventour asserted that 'the party is facing disintegration'
with many comrades being overworked and 'showing signs of resignation'.
The Militia was 'nonexistent' and he noted the popular support given to the
American position on the incident the previous fortnight involving the
interception and destruction by the Soviet airforce of a Korean airliner. 'The
people', he said, 'are getting their lines from the Voice of America.' Cornwall
agreed: 'the honeymoon of the revolution was over' and the committee must
formulate a 'perspective on how the revolution must develop'. Bartholomew
complained of 'timidity' of leadership, and the 'arrogance' of the disciplinary
committee. The mass organizations were poorly led; the NYO, he said, stood

for 'Not Yet Organize'. Phyllis Coard interjected by saying that 'party comrades display a harsh attitude to the masses, who are demoralized because of the party's failure to manners the situation'. Selwyn Strachan questioned 'whether we want to build socialism or just chant slogans?'

Bishop, by now very tense and smoking heavily, intervened to try to regain control of the meeting. He was 'struck by the levels of thought and preparation of Comrades as evident in their various contributions', and, although many of the conclusions appeared to him to be 'rather premature', they were largely correct. He admitted that the main problem was the Central Committee. Its bureaucratic formalism in its dealings with the masses contrasted with the *ad hoc* approach taken to its work. 'Visits to work places have disappeared, increasing non-attendance at zonal councils and parish meetings, visits to communities to meet people at an informal level, decrease in the number of discussions and meetings with people in all areas of work, failure to participate in public activities. Village meetings have disappeared.' (Extraordinary Meeting of the CC, NJM, 14–16 September 1983, p. 10.) Louison agreed with this 'clear lack of contact' with the masses: in the meantime 'the middle-class types have been coming to the revolution for jobs'. But the overall situation was not as bad as had been painted. 'Some Comrades', he remarked, 'give a panicky impression in the way they make their points.' Whiteman's point was that the committee spent too much on small issues instead of 'fundamental issues' like the church, for which no party policy existed. He suggested a lower-level second-leadership structure 'to read and summarize reports' to leave the overburdened leadership time for strategic decisions.

At the end of the first day, Bishop tried to draw conclusions which were not too unfavourable to him. The 'deep crisis' in the party and revolution was due to the poor functioning of the committee, compounded by 'the weakness of the material base', such as unrepaired roads, electrical outages and 'retrenchment' of employment. Only vague solutions were offered, centring upon the establishment of 'meaningful channels of communication' and action based on 'Marxist–Leninist criteria' to guide 'the work in the future'.

His critics returned to the atack the next morning by proposing their own conclusions to the preceding discussion. For the first time, Bishop was directly and personally criticized. James considered that the 'fundamental problem is the quality of leadership of the Central Committee and the party provided by Comrade Maurice Bishop'. His charisma was not enough: what was required was 'a Leninist level of organization and discipline', a 'great depth in ideological clarity' and 'brilliance in strategy and tactics'. Bishop had none of the qualities needed to fulfil these tasks 'at this time'. Layne, Cornwall and Ventour agreed: the party could not be put onto a Marxist–Leninist footing under Bishop's leadership. De Riggs warned, however, that while there was a need to reorganize the leadership, 'the removal of any Comrade on the Central Committee will not help the situation'. Bartholomew was thankful that, at last, comrades were no longer 'hesitant' to make criticisms about Bishop's 'vacillation'. The severest attack came from Phyllis Coard. She criticized 'the idealism, the voluntarism and the failure to face up to hard decisions' by certain committee members. Bishop was 'disorganized very often', avoided responsibility for mistakes and was 'hostile to criticism'. He had opposed both the closure of *Torchlight*—which was decided in his absence overseas—and the prosecution of the 'Gang of 26'. *Sotto voce* whispers reminded members of his hesitancy over the seizure of power in March 1979. Fortunately, she said, Comrade Strachan had taken 'the full responsibility to hold the party together' and 'must be complimented for the proletarian qualities which he has displayed'.

Bishop's supporters tried vainly to come to his rescue. Bain, while agreeing with the criticisms, warned of 'over-hasty decisions'. Louison said that the quality of leadership was 'not the only problem'. Whiteman echoed him. 'We have to be careful', he warned, 'that we don't shift too much from the Central Committee collectively.' When Bishop entered the discussion, he thanked comrades for their 'frankness in their criticisms'. He was disappointed that they had not been raised earlier and appreciated members' concern for the need for 'correct strategy and tactics'. However, he had 'several problems over the years, especially with the style that entails consensus and unity at all costs, which can result in blunting class struggle'. He concluded by asking for time 'to think of his own role', and again recommended that members 'develop and maintain links with the masses' and, within the committee, 'develop mechanisms for accountability' (op. cit., pp. 18–19). The attack resumed. 'We need to find the root of the contradiction', insisted Layne, paving the way for James who then surprised pro-Bishop supporters by suddenly proposing joint leadership to be shared between Bishop and Coard. Bishop would 'direct work among the masses, focus on production and propaganda', be responsible for the work of the 'organs of popular democracy' and the mass organizations, militia mobilization and regional and international work. Coard, in turn, would be responsible for party organization, ideological development of party members and party strategy and tactics. Bishop would preside over the Central Committee and Coard over both the Organizing Committee and Political Bureau. The latter two would meet weekly. De Riggs followed with a proposal to replace Hudson by Layne as PRA Commander, with Cornwall being chief of political and academic work in all the armed forces, including the police.

There followed a concert of approval on the respective qualities of Bishop and Coard. Coard, said Layne, 'had given ideological and organizational leadership and had elaborated strategy and tactics even outside the Central Committee'. Others agreed. But there were reservations. Louison, although he supported Coard's return to the committee, thought the proposal had no 'theoretical basis'. What was wanted was 'collective mannerizing' by the committee to ensure that Bishop could build up the qualities required. Whiteman thought it would be better if Coard were given 'specific functions' as Deputy Leader. Bain was sceptical and had 'difficulty in conceptualizing' how it would work in practice. However, they were lone voices. The only successful objection related to Austin. It was agreed that it was not his fault that the army was in a 'state of rut and demoralization', suffering from 'ideological drift' and literally hungry due to low food supplies. Whiteman proposed a salary increase. Bishop's reply was cautious. Noting comrades' ideological growth, he stressed that he never had a problem sharing power or accepting criticisms. He had worked well with Coard from schooldays and had always defended him even when, from 1977, Coard had been accused of aggressiveness and 'wanting to grab power'. But he was concerned about the 'operationalization' of the proposal in terms of strategy and tactics; he certainly wanted to hear Coard's point of view. 'We will have to decide', he went on, 'how we will articulate this to the party and masses.' The image of the leadership was at stake: the world would see it as a power struggle, and a vote of no confidence in him. James replied that Bishop would still be Prime Minister and Commander-in-Chief and sign all Central Committee documents. He was at pains to emphasize that Coard would not decide strategy and tactics 'all by himself' and the committee would have to ratify all his proposals. In fact, anger was directed more at Louison than Bishop as Louison became emotional in his continuing defence of the prime minister.

Layne summed up the debate. There was a 'creative' theoretical basis for joint leadership since 'the form of leadership is scientifically decided, based on the situation we face. We have used the example of the Soviet Army where the concept of Political Commissar and Military Leadership had developed and worked' (op. cit., p. 33). The matter passed to the vote, a most unusual procedure as CC decisions were always reached by consensus. James's proposal for joint leadership attracted nine votes. Two abstained— Bishop and Austin—and two, Whiteman and Louison, voted against. It was also agreed not to publicize the vote. Bishop was now in a corner. He opposed a move to invite Coard to the meeting as he wanted time to reflect personally on the issue. He still found the 'practicalities' of the resolution to be 'unclear'. He wondered about his own role, and hinted that he feared becoming nothing more than a figurehead. It was reluctantly agreed that the meeting would adjourn and reconvene the next day with Coard present. Bishop would be absent since he and Whiteman had to attend the independence celebrations in St. Kitts–Nevis.

The next afternoon, Saturday 17 September, Strachan explained the position of the committee to Coard and outlined the proposed operationalization of the resolution. De Riggs asserted that the decision was made 'from a standpoint of love and deep respect for the Comrade Leader' and defended Bishop's request for time to reflect as it represented a 'moral crisis' for him. Layne, however, made clear that frankness was essential and that Bishop's reservations would 'intimidate comrades and harm their Leninist advancement in the party'. Coard's reply was positive. He agreed with all the criticisms of Bishop's leadership and of the operation of the Central Committee. The party needed 'a fundamental package of measures' to survive. Although insisting that he never undermined Bishop's leadership, he admitted 'petty bourgeois conduct' as he did not 'manners the Comrade Leader years ago'. He would, none the less, accept joint leadership 'to save the party and revolution'. But the practicalities of the concept must satisfy Bishop and a 'timeframe' be established for informing the masses 'and to start the work internally and hitting the ground scientifically and organizationally'. Although he did not mention it, he had had a private meeting with Bishop on the matter immediately prior to Bishop's departure.

After the intervening weekend, the Central Committee under Coard's chairmanship went to work with a zest. In an intensive series of meetings held over the following two weeks, it agreed on a series of measures to solve the problems. Coard presented a number of proposals. In order to rebuild the party's image amongst the masses, they included more political education, the allocation of 'small but achievable' tasks for individual members, the utilization of the talents of non-party people, more efficient and widespread distribution of party publications and a restructured Party Secretariat to ensure 'everything is implemented . . . on a more professional footing'. The masses should be involved in the selection and promotion of party members. The NJM needed both cadres and militants: the former were to be the organizers and leaders, while the latter would fight for the party in the workplace or community. All must be subject to regular assessment, Layne insisted, and a comprehensive personal filing system established. Every member of the Central Committee would be obliged to study Marxism-

Leninism 'very seriously', and learn from the experience in party building in other socialist countries. There would be an examination every two years. To help the process, a party school would be established. Selected teachers would be sent to the Soviet Union for in-depth training for between three and five years. All members, whatever their rank, had to 'kill all arrogance' in their relations with the masses. 'Open warmth and selflessness' had to be displayed but members were warned 'to sink but not drown themselves' in them (Fifth Sitting of Central Committee Plenary, 19 September 1983, pp. 3–5). Of equal importance was the need to restructure the party on Leninist principles. The duties and responsibilities of every party organ were discussed and procedures established. The quantity of mass organizations and parish and zonal council meetings was to be sacrificed in favour of quality. Meetings were to be well prepared and held at regular intervals, with a reporting system between and across levels.

There was no disagreement in principle to these proposals. Ventour particularly wanted the party 'to take sanctions against comrades who show hostility to criticism'. Strachan welcomed the fact that, 'for the first time' the party realized that 'party building is a science'. Coard stressed the necessity for planning. 'The party', he said, 'must emulate the state and ensure that it has an overall national plan, and sectoral and geographical plans based upon this overall national plan' (Sixth Sitting, 20 September 1983, p. 9). Further planning went hand in hand with supervision and control. Strict prioritization of tasks was necessary: the party had been guilty of 'unbelievable idealism' since new tasks had been constantly added to those already being carried out by party members, without any consideration of manpower resources in the party and individual abilities. Similarly, the work to be done by 'internationalist workers' from socialist countries would be carefully planned to gain maximum benefits. Although the importance of the National Council of Delegates was recognized—the forum where delegates from mass organizations and parish and zonal councils met at least annually to discuss specific matters such as the budget—Coard was anxious both to decentralize the work of the party and its institutions further, and to redirect it. The first task was to establish branches at the workplace, whether manufacturing, commercial, estate or governmental. 'For our entire history our party has operated on the territorial principle', he explained, 'then after the Revolution, on the sectional principle. This was correct because we had a very high unemployment problem and needed to reach people where they lived' (Seventh Sitting, 21 September 1983, p. 12). Now was the moment to change. Not only would the establishment of workshop branches result in increased production but it would also assist the mobilization of workers for the

Militia, help improve management and industrial organization, strengthen trade unionism and ensure that 'the working class composition of the Party is strengthened'. The 10,000 workers in workplaces of fewer than ten needed to be organized on a class basis and, through the trade unions, mobilized for the revolution.

Simultaneously, party work in the villages had to be strengthened. Fitzroy Bain suggested the principle of an 'inner and outer circle' of members and supporters respectively. He estimated there were about 5,000 in the outer circle. They had been organized before the revolution as NJM party support groups, especially in the countryside. But these had disappeared with the growth of village branches of mass organizations and village-based Zonal Councils. Besides the administrative and other shortcomings of these institutions, there was the problem of multiple membership at the village level, which begged the question of 'how many leaders a village has'. Coard urged close attention to the peasantry and their 'class interest'. '[Before the Revolution] we did most of our work with the peasantry and very little with the working class. It is since the Revolution that we are working with the working class and all this has implications for our structures. However, we have never organized the peasantry as peasantry but as village dwellers' (Eighth Sitting, 22 September 1983, p. 15).

Despite the fact that the Zonal Councils were party institutions, no committee member had attended one for eighteen months: it was no wonder that the party was losing ground to the church in the rural areas. Coard argued that a restoration of pre-revolution village public meetings, as suggested by Whiteman, was not the answer. Rather, reforms of the Zonal Councils were needed, the role of the party in them reasserted and their place in the structure of people's democracy recognized in the forthcoming constitution. There was, Coard insisted, 'insufficient confidence in the masses', which explained a previous hesitancy in strengthening the councils and the mass organizations. This had to be rejected and consideration given in the future to the creation of new institutions of People's Power to replace older structures as and when justified on scientific and material bases. In the meantime, the structure and organization of Parish Councils needed revamping. It was agreed that each of the seven councils, to be elected by parish party members, would be identified as party institutions. Each would be chaired by a Central Committee member who would live in the parish.

With the party in firm control of Parish and Zonal Councils, and the mass organizations, the risk was that non-party members would find it difficult to be properly represented. The answer lay in the Village Co-ordinating Bureaus. Their role as the link between the village Zonal Council and the local branches of the mass organizations was to be reinforced and their functions broadened. The meeting agreed with Phyllis Coard that:

the Bureaus should be bodies that the entire membership should relate to, whether they support the Party or not, and anyone who wanted to can become a member. This will help incorporate the stronger elements in the village into the nucleus of local government. [They] will have no party function. The village council will also evolve into a state body to monitor, supervise, control, and to ensure the implementation of the revolution and state as it affects the village and community. They also must have no party function but the Party should function inside them, to supervise and guide them. [Sitting of Central Committee, 28 September 1983, p. 6.]

As before, they could 'manners bureaucrats' as well as undertake 'house-to-house' mobilization. It was expected that, in time, the Bureaus would evolve into executive bodies 'with committees and commissions to do the work in all areas, for example, water, health and housing'. There was one note of caution. The party had to ensure that 'the bourgeois be kept from these bodies because they will seek control'. Coard said that this would be handled by invitations being issued by parish chiefs, based upon a percentage 'giving the majority to the working class'.

There remained two other matters. Propaganda had never been approached by the party 'as a science'. Phyllis Coard was anxious to see it scientifically developed, spreading 'from the inner core to outwards', linked to the 'mass work' and being better co-ordinated and directed by the party.

We need to see propaganda not as flinging things at the masses but to deepen day by day the understanding of the working people in terms of long-term and short-term goals. Deepening the understanding of the working people has to be done little by little with repetition . . . placed in different areas [to] have a cumulative effect . . . and with a variety of forms. [Central Committee Plenary, 23 September 1983, p. 4.]

The Centre for Popular Education obviously had a role to play in this and Strachan's suggestion that it be more village based was adopted. Then there was the question of membership. Some 1,400 party militants were estimated to be required. But how could such a number satisfy more stringent entry rules as were proposed by Coard, comply with minimum work schedules and be regularly assessed? Clearly, the question of the selection of cadres needed further study (Central Committee Meeting, 30 September 1983, pp. 9–10).

The committee was under no illusions at the extent of the task to which it had committed itself. But its morale was high and Coard assured the members that what was proposed was attainable. 'The standards we are aiming for are out of harmony with the level of development of the productive forces of our country but because of the existence of world socialism and the links we are developing with world socialism, this is possible'. (CC Plenary, 23 September 1983, p. 4.) It was further encouraged by the successful outcome of a packed general meeting of Full members held on Sunday, 25 September at Butler House which punctuated the committee's series of discussions. Bishop had returned from St. Kitts–Nevis late on 22 September. He had been asked to attend the plenary meeting early the next morning, but declined on the grounds of tiredness and the continuing need to reflect. He arrived for a scheduled meeting on the following day, Saturday, but this had been cancelled as documentation for it had not been fully prepared.

When they met, party members had been circulated with the Central Committee minutes of the meetings of October 1982 and 14–17 September. A report on the background to the crisis and the decision was also distributed. Uncompromising in its terms and language, 'crisis', 'opportunism', 'demoralization' and 'quality of leadership' peppered the text. It concluded that the 'model of Joint Leadership is an attempt to bring a creative and scientific solution to the leadership question in our concrete circumstances and most fundamentally ... it is the formal recognition of the leadership of our party for the first ten years ... up to one year ago.' (*Why Meeting?*, 25 September 1983, p. 11.)

Bishop refused to attend the meeting, again for the reason that he needed time to consider the concept. Because of this, Coard felt it inappropriate that he attend 'since this may inhibit free and frank discussion'. He would come, however, if requested. The meeting was virtually unanimous in demanding the presence of both. Layne reported that although no message from Bishop had been received, he was continuing to fulfil the duties of Prime Minister: 'this', he said, 'could only be seen as contempt for the Central Committee, contempt for democratic socialism'. If his 'road of opportunism' was chosen, he warned, committee members, as 'aspiring communists and Leninists', would have to resign from the committee on principle (Extraordinary General Meeting of Full Members, 25 September 1983, p. 2).

A vote of forty-six against one called for Bishop's presence. Coard arrived quickly. In response, Bishop sent a message that he still wanted time 'to formulate his position' and that he had accepted joint leadership since March 1973 when, as joint co-ordinating secretaries, he and Whiteman were appointed to lead the then emergent party. Eventually, he arrived. Explaining that he was 'relatively confused and emotional', his main concern was that as the masses in the Caribbean tended to 'build up a personality cult around an individual', their perception of the crisis as a power struggle had to be considered. To his mind it appeared as such, for he questioned 'the real meaning' of the committee's decision. If the qualities needed to carry the party forward were the ones that he lacked, 'I am suspicious that Comrades have concluded that the party must be transformed into a Marxist–Leninist party and I am the wrong person to be leader'. This was 'unprincipled' and he demanded to know 'the genuine substantial preference of the comrades'. James thought this 'emotional' and made plain that Central Committee decisions were binding on all. Layne was blunt. Quoting Lenin's dictum that 'open criticism of its own defects is not a sign of the weakness but of the great strength of a Marxist party', he went on to accuse Bishop of thinking there was 'a plot and conspiracy to remove him'. He was forced to conclude that 'this is gross contempt for the intelligence of the Central Committee. For him to feel that under every chair, under every window there is a conspiracy going on is nothing but contempt.' Whiteman, however, spoke up in support of Bishop, reiterating his argument 'wherever a leader is missing qualities, collective and joint leadership solves the problem'. Fitzroy Bain warned that 'left opportunism' could replace 'right opportunism' and urged that members who had genuine disagreements should not be victimized. He also accused some members of 'caucusing' aimed at Bishop, which could 'mash up the revolution'. But, as in earlier meetings, comments were overwhelmingly supportive of the committee's position and in favour of 'resoluteness' and 'firmness'. Gahagan and Redhead, both PRA officers, were 'shocked' at Bishop's position. 'No-one', added Ventour, 'is president for life.' As for a conspiracy, one member wrily remarked that the only conspiracy is that of the committee against democratic centralism and the party rank and file.

Finally, Coard and Bishop summed up. Coard remarked upon the 'qualitative difference' of Central Committee meetings since 19 September. The same applied to the membership whose words were sincere and showed 'a genuine commitment to struggle for socialism and lay the basis for the eventual building of communism'. He would work, he said, with Bishop, for the party, the revolution and the Grenadian working class. To great applause, Bishop then embraced his new co-leader. Since the meeting had endorsed the committee's analysis, 'this has satisfied my concern ... [and] ... I sincerely accept the criticism and will fulfil the decision in practice'. He pledged 'to erode his petty bourgeois traits' and the past was now behind him. Like Coard, 'his whole life' was for the party and revolution. The meeting ended on a highly emotional note with the singing of the *Internationale*. The crisis, it was thought, was over and the revolution saved. Trevor Munroe, a close friend of both men and chairman of the Worker's Party of Jamaica, arrived that day to advise on the operation of the policy 'according to revolutionary principles'.

The Climax

The next morning, Bishop and Whiteman led a delegation to Czechoslovakia and Hungary on an economic aid mission, preceded by Louison. Bishop's security staff were led by his faithful bodyguard, Cletus St. Paul. On arrival in Budapest, Bishop confided in St. Paul. The crisis, he repeated, was a 'power struggle' and 'no state had joint leadership'. He agreed with Whiteman's contention that collective leadership with himself as *primus inter pares* was both practical and proper. Louison told Grenadian students in Hungary that joint leadership would 'mash up the revolution'. As an issue, it was 'not settled' and 'still under discussion'. Bishop agreed as he had changed his mind and had decided to resist. The party returned via Cuba where they were delayed for twenty-four hours. Bishop had a long meeting with Fidel Castro in Cienfuegos but Castro later firmly denied that Bishop even mentioned, let alone discussed, the problem.

On the day before the party had been scheduled to arrive back in Grenada, Thursday 6 October, St. Paul rang from Cuba to say that Bishop had rejected joint leadership and hinted darkly that 'blood will flow'. This was taken to mean that Bishop was plotting the deaths of the leaders of his zealous critics. The Coards left home the following morning, 7 October, expecting Bishop to arrive later that evening as arranged. They stayed the night at the home of a Guyanese 'internationalist' friend. Others took similar precautions. When Bishop finally arrived on Saturday 8 October, only a casually dressed Strachan was there to meet him. Previous arrivals from state visits overseas had seen most of the Cabinet, and many others, there. St. Paul was so worried that he made Bishop disembark in the middle of the delegation and not at its fore, out of fear of possible assassination. Bishop confirmed that he wanted the issue to be placed back on the agenda as 'certain points had to be reviewed'. In the course of a four-hour meeting at Pearls airport and then St. George's, Bishop refused to elaborate but insisted upon collective, and not joint, leadership. He would, he said, discuss the matter at the next scheduled Central Committee meeting, due the following Wednesday, 12 October. Strachan briefed Bishop on what the party had decided upon in his absence and Bishop joked about one or two aspects. Coard was then informed by Strachan. Bishop, he said, was 'sarcastic'; Louison, however, reported that Strachan gave a 'distorted and exaggerated' account of the conversation. Another, and very bizarre, interpretation of the meeting was given later by the Antigua Caribbean Liberation Movement (ACLM) in its paper, *Outlet*. In a column written personally by ACLM leader Tim Hector, whose relations with Bishop were close, Strachan was denounced as a CIA agent whose role was 'to foment the leadership struggle into a clear political division' (*Outlet* 28 October, 1983). If this was indeed true, Strachan's meeting with Bishop was described by a Trinidad paper 'as an act of a modern Judas' (*The Bomb*, 31 October 1983).

The Central Committee met in emergency session on Monday 10 October and flatly refused to reopen the question. Bishop sent St. Paul to the meeting to discover the general mood of the members: he was told of their deep anger. He was isolated as the committee decided not to contact or have dealings with him except on their terms, although Education Minister Jacqueline ('Jackie') Creft, his former mistress, met him privately. Austin saw St. Paul the next day, Tuesday 11 October, and warned him to be 'very careful'. St. Paul, however, decided to take Bishop on an impromptu drive around the country-side. As usual, Bishop was very well received and it clearly lifted his spirits (interview with Cletus St.Paul, April 1984). In the meantime, the PRA members of the committee were also busy. Briefings on the issue were given to other officers, commissioned and non-commissioned, plus selected troops. While Bishop was on his tour, a resolution giving full support was passed unanimously by the NJM branch of the PRA. 'Never will we allow the desires of one man to be imposed on our party', it asserted. 'Therefore we call on the Central Committee and the entire party to expel from the Party's ranks all elements who do not submit to, uphold and implement in practice the decision of the Central Committee and party membership. The People's Revolutionary Armed Forces Branch of NJM awaits the decision and orders of the Central Committee!' There was only one dissenter: Chief of Staff, Major Einstein Louison, one of George Louison's brothers. His dismissal was demanded.

Just before the meeting began on the Wednesday morning, Bishop drove to the Cuban Embassy and residence to inform Ambassador Julian Torres Rizo of the divisions within the party. He outlined the history to the surprised Ambassador, and told him of the abortive attempts at solution. He never imagined, he said, that the situation would become so serious during his absence in Eastern Europe. But, as Castro later reported, he 'did not ask for our opinion or co-operation to try and overcome them . . . demonstrating his great respect for Cuban foreign policy and for the internal affairs of his own party'. All he did was 'to report the differences' (*Statement by Cuba*, 1983, p. 3). He then drove to the PRA base at Fort Rupert: the meeting was to be held in the highly restricted Operations Room. Sensing the high tension, he imme-diately went on the offensive. 'Attempts were being made to marginalize him' and he had expected Coard to meet him at the airport to discuss the issue with him (Central Committee Meeting, 12 October 1983, p. 6). He asked for an explanation as to why his assistant security guard, Errol George, had been mysteriously called to two meetings of the personnel security division in the PRA headquarters at Fort Frederick at 1 a.m. and 7 a.m. that morning 'on a matter regarding the Prime Minister' of which he knew nothing, and from which St. Paul had been excluded. However, as regards the critical issue, he had been in a state of 'high emotion' at the members' meeting on 25 September and, on further reflection, declared himself to be against joint leadership. By his tone, he clearly revealed what he had confided to St. Paul the previous day: it was a ruse by which Coard and the committee would ease him out of power. He had some justification. The PRA resolution was reported amid applause and army spokesmen called for 'firm action'. A vote of nine to three reconfirmed joint leadership as being essential. It was decided to adjourn and to consider the separate case of George Louison later.

While the meeting was taking place, there was another development elsewhere. A rumour was spreading around the town that the Coards were planning to kill Bishop. It was to be of critical importance. Austin ordered an immediate investigation after the adjournment. Very soon afterwards, he and Captain Chris Stroude arrived at Bishop's house and told him that the rumour had been traced to him and that Bishop's mother, 'Ma Bish', also seemed to be involved. Bishop denied all knowledge but in the early afternoon, security guard George was questioned by counter-intelligence officers. He eventually swore a statement that he and St. Paul were responsible but had acted on Bishop's instructions. They had had to draw up a list of fifteen 'trustworthy' supporters who would be told of the plot: they would be asked to 'notify the masses' if Bishop was physically threatened or killed. George said that 'he could not bring himself to repeat the lies' and had reported them instead to the security forces. He also alleged that St. Paul had advised Bishop to kill or arrest his critics (Radio transcript, 18 October 1983). The meeting hastily reconvened and both St. Paul and Bishop were questioned. Despite his denial, St. Paul was arrested and taken to the Fedon camp at Calivigny for further questioning. There was to be no more interrogation, however, and he was later transferred to Fort Frederick, an old British cantonment occupied by the PRA overlooking the town and harbour of St. George's. Bishop was told that he would have to broadcast a denial of the rumour and accept once and for all the decisions of the committee. He refused and left the meeting. His house arrest was then ordered by those still present. There seemed no alternative if Leninist discipline was to be preserved. It was also stated to be for his 'own protection' against counter-revolutionaries 'who might take advantage of the situation'.

The next morning, the committee reconvened at Coard's house and the house arrest was announced to those absent the previous evening. It was decided to call a meeting of Full members for that night, to which Bishop would be summoned. He arrived under guard and Chairman Ventour immediately went to the heart of the matter. Did he deny both the rumour and joint leadership? Bishop gave an affirmative answer to both in a 45-minute speech. George then repeated his statement. Bishop declined his right of reply which he had earlier requested. He remained silent when called upon to speak. The general opinion was that this indicated his guilt. Members denounced him: he had 'disgraced the party' and was 'beyond redemption'. Strachan then announced the committee's decision on house arrest, and also Louison's expulsion. It prompted one member to question whether Bishop should be allowed 'to remain a private citizen' or 'arrested and court-martialled'. But demands for his expulsion from the party were resisted by the committee: what was required was a resolution of the crisis, not its escalation. To that end, meetings would be held with Bishop's major supporters, Louison in particular, and mediation attempted.

But deadlock persisted. Not only was Bishop convinced that he was to be poisoned and so refused food, he also refused to negotiate. With all the Cabinet now involved in the crisis and with Central Committee meetings in Coard's house taking place virtually every day, government gradually slowed down. In these circumstances, the decision not to inform the masses of the crisis could not be sustained for long. Indeed, rumours began and tension rose as house searches were conducted, starting with that of 'Ma Bish'. Suspicions as to her alleged role in spreading the rumour seemed to be justified following a raid on the militia armoury in St. David's parish, Bishop's former constituency and close to her house. Although Bishop's supporters were disarmed and denounced as 'known criminals' and 'Gairyites', and their leader shot dead—it proved to be an accurate indicator of public feeling.

The Masses Take Charge

As agreed, Louison and Whiteman met Coard and Strachan over three days in an effort to resolve the crisis. Coard insisted that Bishop's arrest was correct and was a logical consequence of his actions: he was 'entirely responsible' for the crisis and should be removed as party leader and Prime Minister. 'I have heard many options but the best one is for him to go to Cuba and cool it for a few years.' He and Strachan dismissed probable public reaction. 'Let the people march', Coard said, 'they marched in 1974 until their feet tired out. They accepted the situation and lived with it then. It will be no different now.' Louison later recalled that Coard's manner was 'sharp and impatient and his eyes blazed with intensity' (interview with George Louison, February 1984).

None the less, he agreed that the crisis had to be resolved with the least damage to the party's public image and reputation. Both promised that a compromise formula would be worked out by 18 October.

The time that was being spent on discussions in complete disregard of growing public concern was indicative of the very deep sense of crisis felt by members of the committee and of their isolation from the masses. It was Radix who first confirmed the rumours of house arrest when he spoke to some senior civil servants on Friday 14 October. The news spread rapidly. Greeted at first with a mixture of disbelief and amazement, fear and foreboding grew with the widespread deployment of PRA patrols. An indication of public anger was shown with the physical manhandling of Strachan when he went that afternoon to the offices of the *Free West Indian* in the centre of St. George's and announced that Coard was Prime Minister. Reported to the world press by Alister Hughes, the incident was immediately denied by the Ministry of Information. But it may have helped to prompt Coard's resignation later that day on the grounds that he had no personal ambition to be Prime Minister (Phyllis Coard also resigned). He was replaced as Finance Minister by his former Permanent Secretary, the economist Victor Nazim Burke, a strong supporter of Coard's position.

Encouraged by signs of popular support for Bishop, his allies in the government and the party began to organize themselves. Whiteman resigned, as did Jackie Creft and George Louison. Fitzroy Bain resigned from the Central Committee. On hearing of the house arrest, Whiteman had made a dramatic return from New York where he had been attending the United Nations General Assembly meeting. Radix was particularly active. He organized a rally in St. George's market square where more than 300 heard him denounce Coard as 'a man obsessed with power'. He told them, and a group of businessmen later, that if they wanted to free Bishop, they 'should seek out Coard'. On the same day, Saturday 15 October, Castro sent a personal letter to the Central Committee. Although Cuba would not under any circumstances interfere in Grenada's internal affairs, he feared that the split 'could considerably damage the image of the revolutionary process within the country and abroad', and hoped that the crisis would be overcome 'with the greatest wisdom, calm, loyalty to principles and generosity'. Some inkling of his opinion was to be seen with a closing comment. 'Even in Cuba', he wrote, 'where Bishop is very well regarded, it will not be easy to explain the events.'

Sensing that the situation was deteriorating, the PRG authorized Austin to broadcast a long statement on Sunday 16 October. That he was nominated was interesting. It showed the dramatic rise of the influence of the PRA within the government. He was also popularly regarded as being very loyal to Bishop. Perhaps it was felt that this would help defuse public anger. In any event, his level of intelligence rendered him open to manipulation by stronger personalities. His broadcast appealed for calm because 'the New Jewel Movement is making every effort to settle this problem' and admitted that it had been 'a mistake not to have informed the masses earlier'. It had little effect. By the next day, all the heads of Grenada's overseas missions, bar those in Havana and Moscow, declared for Bishop. Worse, demonstrations began on the following Tuesday. Schools went on strike and in Grenville a march was organized to Pearls airport. To shouts of 'No Bishop, no school', one flight was delayed. The demonstration helped prompt Louison and Whiteman to take matters into their own hands. Louison made several unsuccessful attempts to reach Coard by telephone to discover the compromise terms promised by that day. That afternoon he resigned his post as did Minister of Tourism Lyden Ramdhanny and Minister of Housing Norris Bain. By his own admission, Louison began mobilizing people and was arrested. Whiteman avoided his captors and made contact with regional radio journalists representing stations in Barbados, Trinidad and Martinique, as well as Radio Antilles, the private regional station in Montserrat. Since all were audible in Grenada, he was able to make plain his opposition to the Central Committee, give his version of events and generally appeal for support for Bishop. The very strictly controlled information from Radio Free Grenada was thereby effectively bypassed. Painted slogans appeared, 'Coard means Oppression' and most commonly, 'No Bishop, No Work, No Revo!'

The proposals were, in fact, being slowly hammered out. The Central Committee finally decided on them late that night at Coard's house. Bishop would be re-confirmed as Prime Minister and as party leader—'in charge of the entire process' as one member put it—on the condition that he made a broadcast acknowledging his error in spreading the rumour regarding the Coards and stating that the Central Committee was the most important political institution in the country. Joint leadership was deliberately fudged: although it was reiterated that Coard had to direct party organization and work, it would be within a framework which acknowledged at one and the same time the importance of Bishop's position and of collective decision-making. 'The "J" for Joint in JEWEL is critical', remarked Strachan. It was further agreed that he would appeal for calm in the broadcast and announce that a settlement was in sight. He would meet Coard to thrash out differences and, if necessary, agree on Cuba as a mediator. In these circumstances, his behaviour since his return would be overlooked and the implicit threat of expulsion from the party lifted. Mediation had, in fact, already been attempted through the efforts of Michael Als, leader of the tiny Trinidad and Tobago People's Popular Movement and Rupert Roopnarine of the Working People's Alliance. Munroe was unable to travel to the island. It was not successful, perhaps not surprising in view of Als' firm pro-joint leadership position. Als sadly reported Bishop's intransigence. 'Boy', he reported Bishop as saying, 'dem men tough as hell and I just as tough, we go see.' (*The Guardian*, 11 November 1983.) Nor was Bishop alone. Jackie Creft had joined him although she had been told by Lt. Abdullah (also known as Calistus Bernard), who commanded the guard, that if she entered the house she could not leave. It was as well she was there for as Als reported, Bishop 'was smoking incessantly and appeared to be in a state of mental agitation'.

The final terms were put to and confirmed by a tense meeting of 'selected members', chaired once again by Ventour. Significantly, it was suggested without disagreement that should the compromise fail, there was no real alternative to a temporary imposition of martial law. Only this drastic step would bypass the paralysis which was slowly gripping the committee. Armed with this endorsement, a delegation consisting of Layne, Austin, James and Bartholomew was dispatched to deliver the proposals to Bishop. Bishop said he needed time to think them over but agreed in principle to a broadcast. However, he wanted Whiteman and Louison to help him draft the text. He also agreed to meet Coard the next day, and to give the same delegation and, if necessary, Als, his final answer.

But there was to be no such answer as events quickly slipped out of the control of both Bishop and, above all, the committee. Early the following morning, Wednesday 19 October, a huge crowd of up to 15,000 assembled in the market square. All shops and offices were closed, their employees on strike. One observer said it was as if 'an underground telegraph system had worked all over the island . . . trucks and buses poured in from everywhere . . . it was much more crowded than Carnival'. At about 9 a.m. some 3–4,000 in the crowd, mainly schoolchildren, broke away and, led by Whiteman and some businessmen, marched up the steep streets to Bishop's house. Their chant reverberated around the houses: 'B for Bishop and betterment; C for Coard and communism'. They wanted him to speak at the square, the traditional meeting place. The PRA guard was quickly reinforced to over one hundred plus two armoured cars. The Central Committee was meeting in Coard's house, adjoining Bishop's, but several members were in Bishop's large front courtyard waiting for his decision. Austin and Layne tried to reach Bishop to ask him to speak to the crowd and start negotiations immediately but the crowd, the gates now smashed, was too great. Shots were fired into the air and many people, loudly booing, dared the troops to shoot them. Layne and Abdullah ordered a withdrawal. Some guards had rushed into the house and had tied up Bishop and Creft in separate rooms and stripped both to their underclothes. The crowd found them in this state: both were weak and Bishop was crying. One witness reported: 'He couldn't speak and all he was saying was "The masses. The masses. The masses". It was all he was saying. Tears wash down his face.' (*The Guardian*, 8 November 1983.) It was 10.35 a.m.

Both were taken by truck downhill into the town. They were expected to go to the market square to address the huge crowd but Bishop wanted to go to Fort Rupert to use the army transmitter to broadcast to the people. He also wanted medical treatment from the nearby hospital. As the crowd reached the fort, cramming the steep narrow access road to capacity, the PRA guards did not fire and gave up their weapons on Bishop's orders to the base commandant, Captain Stroude. The magazines were emptied. The crowd also, however, loudly abused some women soldiers who resisted. Stroude ordered the women to change into civilian clothes. By this time, Bishop had been carried shoulder-high to the operations room on the upper floor of the two-storey communications building facing the first level square and the access road. After acknowledging the cheers of the crowd, he announced to Stroude that Hudson Austin was replaced as Commander of the PRA by Einstein Louison. Noel then asked who in the crowd were trained Militia. He and Einstein Louison, who had been given the armoury keys, began distributing weapons, whereupon several soldiers shed their uniforms and said they wanted 'no part in such madness'.

While this was happening, the Central Committee retreated to the safety of the other PRA base of Fort Frederick. It reconvened in a large tent with PRA officers and reinforcements were summoned from Calivigny. Attempts were made to contact Bishop by telephone but Bishop, although urged by Lt. Lester ('Goat') Redhead, Stroude's deputy, to negotiate and to get the people off the fort, refused. Instead, he ordered telephone engineers to fix a landline to a radio transmitter, dispatched a search party to locate a public address system and demanded the arrest of the PRA leadership. Whiteman spoke on his behalf to Fort Frederick. 'No negotiation, no compromise', he shouted, 'we want manners for all of you.' Stroude kept his superiors informed, particularly reporting the distribution of arms. The civilian members of the committee seemed paralysed: to the PRA leaders, the military and political position was intolerable and untenable. They concluded from the information they had received that orders had been given by Bishop to eliminate them, that the Central Committee was to be arrested and an armed assault mounted on Fort Frederick. Austin was told that the only way to restore order and save the revolution was for the army to take over Fort Rupert and establish military rule for a short period. He disagreed but could offer no alternative. The Central Committee was consulted. A detainee in a nearby cell alleged that he overheard the order to execute in between shouts of 'Long live the Central Committee!' But when three armoured vehicles arrived from Calivigny under the command of Officer-Cadet Meyers, he and two other officers, Lts. Abdullah and Nelson were ordered each to command a vehicle. It was later alleged that they were briefed by senior PRA personnel to take Fort Rupert with the minimum of force and to storm the communications building and, if possible, capture Bishop and his allies.

Meanwhile, Bishop and his supporters—sometimes amounting to thirty to forty people—had crammed into the operations room. Drinks, cigarettes and some food arrived. Merle Hodge, a Trinidadian who worked in Grenada during the revolution, was present throughout and reflected afterwards:

With the whole country coming down to town to support Maurice, you wouldn't think that it would enter anybody's head to try and take power in the face of all that. Because you'd be fighting the whole nation. Jackie said to me the other side had the radio station. She talked about the possibility of the army sending a detachment so she said to me that when we go outside, we should make sure that the people stay around, because then they wouldn't shoot. Maurice was just kinda smoking and pacing. . . . [*The Guardian*, 8 November 1983.]

The Massacre

At about 1 p.m., the three vehicles arrived from Fort Frederick. At first, some of the crowd were under the impression that the troops were going to join them but their belligerent attitude soon made them change their minds. Some in the crowd began shooting: the reply was a devastating barrage of rocket shells and bullets as the troops fired from the armoured cars to the order 'fire your way through!' Redhead and another soldier were with Bishop; as they gave the order to lie on the floor, they smashed through a back window to go into the inner courtyard and the armoury behind the building. Stroude ordered the issue of weapons to all PRA personnel. One rocket shell hit the operations room. Among the wounded and dead, Bishop shouted, 'My God, my God, they are using the guns on the masses'. The defenders returned the fire as best they could with Noel and Whiteman defiantly shouting 'No Compromise, No Negotiation!' Noel fell to the ground, his legs shattered. Two hand grenades thrown into the crowd caused panic and a burning car was overturned, adding to the confusion. As Merle Hodge again remembered, 'there was a discussion among Maurice and some of the fellas to the effect that what we had to do was to go out and say we surrender, that anything else would be suicide'. That indeed was the case: despite several losses (including Meyers), the troops advanced. Those in the crowd who found their exit cut off ran into the inner courtyard and up on the eighteenth-century battlements of the old slave fort. There lay a grim choice: a jump over the edge—a fifty to ninety foot drop—or being machine-gunned down. Bishop shouted that he was surrendering and led the survivors down the steps. He ordered that a child with a gaping head wound be held up in full view. As he walked across the courtyard, Redhead appeared out of the tunnel which burrowed under the battlements between the higher, and inner, courtyard and the outer square. He ordered him and the politicians to put their hands over the back of their heads and return with him up the steps and through the tunnel. Redhead, with Abdullah's help, ushered them through, at the same time ordering the remnants of the frightened public away. Their last view was of Bishop in dark green shorts and a jumper, and Creft in yellow shorts and a white jersey, contrasting sharply with the grey stone and lingering smoke.

Abdullah broke away at the tunnel's entrance and returned to the communications room to consult Stroude and others. Stroude had just returned from refusing a plea by Fitzroy Bain to save his life. A red flare was then seen to be fired in the air from Fort Frederick. In the inner courtyard, Redhead ordered his captives to line up and face the west wall with its slogan 'Towards a Higher Discipline in the PRA'. He saw three other Bishop supporters; he ordered them also to face the wall saying 'you are all bourgeois'. Abdullah then arrived and told the eight—Bishop, Creft, Whiteman, Fitzroy Bain, Norris Bain and the unfortunate three—to face him. He announced that their execution was ordered by the Central Committee. He called two soldiers down from the battlements to join the firing squad consisting of himself, Redhead and another, and ordered two others with machine guns on the upper wall also to fire on his command: disobedience would be summarily dealt with. All except Creft were ordered to strip to the waist and to face the wall again. Jackie Creft shouted that she was three months pregnant. 'Comrades, you mean you're going to kill us in truth?', she cried disbelievingly. Her plea was met by a torrent of abuse. 'You f- bitch', shouted a soldier, 'you are no f- comrade! You're one of those who was going to let the imperialists in!' Bishop refused to turn, remarking that he was not going to be shot in the back like his father had been. He wanted to see who would pull the trigger. He folded his arms and stonily faced the squad. Abdullah gave the order. Bishop was the first to be hit, his head splitting open. Amazingly, even after 500 or so rounds had been fired, Fitzroy Bain showed signs of life. Redhead, who apparently did not fire his gun, curtly ordered his disposal. A soldier administered the *coup de grâce* with a shot through the head. For good measure Bishop's throat was then allegedly cut and a finger cut off to remove a ring (Coard, 1984, p. 6). Shouts of 'Long Live the Central Committee!' and 'Forward Ever, Backward Never!' ended the scene. Outside, Vince Noel lay badly wounded. Abdullah, leaving orders for the bodies to be laid out on sheets ready for transport to Calivigny, was dissuaded from shooting him. He was subsequently lifted to the rear of the communications building where he died (interviews).

The killings were over by 1.15 p.m. A yellow-white flare was fired into the air from Fort Rupert. The whole ghastly episode had taken about twenty minutes in its entirety. The crowd had vanished; all that were left were the wounded who, assisted by friends and relatives, tried to make their way down the hill to the hospital or a rapidly emptying St. George's. The exact number of deaths that took place around the fort will never be known. There was thereafter an extraordinary reluctance among the public and the post-invasion government alike to determine the exact number of deaths on that day. It was as if there existed a collective exorcism of the tragedy. Despite numerous pleas from distraught parents for information on missing sons and daughters, nobody would venture to go beyond the subsequent PRA announcement of twenty-four dead, including those executed. Discounting fanciful estimates, reliable eye-witness accounts agree that between sixty and seventy met their deaths. Fort Rupert now cleared, Stroude addressed the troops to explain the situation while Abdullah reported officially to the army command at Fort Frederick. Austin could no longer ignore reality and agreed to form a military government.

The Revolutionary Military Council

At 3 p.m. that afternoon, General Austin announced the formation of a sixteen-man Revolutionary Military Council, which would rule 'until normality is restored'. The PRG was dissolved and all Cabinet ministers dismissed. However, continuity was assured since five of the sixteen were also members of the NJM Central Committee—Austin, James, Layne, Bartholomew and St. Bernard. A few hours later, Austin broadcast to a shocked population. He announced Bishop's death but said that he had been killed in shooting initiated by his supporters. As for the future, he made clear the intention of the RMC to 'govern with absolute strictness'. Anyone who sought to demonstrate or disturb the peace would be shot. A four-day curfew was imposed as from 9 p.m. that night to 6 a.m. the following Monday. 'No-one is to leave their house. Anyone violating this curfew will be shot on sight. All schools are closed and all workplaces . . . until further notice.' The PRA, he stressed, was 'totally united' and ready 'to protect and defend our country against any attack by imperialism'. A military invasion was possible—which would result in 'deaths of thousands of our people'—and he pleaded for unity.

This was a forlorn hope. With much of the telephone system immobilized and Radio Free Grenada broadcasting only music, rumours multiplied. Some of the RMC's actions over the next four days exacerbated them. As one Washington analyst put it, 'the politics of hysteria have taken over Grenada. As [the RMC] see it, they have no alternative but to kill all of those who might try and take over from them. In the eyes of General Austin, it's a simple matter of self preservation.' (*New York Times*, 21 October 1983.) Justified by a fear that the 'hostile bourgeois press' whose 'interests were not of Grenada' would 'manipulate the crisis', the news blackout helped create a regional and hemispheric atmosphere of suspicion, speculation and anger, and did little for the image of the RMC, domestically or internally. Foreign journalists were expelled or prevented from entering Grenada when they arrived at Pearls airport. All telex and communications facilities were denied. Not surprisingly, the foreign press turned to American and other hostile regional sources who readily interpreted the military takeover and executions as being Cuban-inspired. Bishop, the press said, had been removed by Cuba and Russia as he stood in their way. Coard's personal ambition, pro-Moscow sympathies and plotting was behind it all. This, and similar stories, seeped into Grenada through radio broadcasts from neighbouring countries. Shocked and dazed Grenadians could easily believe it. A typical example of the prevalent press attitude outside of the socialist states was that of the British populist tabloid newspaper, the *Daily Express*. The 'Russian and Cuba-backed coup', it screamed, 'has turned Grenada into Moscow's base'. Bishop, 'who stood in the Kremlin's way' had been 'liquidated' because Grenada's position was very strategic to the Soviet Union being 'so close to the oil shipping lines from nearby Venezuela'. To America, it was 'an island Afghanistan'. Coard was 'Moscow's man' and would not permit 'the Kremlin to do whatever it wants through its Cuban clients' (*Daily Express*, 22 October 1983). To the tabloid *New York Post*, the RMC were 'communist scum' and 'Andropov's angels' led by 'a man [Coard] who would sell his mother for a nickel and his country for a dime of Red money' (23 October, 1983).

In fact, Cuba had reacted to the news of the killings and the RMC take-over in a very hostile fashion. In a statement issued the day after, it condemned what had happened in no uncertain terms:

No doctrine, no principle, no opinion calling itself revolutionary and no internal split can justify such atrocious acts as the physical elimination of Bishop and the prominent group of honest and dignified leaders who died yesterday. The death of Bishop and his comrades must be cleared up. If they were executed in cold blood, the guilty should receive exemplary punishment. [*Granma*, 20 October, 1983.]

Clearly penned by Castro himself, the announcement named Bishop as 'one of the political leaders best liked and most respected by our people because of his talent, modesty, sincerity, revolutionary honesty and proven friendship with our country. . . . The news of his death deeply moved the party leadership.' Ominously, Cuba's political relations with the new leadership of Grenada would have to be 'subjected to a profound and serious analysis'. However, as before, Cuba would not interfere in Grenada's internal affairs and 'above all we will take into account the interests of the Grenadian people as to economic and technical cooperation, if such cooperation is possible in the new situation'.

The RMC and its supporters heard this with deep dismay. They had slowly realized the international implications of the tragedy. As Castro correctly forecast, the risk of exploitation by imperialism was high. Rationalizations of the outburst of ultra-leftism—such as that of one of those involved to whom the action had been necessary 'to arrest the Mao Tse-Tung line adopted by Comrade Maurice of bypassing the party in a criminal fashion and appealing to the unscientific spontaneity of the people'—seemed increasingly irrelevant. The first priority was to restore normality. But this was undermined by an extraordinary degree of political ineptitude caused by a mixture of long argument and insensitive application of military discipline. The curfew was lifted for four hours on Friday 21 October to enable people to obtain food. The shops opened but not the market as transport could not be arranged in such a short time. Fresh produce, the livelihood of many people, rotted in the fields. All inter-island boat traffic ceased and the fruits destined for Trinidad shrivelled up. Passenger flights into Pearls airport were very strictly controlled, adding to the sense of siege. However, the curfew was lifted for employees in essential services, who were issued with passes and travelled under escort. In the country, peasants and others could obtain water from neighbourhood standpipes and could feed those of their animals close to their house. In some instances, PRA patrols helped them, anxious to restore good relations. But mothers of newly-born babies had to fend for themselves and those who died at home were left unburied. To a peasant population with strong religious foundations and used to living in open and closely-knit village environments—on the doorstep as it were—the situation was intolerable. They were under house arrest just as their hero had been. There was no PRA 'rule of terror' in that nobody was killed, but there was no need of one to ensure compliance. The deep collective sense of trauma saw to that.

Under cover of the curfew, troops removed the bodies from Fort Rupert. A convenient pit already existed by the latrines at the Calivigny camp and the bodies of the executed were burnt in it under Abdullah's direction with old tyres, petrol and boarding. As the heat was insufficient, several remains were later dug up but only those of Jackie Creft were recognizable. As for the other dead, information obtained from soldiers suggested that the majority were disposed of at sea off Point Salines, where the current is particularly strong (*Latin America Regional Report: Caribbean*, RC–83–10, 9 December 1983).

Inevitably, resentment turned to deep anger; apprehension to fear. The closure of the churches was particularly felt. News of further arrests came. Alister Hughes, Einstein Louison, prominent business men and others identified as 'counter-revolutionaries' were dispatched to Richmond Hill and the Ministry of Information worked strenuously to counter allegations by neighbouring radio stations that they had been executed. By 21 October, the prison was overflowing and conditions deteriorated. Hardly any food was delivered due to administrative confusion. George Louison and Radix had been removed the previous day to a dungeon at Fort Frederick. St. Bernard told them that they were to be executed and a 'shot while in cross-fire' story concocted. However, saner counsels prevailed, and they were left alone, but without food or water. After two days, on Saturday, the two dissidents were fed but by this time Radix, a diabetic, was in a coma. After much argument, he was taken to hospital and Louison transferred back to the prison.

In fact, several of the RMC and all of their advisers, notably Coard, were acutely conscious of the extent of hostility at home and abroad. On the day following the appalling chain of events, the Council met to consider three pressing needs: to explain the position, as it saw it, to the people; to prepare economic survival plans to counter the OECS and CARICOM trade, fuel and transport embargo that had been swiftly imposed; and to stave off the growing threat of military intervention by making contact with neighbouring and other countries. The restoration of good relations with Cuba was considered paramount. Intensive discussions lasting over twenty-four hours finally resulted in a decision to create a 'broad-based' civilian government within two weeks, a process that would begin with the deliberate co-option of, in particular, business men, bank managers and hoteliers in order to restore confidence both domestically and internationally. In addition, all workplaces were to reopen on Monday 24 October.

The 'Political Department' of the RMC, headed by James and Stroude, was charged with public relations. The first statement was issued to the army on Thursday 20 October and detailed the heroism of those who had defended the revolution at Fort Rupert, especially those who had died.

Comrades, the masses had no intention to cause bloodshed and in their confusion they were led by Maurice Bishop and his petty bourgeois and bourgeois friends as cannon fodder to cause bloodshed ... [They] had deserted the working class and working people of Grenada. He instead pushed them in front to cause trouble and bloodshed in the country. [*Bulletin*, Revolutionary Military Council, 20 October 1983.]

This attempt to boost morale was bolstered by a 15 per cent salary increase, so raising a private's pay from EC$200 to EC$230 per month. The second statement was broadcast by RMC Chairman General Austin later the same day. Bishop was to blame because he led the crowd into a military camp rather than to the market square. He alleged that 'Noel and his group' fired first which necessitated a restoration of order by the army. Further, 'it is now known that it was the intention of Maurice Bishop to have all the officers present at Fort Rupert executed almost immediately'. He asserted that allegations that Bishop was murdered, rather than shot in 'the heat of the moment' in the crowd, were 'a lot of lies'. Also, talk of a power struggle in Grenada put out by 'exploiters of the Caribbean masses' such as Adams and Eugenia Charles was nonsense (radio transcript, 20 October 1983). A further statement the following day announced the intended formation of the civilian government. It also insisted that seventeen civilians had been killed although 'it was never the intention of the armed forces of the people to shed the blood of the people'. The remaining seven were soldiers, whose example the Grenadian people were urged 'to emulate'.

On the economic front, Nazim Burke drew up an Emergency Economic Programme with Coard's assistance, although Coard kept himself firmly in the background. It recommended an Emergency Economic Commission headed by a 'Political Leader/Minister' who 'would give guidance to the Commission and convey its news to the Government'. The Commission would be responsible for the overall direction of the economy and supervise any controls deemed necessary. Each area of the economy was to have a co-ordinator. It was to be primarily concerned with the state sector and to maintain a 'low profile'. Managers of state enterprises and senior bureaucrats would be given responsibilities and report to Commission members 'but would be given only limited information'. All requests by the Commission were to be given top priority. As for the private sector, only 'appropriate briefings' were thought necessary (Emergency Economic Programme, 22 October 1983, pp. 2–5). A lower level of management was also established in a smaller Council. Chaired by Nazim Burke, there were to be nine members, two of which, including Roopnarine, were co-opted 'internationalist' workers, responsible for money and banking and foreign exchange.

Once established, the Commission and Council drew up detailed task and work programmes aimed at conserving food and fuel supplies including rationing—ration cards were designed and ready for printing—and at restoring international transport and postal services. The PRA, however, was to have priority in all supplies. Treaty obligations were to be observed, but dismay was expressed at the extent to which Grenada was dependent upon the multi-national Cable and Wireless Company, both in St. George's and elsewhere in the region, for its international telecommunications. 'The attitude of radio operators' had to be assessed, as some might sabotage equipment. Should any international organization of which Grenada was a member move towards taking sanctions, 'as a priority we must get in touch with [them] . . . and insist on our right to be informed of any meeting and to be heard'. Further, the Commissioner for International and Regional Organizations, Merle Collins, was ordered to 'identify countries on whom we can hope to depend in the coming period. As soon as is possible we must contact them. At whatever stage our emergency programme has reached, we must inform them of our needs and seek assistance' (Emergency Economic Plan, s.6(4), p. 6). As the proposed measures meant serious disruption to the everyday lives of many people, 'clear guidelines for public education and propaganda programmes' were called for. A programme 'of bringing various areas of private property under Martial Law', especially 'key enterprises', would have to be justified. Also, since the fruit and vegetable trade with Trinidad was suspended, 'farmers who lose need to be dealt with', and a policy towards the hucksters—the small traders—'has to be worked out'. A Council on Employment was to be established and no worker laid off without it being reported. Finally, an Economic Monitoring Emergency Desk began work in the Ministry of Finance, to which all co-ordinators were linked by telephone.

While this activity went on at the functional level, the RMC tried to get overseas support as the American military build-up became clearly apparent. Prime Minister Cato in St. Vincent sent a message to Austin on 21 October asking for a meeting. After some delay, Austin agreed but was too late as Cato had left the next day for a CARICOM meeting in Port of Spain called to decide on a response to the crisis. Another message suggested Carriacou as the site but went unanswered in St. Vincent as the first American warship arrived in Kingston harbour. As for Cuba, the RMC was sharply critical of Castro's response. It deplored 'the deep personal friendship between Fidel and Maurice which has caused the Cuban leadership to take a *personal* and not a *class* approach to the developments in Grenada'. It was clear that Castro knew nothing of Bishop's 'dishonesty' and that 'Cuba's position creates an atmosphere for speedy imperialist intervention'. It was resolved to ask for military assistance and to work for 'the best relations' based upon the 'principle of proletarian internationalism' (RMC Meeting, 20 October). This bitter reaction disguised a revolution within a revolution. Coard had worked energetically, seemingly in all directions. Besides advising Nazim Burke, he helped draft the radio statements and was busy maintaining morale. But he failed to obtain a badly needed EC$5 million loan from Cuba to pay civil servants' salaries: the confusion had left the Treasury virtually penniless and the banks remained closed. His further request for Cuban military reinforcements was angrily turned down by Castro. To add insult to Castro's injury, a demand was made that Cuban troops had to be placed under Grenadian military command once on the island. The RMC also wanted the construction personnel to be subordinate to the PRA. Once the impossibility of these demands was realized, Coard was seen as a liability. As he was dropped by a now desperate junta, Austin was heard to shout, 'Coard caused everything here, not me!' (interviews, April 1984). Coard and his wife retreated to a house in the country over the weekend, their children having earlier been dispatched to Jamaica. The junta's worries did not end there. Overtures to selected civilians to form a government met either with blank refusal or, at best, reluctance. Leaving aside the image of the RMC, when would the next firing squad be? Mario Bullen, Ambassador to the European Community, for example, refused to consider the request in Brussels; he would only discuss it in Grenada at a time of his choosing.

Castro had, in fact, sent a message to Ambassador Torres Rizo on the Saturday. Most of it was to be relayed to Austin and Layne. It argued that any evacuation of Cuban personnel 'at a time when US warships were approaching' would be 'highly demoralizing and dishonourable' for Cuba's honour and prestige. But all were urged to 'vigorously defend' themselves if *directly* attacked. As for reinforcements, they were 'impossible and unthinkable'.

The political situation created inside the country due to the people's estrangement on account of the death of Bishop and other leaders, isolation from the outside world, etc., considerably weakens the country's defence capabilities, a logical consequence derived from serious errors made by Grenadian revolutionaries. That due to [this] situation, the present military and political conditions are the worst for organizing a firm and efficient resistance against the invaders, an action which is practically impossible without the people's participation. [*Statement by Cuba*, 1983, pp. 7–8.]

He repeated in a later statement that the 'Grenadian revolutionaries themselves are the only ones responsible for the creation of this disadvantageous and difficult situation'. Furthermore, he later recalled that they 'continued to insist on plans that ... were, in some respects, unrealistic and politically unsound'. He concluded on a firm note: 'instructions regarding what the Cuban personnel is to do in the case of war can only be issued by the Government of Cuba' (op. cit., pp. 9–10). A small group of military experts did, however, arrive on 24 October to organize defensive positions around the Cuban workers' camp.

Castro's second statement never reached the RMC as the invasion intervened. Castro had authorized a Note to the American government on 22 October stating that Cuba was not interfering in internal affairs in Grenada, that he shared Washington's concern over the safety of foreign nationals, both American and Cuban, and offered to maintain contact to resolve any difficulty that might arise relating to their security. It was ignored, as were Austin's energetic efforts to reassure American nationals, particularly the 500 or so students at the St. George's University medical school, whose main campus was right at the end of the Point Salines runway. They and other foreign nationals were told that they could not be harmed and that anybody who wanted to leave could do so since it was planned to reopen Pearls airport as soon as possible. A highly conciliatory message was also sent to the American Embassy in Barbados. It read in part:

We are for peace, friendship and for maintaining the historically established ties between our countries and hope they would grow and strengthen ... The RMC has no desire to rule the country ... a fully constituted broad-based civilian government is [being] established ... expressing the interests of all social classes and strata in our country. [It] will pursue a mixed economy and will encourage ... foreign investment. ... The Revolutionary Military Council of Grenada takes this opportunity to reassure the honourable ... USA of its ... highest regards. [Radio transcript, 23 October 1983.]

A conciliatory message was sent also to the British High Commission and given personally to the Deputy High Commissioner when he arrived on 24 October.

On Monday 24 October, shops and offices reopened and an air of normality was restored. The airport was opened, closed and opened again for the few aircraft still operating a service as a result of poor communication within the RMC. PRA armed patrols were withdrawn from the streets and discreetly confined to strategic locations. However, schools were ordered to remain closed for the week and the curfew was reimposed from 8 p.m. to 5 a.m. Some twenty minutes after the end of the first overnight curfew ended, the invasion began. The Revolutionary Military Council, and with it the tattered remnants of the Grenadian revolution, was to have only a few hours to live.

The Aftermath

The brief rule of the Revolutionary Military Council was unloved and, although it never had a chance to redeem itself, its passing was unlamented by the Grenadian people. Their anger and fear was deep and even NJM supporters saw the descending paratroops as saviours. The Pentagon claimed that only sixteen American military personnel out of the 6,000 that landed were killed in action, over half by error; if Bishop had been alive, PRA and popular resistance would have told a much more grisly tale. Most of the PRA threw away their arms and fled, but many were also killed. A day after the invasion, on 26 October, prison guards fled Richmond Hill prison. The tales of the detainees, combined with the discovery of the arms warehouses, the details of the military agreements with the Soviet bloc, Cuba and North Korea, and the emergency economic and rationing plans of the RMC, served only to intensify the feelings of relief. The emotional, even hysterical, scenes that greeted the American forces—and those of Washington's West Indian allies who flew in once the fighting was over—were accompanied by widespread slogan and letter-writing in praise of 'Daddy' Reagan and the constant refrain that 'we must never let it happen again'.

In sharp contrast, Castro saw the invasion as a monstrous crime, possible only on the pretext provided by Bishop's death and by deliberate lies told by the Reagan government.

The invasion of Grenada was a treacherous surprise attack . . . presented to the US people as a great victory for Reagan's foreign policy against the socialist camp and the revolutionary movement [and] linked to the resurgence of the United States as an influential power on the world scene. A dirty, dishonest appeal was made to US patriotism, to national pride, to the grandeur and glory of the nation. . . . The deplorable, truly dangerous fact is that, when world opinion unanimously denounced the warmongering, aggressive, unjustifiable action that violated a people's sovereignty and all international norms and principles, most of the people of the United States—manipulated, disinformed and deceived—supported the monstrous crime committed by their government. [Castro, 1983, p. 13.]

Eulogizing the Cuban dead on their arrival in Havana, he vented his feelings against the 'hyenas' who had 'emerged from the revolutionary ranks'. By invoking 'the purest principles of Marxism-Leninism' to support their 'allegedly revolutionary arguments', and their accusations against Bishop, the result was one in which 'the CIA could not have done better'. As for his fallen friend, 'it was impossible to imagine anyone more noble, modest and unselfish. He could never have been guilty of being authoritarian; if he had any defect, it was his excessive tolerance and trust' (op. cit., p. 3). It was a clear indication that those he held ultimately responsible for the victory of imperialism could expect no aid or succour from Cuba. Such was his anger that Ambassador Rizo was subjected to disciplinary action on his return, Castro presumably thinking that he had known far more about the crisis from Coard than he reported. The Soviet Union was, on the other hand, more supportive of Coard and his colleagues and Cuban–Soviet relations duly suffered (*Caribbean Insight*, November 1983). The disagreement did not, however, last long: Cuba dispatched a very high-level Central Committee member to head its Embassy in Moscow, and the Soviet Union, in deference to its ally, agreed not to consider any request for aid by any NJM stalwart if put on trial, should a request be made (interview with Gaston Diaz, March 1984).

On the ground in Grenada, the Americans realized that the invasion was but a prelude to a set of complex and expensive problems. There were three tasks. First was the urgent need to erase whatever remaining sympathy Grenadians had for the revolution. Particular emphasis was put upon denigrating Bishop by a hurriedly assembled Psychological Warfare force. Damning documents with many statements taken out of context were publicized. Besides the 784 Cubans found on Grenada, including some twenty dead, who were summarily deported together with all Soviet bloc and Libyan diplomatic personnel, internationalist workers were dispatched to their respective countries. The 'communist orientated' CPE was quickly wound up as were the Ministries of National Mobilization and Culture. The Ministry of Women's Affairs was 'reorganized'. American trade-union advisers also flew in. The second, and equally urgent, political task was the establishment of a new government. An Advisory Council—popularly known as the Interim Administration—was with some difficulties finally put together in three weeks. Technically it was to advise the Governor-General, Sir Paul Scoon. Scoon was the one constitutional link with the pre-revolutionary past and the invasion was legalized by his signature of a pre-dated appeal for assistance while on an American warship two days after the invasion. The Council had some difficulty asserting itself as the United States was clearly in charge of security and influenced much else. However, as life returned to normal and particularly after the bulk of the American troops left in mid-December, American political influence lessened. It was happy that it did as helped to deflect overseas criticism.

It was not until 5 December 1984 that the long awaited and promised election took place, which restored Gairy's rival, Herbert Blaize, to power. He had been seventeen years out of office and immediately, his age and infirmity gave rise to speculation that he would not last long as leader. The reason for the delay was to ensure a viable political force able to withstand both the challenge from Gairy and from the remnants of the NJM. Gairy was a credible force to be reckoned with. He returned to Grenada in January 1984 and re-established the Grenada United Labour Party. But many of his mainly rural supporters were ageing and considerable publicity was given to the strong-arm tactics of his more enthusiastic younger henchmen to impose their leader's wishes. On the left, Louison and Radix attempted to capitalize on Bishop's image. They helped create first, the 'non-partisan' Maurice Bishop Foundation, designed to receive funds to finance, *inter alia*, a memorial and scholarships, followed by the Maurice Bishop Patriotic Movement (MBPM). Funds, mainly from over-seas sympathizers, helped finance a newspaper, *The Indies Times*, whose views stood in stark contrast to those expounded by the strongly pro-American *Grenadian Voice* edited by ex-detainee Leslie Pierre with the help of Lloyd Noel and others. The MBPM, however, had a rival by October 1984 when Ian St. Bernard, newly released from custody, announced the relaunch of the NJM. Calling vigorously for the removal of all occupation troops, its statements stoutly denounced the 'traitorous' and 'opportunist' activities of the ex-PRG ministers in the MBPM. The deep split was mirrored in all those cities with a Grenadian population: London, New York, Toronto and Port of Spain.

Ranged against the two ends of the political spectrum were a number of centrist parties. The biggest was the old Grenada National Party of Blaize. A very vigorous rival appeared in February 1984 with the birth of the National Democratic Party, led by George Brizan. Blaize spent much time denouncing Brizan's former involvement in the NJM and accused him of being a 'com-munist', a charge which led Brizan to try to prove that he was more anti-communist than his accuser. Also in the arena was the Grenada Democratic Movement. Formed in 1980, it consisted of different groups of exiles. The biggest was in the United States, led by Keith Mitchell in Washington; another was headed by Francis Alexis in Barbados. Both were university teachers. A third, in Trinidad, eventually linked with yet another party, the Christian Democratic Labour Party of Winston Whyte. Despairing of any unity between the warring groups—several attempts at unification had failed mainly on Blaize's insistence that he had to be leader and personally approve all electoral candidates—several of the regional prime ministers involved in the Caribbean Peacekeeping Force finally forged an alliance at a meeting at the end of August 1984 on Union Island. The New National Party emerged and although Whyte's faction left it soon afterwards, it went on to capture 58 per cent of the vote, and fifteen of the sixteen seats. The GULP won the remaining seat with 36 per cent, coming second in all other constituencies. The MBPM captured only 5 per cent, all its candidates bar Einstein Louison losing their deposits. Whyte's tiny party barely survived with 1 per cent. The NJM refused to participate in a poll dominated, as it saw it, by imperialism. This was no rhetorical matter for Reagan himself admitted that well over US$250,000 was donated to the NNP by the Republican Party and the American private sector. Funds included provision to defray the expenses of experienced political workers drafted in from Adams' Barbados Labour Party and, above all, from Seaga's Jamaica Labour Party. Taxi drivers, for instance, were paid up to US$250 on the day to ferry people to polling stations in shifts.

The third post-invasion task was that of economic reconstruction. US$3 million was quickly granted as emergency aid, both to provide badly needed cash and to generate some employment for hundreds of people suddenly thrown out of work with the wrecking of many enterprises, mostly state-owned, either through war damage or by wanton destruction. Another US$6 million was allocated as war damage compensation to the private sector and householders. Despite much effort, the Agency for International Development—whose Grenada office was soon larger than that of Zimbabwe—found very few private American investors ready to help reduce the unemployment rate of 35 per cent, despite Grenada's new-found inclusion in the Caribbean Basin Initiative. Instead, it was forced to underwrite most of the capital budget deficit of US$11.8 million announced for the 1984–5 financial year, which was aimed at infrastructural improvement. In addition, US$19.1 million was allocated to complete Point Salines airport, which finally opened virtually one year after the invasion, with another US$2.1 million set aside to compensate Plessey Ltd, most of whose assets had been destroyed by the military action. Other donors also stepped forward. Canada granted US$6 million to the airport and another million for other projects. Venezuela, Australia and the Caribbean Development Bank also played a part. Britain allocated US$7 million, split between loans and a grant, in addition to considerable assistance in the rebuilding and training of the police force. Since Congressional legislation precludes American aid for police forces, a section of the police was designated a 'Special Service Unit'. A paramilitary force of over one hundred men, its aim and structure was similar to others established by the United States and trained by American paramilitary specialists. Reinforced by newly-planned regional defence agreements, their purpose was to ensure that no armed group, of whatever background, could with impunity overthrow any one of the island governments again. Despite this assorted help, the US$98 million capital expenditure plan for 1984–6 was by mid-1984 short by some US$22 million. Finance Ministry officials were not disappointed. As one put it, 'the US wants to make Grenada a showpiece of democracy and it will have to pay for it' (*Latin America Regional Report: Caribbean*, RC-84-05, June 1984).

Fourth and last was the arraignment of Coard and nineteen others on charges of murder. Coard and Austin were captured some days after the invasion, and some reports alleged that they had attempted to bribe yachtsmen to take them to Guyana where they hoped to obtain asylum. It was also alleged that a very substantial sum in US dollars was found on Phyllis Coard's person when she was arrested. The preliminary inquiry into the charges began after many adjournments in May 1984 and ended two months later. All bar one, St. Bernard, were subsequently charged and the trial set for 1985. Some other detainees were also charged with physical assault of prisoners in Richmond Hill and elsewhere in early 1980. A few, however, were released. Chris de Riggs, who had been sent to New York by the Central Committee after Bishop's house arrest to justify the line taken to Grenadian communities in North America and who had been arrested on returning after the invasion, was one. He subsequently sought refuge from harassment in Sweden. Basil Gahagan was another: he was a professional soldier who had been concerned solely with the defences of Fort Frederick.

The combination of trauma and American largesse brought the Grenadian people back to pre-revolutionary 'normality'. It is doubtful, however, if many had really deviated from it. Few disagreed with Blaize's demand that American troops remain in Grenada for 'at least' five years; 250 remained by the close of 1984. They and their less popular West Indian colleagues-in-arms were due to be evacuated in mid-1985. To some, particularly young people, the invaders had clearly outstayed their welcome; as the voter registration statistics showed, they were not going to participate in sham elections. An estimated 5,000 eligible Grenadians could have been added to the 46,000 who registered. Certainly, many objected to the compulsory photograph, a totally new departure in Commonwealth Caribbean elections, which, it was argued, was justified to avoid any repetition of the type of fraud that had characterized Gairy's Grenada. In the security-conscious atmosphere, objectors feared their use by the police and American forces. However, it was just as probable that this protest came from a deep disillusionment with *all* politicians after the heady experience of revolution that went wrong. It was not so much that neo-colonialism had been re-imposed, which Castro warned would be Grenada's fate if the NJM's internal differences were not solved. Rather, the West Indian condition had re-asserted itself and triumphed. And the path mapped out by the United States will be followed, to the relief of Washington. As one spokes-man put it, 'Grenada has disappeared off the radar screen; nobody talks about it much. It is now sinking gradually into the oblivion we reserve for our friends' (*Newsweek*, 30 January 1984).

Arguments leading to the dramatic end of the Grenadian revolutionary experience pose fundamental questions for political activists and theorists alike, and especially to those on the Left. There is much to be learnt, as much by the black descendants of the slave experience as by the wider Third World. It is no exaggeration to assert that the post-mortem extends to the critical mass of Marxist-Leninist theory. The experience and the tragedy point to the necessity to rethink and possibly to revise the Marxist-Leninist model of political strategy and organization as it has been embraced by Third World political movements in particular.

That this is a necessity is self-evident. Marxism–Leninism of the Moscow-preferred orthodoxy was edged out of Western Europe by the less centralized and authoritarian theory and practice of Eurocommunism. Orthodoxy's new home, is, in the main, in the Third World. This is not surprising: it provides at once an explanation of continued under-development and a ready justification for sacrifices in the name of patriotism, the future and the oppressed. It also rationalizes, as and when necessary, outbreaks of authoritarianism and repression, whether in alliance or not with the military. In the worthy cause of 'anti-colonial' nation-building and 'revolutionary reconstruction', firmness is required. More practically, it taps an alternative and valuable source of aid and largesse, that of the Soviet Union, although most Third World states who have embraced the doctrine are careful also to maintain relations with international capitalism. The shortcomings of Soviet bloc assistance—few consumer goods, capital equipment of sometimes indifferent quality and a lack of convertible currency being among them—can be embarrassing. The alleged claims and demands of Marxism–Leninism can also be a useful smokescreen to disguise economic and political mis-management for as long as possible. When this can be hidden no longer and Soviet bloc aid of the type demanded is unavailable, recourse to international capitalist institutions becomes necessary. The alternative is either a palace coup or a military take-over. Taken as a whole, Grenada's experience was not far removed from this broad pattern.

But the orthodoxy is deeply entrenched and any enquiry into its efficacy can be expected to be resisted. Power structures would be challenged and the confidence of revolutionaries in the rightness of their cause and actions rudely disturbed. Marxism–Leninism, after all, has a comforting embrace precisely because, like messanic religion, all is explained and justified, and was proved 'correct' in Petrograd in late 1917. Their number included the members of the New Jewel Movement whose mimicry of Leninism was uncritical. That is not to say that the methodology of dialectical and historical materialism as expounded by Marx and Engels is no longer relevant. It most surely is. The analytical insights of Marx the philosopher remain, as they have been for over a century, intellectual tools of incalculable value. What is at issue is the application of organizational and mass mobilization procedures demanded by the eponymous doctrine of Lenin for a time, place and society far removed from the West Indies and elsewhere in the deprived four-fifths of world society.

The Why and Wherefore of Failure

The attempted application of Leninism was the root cause of failure. From it stemmed six problems which together overwhelmed the revolution. First and foremost was the West Indian condition as manifested in Grenada. The attempt to introduce what was labelled as Marxist socialism, however much watered down, through Leninist application, was doomed to failure. By their actions and statements, the PRG leadership sensed this: assimilated values, entrenched economic relationships and an overwhelming popular attachment to land and chattel ownership needed no emphasis. The Leninist theory assumed that, of necessity, the revolution would be guided by an experienced elite which, because of a theoretical understanding denied to others, would then guide the masses into shaping a new communist society. It was, in these circumstances, unrealistic if not verging on the grotesque. Second was the wider application of the West Indian condition. Grenada's strident pro-Soviet foreign policy and application of 'revolutionary manners' brooked no opposition—least of all from its neighbouring kith and kin. It came as no surprise that, with the notable exceptions of Trinidad–Tobago and Guyana, they either acquiesced in or gave active support to the American-led action after so much blood had been shed in pursuit of a disliked orthodoxy. Allied to this was the third, the determination by the United States to rid the region of a political carbuncle and maverick which had breached the backyard fence. In the new Cold War, the fence had to be fixed; only a good excuse was awaited to satisfy the American public.

The fourth problem was the determination of the People's Revolutionary Government to go beyond ignoring this reality, by positively urging a reluctant Soviet Union to involve itself more directly in the region through Grenada than Moscow thought prudent. Both the Soviet Union and Cuba urged constraint. They realized that the correlation of forces—the struggle between the forces of imperialism and the forces of socialism—had moved in favour of the former from 1980, but this was ignored in St. George's. The Grenadian revolutionaries insisted that they were on the noncapitalist path and so qualified for full Soviet support, without any deep appreciation, it seemed, of class forces within their own society. In any case, it was the Soviet Union's prerogative to determine whether a state was on the correct path, and its theoreticians certainly did not endorse the PRG's claim. Admittedly, Cuba's friendship and aid was generous. But this was possibly as much to do with the close bond that had developed between Castro and Bishop, and the need for allies in an increasingly hostile region, as with theoretical correctness. For all the PRG's efforts, Soviet diplomatic and economic aid was limited. Not only did it mean little in real terms when the crunch came but, far more importantly, it left Grenada in a highly exposed position and a ready target for an antagonized United States. Nor did the application of Leninism stop there: the fifth problem that it spawned was an explosive mix of revolution and militarism. When applied to the sixth, the intimate intermingling of theoretical and personality differences, there emerged a parody of socialism. With such burdens, 'the tune composed by the Grenadian revolutionaries [should] be retitled "false optimism" not "new dawn" ' (Cohen, 1985, p. 463).

Although the end result was the same, it would be misleading to assert that the motives of the United States and its Caribbean allies were, to all intents and purposes, identical. With the clear exception of Seaga, the doyen of the Caribbean reactionary right, they were neither blindly collaborating with Washington nor parties to a grand conspiracy as suggested by some commentators overseas (e.g., *Caribbean Times*, 27 October 1983). Conspiracy theories are deceptively simple and this one was no exception. Nor did they act in political acknowledgement of their economic dependency. Europe rather than the United States is their main export market and only Antigua and, to a lesser extent, Barbados, is betrothed to the United States through the tourist trade. Family and other links are predominantly with Canada, Britain and Trinidad. Nor had they loudly and consistently denounced human rights abuses by the People's Revolutionary Government. Indeed, the respect for the PRG that had gradually developed was most clearly shown at the November 1982 CARICOM Summit in Ocho Rios. The attempt by the host, Seaga, together with a half-hearted Adams, to exclude Grenada from CARICOM by redrafting the criteria for membership quickly collapsed. With little difficulty, the principle of ideological pluralism had been accepted; after all, Seaga wanted Haiti as an associate member. Furthermore, his unwillingness to denounce political and human rights abuses in Guyana, whose record was appalling, was not lost upon the OECS contingent. Another misconception about their motives was one of a 'mission'. As the popular tee-shirt sold in Grenada after the invasion proclaimed, 'Thank You Caribbean Brothers For Rescuing Grenada'. But available evidence indisputably shows that the notion of 'rescue' was encouraged through a broadly co-ordinated media only *after* the invasion. In other words, it was at the prompting of the United States who, in Reagan's words, 'only just got there in time', (*The Times*, 29 October 1983) and was an *ex-post facto* rationalization. Another accusation which circulated mainly overseas but also among the region's intelligentsia was that Grenada represented a threat to their own social and economic structures with its message of socialist reconstruction and that a 'psychotic fear' developed (Lewis, 1984, p. 10). Although attractive, it is untenable. The Grenada economy showed little or no sign of collectivization, the PRG remained in the Eastern Caribbean Currency Authority and participated in world capitalist forums as well as in regional marketing agreements, e.g., WINBAN for its bananas. It was only through its foreign policy that the PRG's Marxist-Leninist preferences were manifested; all internal party organization structure and documentation remained as unknown to the outside world as to most Grenadians.

The reality was that they perceived their participation as being in their own direct national interest. To the extent that they feared Grenada as a staging point for their own revolutionaries and as an armed transit station designed to further Cuban and Soviet designs against them, they clearly acquiesced in Washington's perception of the legitimacy of its role in its sphere of interest and the subsequent logic of its policy. But they were more concerned with the problematic ease by which governments of their size could be toppled. Not that realization of their vulnerability was novel. The 1979 insurrection was welcomed initially and would have been constitutionally forgiven if legitimized by elections. But the three coup attempts against Prime Minister Charles during 1981 involving dissident members of the Dominican Defence Force, mercenaries and agents of highly dubious overseas companies were inexcusable. The Defence Force was disbanded as a result. This prudence seemed to be underlined by the violent takeover by the Revolutionary Military Council, and its subsequent extraordinary political ineptitude. The violence of the People's Revolutionary Army deeply shocked West Indians—and others— in the region and elsewhere; when the United People's Movement in St. Vincent published in its newspaper *Justice* (30 October 1983) what was perceived as a justification by remarking upon the 'regrettable' incident at Fort Rupert, copies were burnt in the streets of Kingstown by angry crowds. The sheer scale of the violence could not be ignored; neither could the widespread unpopularity of the military regime and the clear unwillingness of all those civilians approached to form a new government to do so. In a nutshell, the precedent was intolerable, and both their own defence forces and local radical groups had to be made aware of that beyond all possible doubt. After all, Grenada was too near for comfort and its history, society and economy close to their own. To what extent, the RMC was unlike other military regimes in other parts of the world with far worse records, which West Indian states had generally happily dealt with.

There was also the fact of Bishop's popularity to consider. As with the majority of Grenadians, few realized that he was a Marxist and his personal role in enforcing 'revolutionary manners' either unknown or ignored. Although the leaders were not of their number, they had learnt to respect him as the proceedings of the 1982 and 1983 CARICOM Summits testify, but Bishop never entirely patched up his quarrel with Adams. He developed a good working relationship with Chambers and was ready to listen and accept his criticism regarding the continuing delay over the Constitutional Commission. But whether this relationship was influential in determining Chambers' subsequent position on the invasion is doubtful. What is certain is that although it is easy to dismiss the talk of rescuing Bishop from house arrest as speculative and hypocritical, it was seriously discussed among the OECS leaders. It is not, therefore, out of place to suggest that an element of vengeance was present.

By contrast, the motives of the United States were strategic. The invasion clearly confirmed the hegemonial mantle which it had assumed over the Caribbean Basin as a whole. It endorsed the filling of the vacuum left by a largely uninterested Britain, completing a process formally begun in 1940. By this stage, the United States saw no reason to consult Britain and neither did the two principal West Indian actors, Barbados and Jamaica. It was subsequently taken aback by the extent of the reaction and was unprepared for the accusations and apprehensions of those in another theatre of American national interest, the continental Western Europeans. In the controversy over the stationing of American intermediate-range nuclear weapons on their territory, they feared being frozen out of any meaningful consultation in time of war in their midst, just as the most pro-American British government since 1945 had so clearly been over Grenada. Fortunately for the United States, the British response was more apparent than real as it readily concurred with the invasion. The ruffled feathers of Britain's NATO partners were also suitably smoothed as American diplomats reminded them that, just as there had been close consultation with allies in the West Indies and, indeed, joint action, so the same would apply in a European crisis.

But the differences between the United States and its West Indian allies continued after the invasion. To the United States, arms caches and the search for Cuban *agents provocateurs* and saboteurs was critical, followed by a militarization of the region to help ensure that leftist insurrections would never again be tolerated. But the resumption of the rule of law and free elections, press and expression were the priorities for the OECS states. They feared a return to power of Gairy, clearly indicated by their promotion of the agreement between the four fractious centrist and centre-right parties. The United States, on the other hand, was far more concerned with the possibility of a substantial show of support from, let alone victory of, the self-proclaimed successor to the NJM, the Maurice Bishop Patriotic Movement (MBPM). Therefore, it consistently encouraged moves by the interim administration to impede its development and timed the release of captured documents to ensure maximum impact by a compliant press.

The very poor showing of the MBPM in the December 1984 elections was certainly influenced by these and other discriminatory measures but they were by no means conclusive. The PRG seemed oblivious to the degree of its popular support; weakness could be solved by better organization and an acceleration of plans for socialist transformation, particularly in external affairs and the deepening of relations with the Soviet bloc. Unfortunately, in contrast to Cuba, the Soviet Union was not so willing to reciprocate. It did not need Grenada except for its nuisance value as a useful pressure point against the United States. Admittedly, the Cuban revolution had given the Caribbean region a far greater significance in Soviet ideological and national perceptions, enabling the area and Latin America generally to feature in its foreign policy. Cuba was seen as a catalyst for restructuring inter-American relations, but the Soviet Union only endorsed Cuba's policies when they ceased to be imbued with romantic ultra-leftism, and recognized that specific objective conditions fruitful for successful revolution could not be constructed out of thin air. The enthusiasm of the PRG leaders was doubtless welcome but the risks were considerable. Although their incessant demands for more and more Soviet bloc equipment and aid were expensive, support was worthwhile if it helped engage America's attention and cause difficulties below the threshold of intervention. That is not to say that non-Cuban Soviet bloc aid was given cynically: technical and education assistance was fulsome and generous. But military aid and training far outweighed these efforts. Although a miniscule proportion of the world total of Soviet military assistance, it loomed very large in Grenada. Cuba, on the other hand, gave much economic assistance and clearly made sacrifices. The bitterness of its engineers after their forced return to Havana in humiliating conditions was apparent to all: their professional pride and expertise in helping to develop a small fellow Caribbean country had been cruelly brushed aside. Castro proudly recalled Cuba's contribution after the invasion.

The value of our contribution to Grenada in the form of materials, designs and labour in building the new airport came to US$60 million at international prices—over US$500 per inhabitant. It was as if Cuba—with a population of over 10 million—received a project worth US$5,000 million as a donation. In addition, there was the cooperation of our doctors, teachers and technicians in diverse specialities, plus an annual contribution of Cuban products worth US$3 million, or US$40 per inhabitant. It is impossible for Cuba to render material assistance on that scale to countries with significantly large populations and territories, but we were able to offer great assistance to a country like Grenada. Many other small Caribbean nations, used to the gross economic and strategic interests of colonialism and imperialism, were amazed by Cuba's generous assistance to that fraternal people. They may have thought that Cuba's selfless action was extraordinary; in the midst of the U.S. government's dirty propaganda, some may have even found it difficult to understand. [Castro, 1983, pp. 1–2.]

The Soviet Union could not, of course, make such a claim. Rather, while making their anger very clear, the Soviet leadership saw the assertion of American power in Grenada as justifying the principle of spheres of influence. They quietly acknowledged America's position and clearly hoped that the United States would respect theirs in Poland and Afghanistan. Whether or not the situation may have differed if the insurrection had occurred three to five years earlier is worthy of speculation.

Revolutionary Theory and Practice

It is the remaining causes of failure—militarism and personality—that most dramatically beg the wider question of the appropriateness of Marxist-Leninism to Third World societies. The PRA's arrogance was regularly expressed towards fellow Grenadians and others by heavily armed young men mouthing slogans and ill-digested Marxist dogma. What happened at Fort Rupert was a culmination. It had the effect of clearly associating militarism with socialism in many a West Indian mind. In retrospect, it was a romanticized philosophy which automatically accepted the notion of a 'nation under arms'. No matter what resources were planned for it, and the force of 11,000 which was envisaged beggars belief, it would always have been too small to counter Grenada's only potential invader, the United States. Once the threat of mercenary-led counter-attack in 1979-80 had passed, the growth in the army and Militia appeared to many to have as a major purpose to aid and abet internal control. Ironically, Marx and Engels were strongly anti-militaristic, seeing armed states as enemies of revolution. Gordon Lewis penetratingly analysed the interplay between militarism and revolution.

There is involved here a sort of revolutionary romanticism . . . the concept of 'holy violence . . . It is tempted to think in terms of the 'revolutionary movement', of the quick overthrow of governments, even indeed of the 'revolutionary hero', the strong-man, who will lead the revolution. It thinks in terms of sabotage, underground activities, secret plotting . . . which almost becomes with certain movements, left-wing terrorism. It all leads . . . to the appearance in the revolutionary struggle of the military chieftain [and] ends up in a new form of military socialism. Such a process clearly took place in Grenada, with the emergence of military men like Austin, James and Cornwall. The militarization process of the revolution thus comes full circle. [Lewis, 1984, p. 8.]

It is, he concludes, 'the old story of arms and the man; sooner or later, the one will be used against the other'. It is also one repeated in many Third World countries which have formally declared themselves to be socialist in orienta-tion, if not Marxist–Leninist. Surely, Marx would turn in his grave if he learned what was perpetuated in his name.

The dovetailing of elements of personal rivalry into a primarily ideological dispute was, as events showed, to have tragic consequences when militarism was such an integral part of the environment. The crisis was personified, particularly by post-invasion commentators who, by its simplicity, were able to explain the derailment of the revolution to Grenadians and the world in easily understood terms. The over-simplification was clearly misleading but it did contain a grain of truth. The ongoing *post mortem* was pockmarked by acerbic outbreaks of hyberbolic hysteria and accusations and counter-accusations. They mainly centred upon the easiest explanation for the crisis, that there was a carefully planned conspiracy by the ambitious Coards to seize power, backed by the full support of Cuba and the Soviet Union.

But there is only circumstantial evidence to support this particular con-spiracy theory and absolutely no evidence of undue external pressure. Coard's intense dedication to the revolutionary task was tempered by a clear realiza-tion of the need for public support and mobilization. Although he had a measure of popular appeal derived from admiration, perhaps tinged with fear, of his intellect and resolution (his electoral victory in a socially varied constituency in St. George's in 1976 should not be forgotten), it nowhere approached that of Bishop. Charismatic leadership fitted well in a small island society such as Grenada where there was precious little privacy or insti-tutional impersonality to act as a counterforce. The island polity was also in a region where charisma has been a virtually omnipresent factor in the modernization process since the inauguration of self-government. To the impressionable and psychologically dependent Grenadian populace, Bishop was 'Maurice' and Coard was plain Coard. He could be nothing else in comparison. But within the party, it was not surprising that his strong personality and authoritarian Stalinist streak, which insisted upon obedience and orthodoxy, led to leadership falling naturally upon his shoulders. Lewis characterized him as a particularly complex person whom revolutionary movements tend to spawn.

This type is dedicated, earnest, hardworking, trained at once in the schools of the Black Power Movement and the revolutionary Marxist–Leninist tradition. He, or she, is beyond doubt, dedicated to a degree. But it is this dedication that makes him, or her, also dangerous. For we are here in the presence of the professional revolutionist . . . who along with his dedication is also fatally possessed of a temper of moral unscrupulosity. He is prepared to accept any measures, even the most extreme if he believes—as he often does with real conviction and sincerity—that the measures are necessary for the preservation and furtherance of the movement. It is almost a religious type . . . incorruptible in private habits, except being capable of being corrupted by power. The type was well summed up by Lord Acton. 'It is this combination', he wrote, 'of an eager sense of duty, zeal for sacrifice, and love of virtue, with the deadly taint of a conscience perverted by authority, that makes them so odious to touch and so curious to study'. [Lewis, 1984, p. 9.]

It was unfortunate for him that Grenada's was the 'Improbable Revolution'. Although he urged a quickening of the pace of socialization, he regretfully realized that pragmatism in policy was necessary, whatever his party rhetoric. He had an acute political 'sixth sense', a penchant for careful planning and was in nobody's pocket. Therefore, the subsequent charge of conspiracy was all the easier to make. A more plausible explanation for the clash of personalities stems from what was a natural rivalry between the two which, under extreme pressure, burst into violence in a desperate attempt to follow the correct road. This rivalry was understandable and, indeed, inevitable: both men were highly intelligent, articulate and politically active. It was for a long time highly creative and very beneficial to the Grenadian revolutionary process. But when the revolution was perceived to be losing its way, Coard did nothing to discourage the growing belief that Bishop's approach to work, methods of operation and priorities were primarily responsible. Bishop had certainly let party organization become ossified and, despite self-criticism, had perpetuated methods of decision-making which did not accord with the dictates of the party structure. A high profile, particularly internationally, attracts criticism and jealousy as much as praise and sycophancy. Suppressed resentment at alleged 'onemanism' led to a witch-hunt in which no compromise was possible. To the watchdogs of orthodoxy, it was a matter of principle. As one put it 'There is no middle of the road. This is not a personality question until people make it so. It is a question of principle. Principles are principles. This is what I was taught and we owe it to the Grenadian working class to say so.' (Central Committee Meeting, 12 October 1983, p. 5.)

Bishop, however, saw it differently. He also knew that the mood of the Central Committee would indeed not entertain a compromise. Both he and Coard had been sucked into a situation which ultimately neither could control. None the less, there is little doubt that Bishop's fear that he would be gradually ousted from effective leadership—beyond being a public relations front-man and popular mobilizer at home and abroad as and when the occasion demanded—would have been fulfilled. Coard would have had control of the important sub-committees and enjoy army support. The rivalry would have caused a constant haemorrhage in the years ahead, even if the crisis had been papered over. The revolution was thus lost the moment the joint leadership proposal was advanced and approved.

In Coard's favour, and in those who sponsored and supported the principle of joint leadership, there were the risks of charismatic leadership to consider. Visions of grandeur, leading progressively to mis-management, non-accountability and ultimately corruption, may result unless checked by a strong sensibility of moral conscience and responsibility, or by institutional safeguards. In a one-party state, the risk is especially high. Although he was never mentioned, in deference to the NJM's staunchly pro-Soviet stand, Trotsky's dictum was as applicable in Grenada in late 1983 as it was when originally recorded in 1904 in *Our Political Tasks*. 'The party', he warned, 'tends to take the place of the class, the Central Committee that of the party, and the leader that of the Central Committee' (Trotsky, 1970, p. 121). But a one-party state demands firm leadership and direction to maintain morale and unity. Therein was Coard's problem. To fight the risk of a Stalin-type personality cult, he felt it incumbent upon him to assert himself as the primary ideologue. In doing so, he betrayed his Stalinist tendencies: rigidity, impatience, authoritarianism and not a little cunning. Nor was he prepared to work within the system he eulogized. His resignation from the Central Committee was a serious mistake as it fuelled the fires of alleged conspiracy. It also barred him from legitimately claiming that he had fought—even in vain—for change, reform and progress towards socialism in the party's inner sanctum. It also did not help that he often absented himself from Cabinet meetings on the grounds that a lot of the routine business was of less importance than his own. Therefore, although he was acutely aware of the party's weaknesses—lack of poor managerial control, poor organization and the like—he contributed to them. Further, he preferred to discuss and analyse them within the framework of the formally defunct Organization for

Research, Education and Liberation. In short, neither he nor Bishop were willing to work within the new political system that they had helped to create. Radicalized with each turn of the screw by the United States, the party could not afford any signs of weakness in its leaders. If it did, the revolution as a whole would be at stake.

It was this that was the fulcrum of Coard's concern. The potential vacillation by the bourgeoisie which dominated the party, about which Ulyanovsky had warned, appeared to be materializing. Only the firmest revolutionary leadership would prevent deviation into reformism and social democracy in one direction, or ultra-leftism in the other. In the event, the risk of the former was perceived the greater but the ultimate outcome was the latter. In a study of the applicability of the noncapitalist thesis to the Eastern Caribbean published just prior to his appointment to the post-PRG Advisory Council, Pat Emmanuel wrote with remarkable foresight of what was to happen in the NJM.

The cadres that are expected to undertake ideological work are themselves quite young and recently initiated. An understandable revolutionary enthusiasm too often causes creative revolutionary philosophy to degenerate into a catalogue of abuse and ultraleftism . . . In their anxiety to pass the stern Soviet tests of ideological development, it can so easily occur that petty bourgeois radicals can outdo themselves with new kinds of infantile disorders of the far Left. [Emmanuel, 1983, p. 204.]

The problem was that the NJM left the Grenadian people far behind in its struggle for Marxist-Leninism. The central body of professional revolutionaries was distant and largely unknown. The masses certainly felt no loyalty to it. Even such a respected revolutionary as Munroe criticized the over-selectivity of the party (Munroe, 1984, p. 161). The material basis of the revolution was undoubtedly suffering due to a combination of world recession, falling commodity prices and the diversion of investment funds to the airport project, but the difficulties as articulated by the ideological militants on the Central Committee were grossly and consistently exaggerated. Paradoxically, despite Bishop's undoubted popularity, it is doubtful whether even he realized the extent of the credibility gap that had opened up between the party's aspirations and the consciousness of the masses.

The Future of West Indian Socialism

Although the majority of Grenadians broadly supported, or at least acquiesced in, PRG policies and, in particular, felt a deep bond of attachment to Maurice Bishop, a credibility gap had dogged the party from the beginning. The masses for the most part neither knew nor were explicitly told that the NJM had formally decided to be a Marxist–Leninist party. Even if they had known, few would have understood the implications for their society, no matter how far in the future the transformation process would extend. Elitism prevented any popular involvement in theoretical debate, let alone participation in policy making. Indeed, the shortcomings of the revolution were attributed to unsatisfactory levels of strict Leninist elitism and discipline! Bishop himself made this clear in his *Line of March* speech which had set the tone for the year-long crisis. Leninism itself had no shortcomings and, by the definition of orthodoxy, there was no alternative. That Leninism was, on the contrary, entirely inappropriate for Grenada was an idea that was never discussed. Therefore no thought was given to possible alternative philosophies and practices of organization and leadership which would just as effectively fight deprivation, dependency and mismanagement.

The successful transformation by Lenin of Marxian philosophy into a political action programme was a process that was to have truly enormous impact upon politics, governments and economies. None the less, it is instructive to recall Marx's prescription for political organization. He had counselled in the *Communist Manifesto* of 1848 that Communists should not form a separate party but consider themselves a 'section' of the most militant and resolute section of the working-class movement. As political mobilization and leadership were clearly necessary, however, there had to be genuine democracy with party accountability to the members with struggle against any personality cult. The party, furthermore, had no monopoly over scientific research as 'science' could not be imposed on the working-class movement. One observer's summary is succinct.

Marx's view of the proletarian political party is extremely flexible, sensitive and open . . . [where] the real agent in historical action, in the revolution, is the class. The proletarian political party can never replace it in this role: it must be its instrument and under its control . . . [and] not the 'leader' of the class . . . Its mission is not to take over the leadership of the class, but to help it to lead itself. As Rosa Luxemburg said, arguing with Lenin and faithfully reflecting Marx's thought, 'social democracy is not connected with the organisation of the working class, it is the actual movement of the working class'. [Chaudin, 1975, p. 629.]

Of course, Lenin can be forgiven for making the political and organizational preparation of the revolutionary party a priority: class consciousness and class struggle had to be impressed upon the proletariat as capitalism and imperialism increasingly showed itself capable of improving its lot. Further, the Tsarist Russian experience had shown that 'spontaneity' spelt doom. Without revolutionary leadership and direction, class struggle would degenerate into forms of bourgeois ideology or worse. Revisionism and anarchy had to be fought by professional revolutionaries. His prescription was, through the application of scientific analysis, deemed to be correct; deviation from what he insisted was the revolutionary blueprint for success was resolutely opposed. The Bolshevik victory of October 1917 canonized his theory of the party; all others, particularly that of Rosa Luxemburg, were suppressed, and remain so in the Third World. Luxemburg's attempt at revolution in Berlin in 1919 met a grisly end. With her died her theory of organization, which was the closest to Marx's thoughts. She was opposed to centralism, implicit in which was strict obedience of all lesser party organs to the highest 'which alone thinks, plans and decides for all' and the separation of party from class or, in her words, 'the surrounding revolutionary milieu'. She warned that without elections, and freedom of assembly, speech and expression, public life would atrophy and be replaced by cynicism and bureaucracy. Elitism, she forecast, would lead to arrogance by a 'few score party leaders'. Insisting upon obedience and lauded when necessary by care-fully chosen representatives of the working class and other sycophants, they would 'with inexhaustible energy and limitless idealism . . . direct and rule'. While she applauded the Bolsheviks' victory, she was to add that 'The danger begins only when they make a virtue cut of necessity and want to freeze into a whole complete theoretical system all the tactics forced upon them by these circumstances, and want to recommend them to the international proletariat as a model of socialist tactics' (Looker, 1972, p. 250).

It is clear that the structure and processes of the NJM, faithful as they were to Lenin's blueprint, would have fulfilled her fears. They were in truth the organizational embodiment of a party essentially external to the people. 'Vanguard' spelt isolation and exclusivity. 'People's Power' never meant meaningful popular participation in decision-making despite the brave idealism of the former black power advocates. The party through the People's Revolutionary Government was the ultimate custodian of state power. On its own, it was also the custodian of theoretical truth and consciousness, and the tiny proletariat could not become the revolutionary class without being placed under its leadership. Indeed, in the national democratic stage Leninism dictated that *all* the working classes had to be led. The party therefore claimed to be their representative even if they did not recognize it as such. The most obvious institutional expression of this vanguard leader-ship, the trade unions, was the most conspicuous failure: the party could not quench the spirit of free trade unionism that had emerged from the struggles of 1950-1.

Grenadians—in common with other West Indians—had, despite a bitter history, been reared on a tradition of multi-party parliamentary democracy of the Westminster model. Although much abused and in urgent need of reform, it also included precious freedoms. To argue that freedom of expression, press and assembly were 'bourgeois' and therefore expressive of counter-revolutionary thinking was alien; the denial of human rights by 'revolutionary manners' through such thinking was resented; and to argue that the rule of law was a class weapon aimed at the proletariat was oppression. 'Much of the Caribbean left is set within a mould of hard-line Stalinism', asserts Lewis, failing to come to terms in its rigidity and blind obedience with cherished values (Lewis, 1983, p. 236). Totalitarianism through the dictatorship of the party was acceptable if that was meant by following the orthodoxy. This was totally unacceptable to most Grenadians. In sharp contrast, the Cuban revolution was born in violence and out of an authoritarian past in which, as in Tsarist Russia, the democratic and constitutional tradition was notoriously weak, The gradual takeover of the Cuban revolution by the Cuban Communist Party did not create deep political trauma. The first *émigrés* were largely the rich and the politically influential, fleeing from fear of sequestration and loss of privilege. The poorer stratum followed later protesting the failure of the revolution to fulfil its economic promises.

In short, the NJM was not of the people. Even within it, 'centralism' enjoyed undisputed priority over democracy. Inner-party democracy was substituted by bureaucracy, defined as a centralized, hierarchial and professionally organized structure based in principle upon the specialization of members in different activities of the party. The problem was that even this was not fully operationalized: small size made specialization a forlorn hope and the Central Committee was from the start virtually independent of the party at large. It strove valiantly to avoid the emergence of a personality cult by insistence upon consensus. In practice, many decisions in principle were taken outside the structure. But whatever the method, they were enforced, as was party discipline. In the struggle against Stalinism, the worse features of which Lenin's standard bearers of the Communist Party of the Soviet Union had denounced, Stalinist methods had to be used.

The result was that the close association of socialism with authoritarianism and militarism spread beyond Grenada's shores. As the Working People's Alliance warned in its *post mortem*, while defence against external aggression aimed at suppressing revolutionary advance is necessary, those holding the reins of state power have a special responsibility.

When the denial of human rights takes place under cover of left intent, it opens up the floodgates for rulers with other political intentions to suppress their opposition.

Human rights standards cannot be imposed upon governments of only one outlook
... There should be no difficulty in harmonizing the rule of law with revolutionary
needs. Revolutionaries should not be seen as inconsistent in the defence of fundamental civil, political, cultural and economic rights. [Working People's Alliance,
1984, pp. 5–6.]

Indeed, as Clive Thomas has cogently argued, socialism has helped spawn
political democracy. Individual freedoms have been won by workers'
struggles: 'political freedom therefore cannot be put to stand counterpoised
to socialism' (Thomas, 1976, p. 15).

As for the 89,000 Grenadians, authoritarian socialism had an added
poignancy as it was their kin who suffered at the hands of ultra-leftists on 19
October 1983. Many of the positive achievements of the revolution will be
blotted out by this memory. But despite the singularly unsuccessful attempt
to capitalize on his name in the post-invasion election, Bishop will also be
remembered. He was the most remarkable leader the island—or even
possibly the West Indies—is ever likely to experience. It is highly probable
that after time has erased memory of his shortcomings, he will assume the
proportions of a legend and a hero, with all the mythology that this will
entail.

Whether this will help or hinder West Indian socialist theory and practice
in the future is difficult to forecast. Progressives will doubtless be able to
harness any sense of popular sentiment that it may spawn in the years to
come. But it is highly doubtful whether it can be done within the framework
of an orthodox vanguard party organized on Leninist lines. Such parties are
doomed to languish on the political margin, at least in the West Indies if not
in other polities elsewhere which have progressed well beyond a subsistence
economy and which do not have a heritage of authoritarianism and collec-
tivism. A dedicated group of revolutionary cadres to whom secrecy, discipline and elitist exclusiveness is second nature cannot expect seriously to
mobilize and direct the popular will. Munroe, while fully endorsing Leninism, realized this. Although party members were by definition prepared to
make sacrifices at all times, 'how can such a small group alone carry the load
except with the help of the large numbers who are not prepared to make a
big sacrifice but are prepared to help out in smaller ways?' (Munroe, 1983,
p. 5). His answer was the orthodox: to retain the vanguard nature of the party
and to 'merge' with the people and mass organizations. But 'there is a difference between merge and submerge. You merge with [them] in order to carry
[them] forward, not so that it submerges you, carries you backward. The
more the Leninist party merges with the people and the more the people

with the party, the more neither the party nor the people's struggle can be destroyed' (op. cit., p. 48). The party, he counselled, should not seek to impose its will but rather educate and identify closely with efforts at grass roots level as well as in mass organizations to relieve distress and suffering. In that way, the revolutionary party would show clearly the linkage between imperialism, poverty and underdevelopment, and manifest its solidarity with worker's struggles.

Coard expressed much the same sentiments, particularly when he assumed the chairmanship of the NJM Central Committee in mid-September 1983. But, as in Jamaica, putting the plan into action was a different matter. Popular identification of imperialism as the foundation of underdevelopment was, without doubt, possible. It does not follow, however, that people and non-party mass organizations will be weaned away from allegiances to traditional political parties. However much these bourgeois organizations only galvanize into action as elections approach, there is little chance of developing a personal identification with, or meaningful involvement in, the revolutionary vanguard in the absence of absolute dedication. Coard and his colleagues never addressed this issue. Even 'inner' or 'outer' cores, particularly in small communities, will serve only to create divisions and jealousies. In any event, a small population necessarily means very few cadres and intolerable burdens. In larger communities who choose the orthodox Leninist path there is the risk of creating a new highly privileged class, a phenomenon all too clearly observable.

The West Indian tradition has been to import models of economic, social and political development—and their associated values—from elsewhere, largely without question. The time has surely come to consider the formulation of indigenous approaches to the problems of the sub-region. They must take regard of geo-political realities while at the same time insist upon the key significance of imperialism in all its facets, respect traditional values such as free trade unionism and multiparty activity that still prevail over most of the Commonwealth Caribbean, and, above all, harness the aspirations of the people. The sight of large and grateful crowds welcoming the American soldiers and their West Indian allies to release them from a regime 'who kill we children' told its own story. A political sociologist once noted that 'in no society is there a singly uniform political culture, and in all politics there is a fundamental distinction between the culture of the rulers or power holders and that of the masses, whether they are merely parochial subjects or participating citizens.' (Pye, 1965, p. 15.) That was certainly the case in the NJM's Grenada. Socialist theory must be reworked and reformulated by West Indians to bridge that 'fundamental distinction'. It is surely there that the future lies.

Bibliography

Books and Articles

Ambursley, F. and Cohen, R. (eds), 1983. *Crisis in the Caribbean*. London, Heinemann.

Andreyev, I., 1974. *The Non-Capitalist Way*. Moscow, Progress Publishers.

Bishop, M., 1979. *Declaration of the Grenada Revolution*. St. George's, Government Printery, 28 March.

— 1982a. *Forward Ever! Three Years of Revolution*. Sydney, Pathfinder Press.

— 1982b. *Line of March for the Party*. Presented by Comrade Bishop to General Meeting of the Party, 13 September. Washington D.C., United States Department of State, Grenada Occasional Paper, No. 1, August 1984.

— 1982c. *Selected Speeches, 1979–1981*. Havana, Casa de las Americas.

Bishop, M. and Searle, C., 1981. *Education is a Must*. London, Education Committee of the British-Grenadian Friendship Society.

Brizan, G. I., 1979. *The Grenadian Peasantry and Social Revolution, 1931–1951*. Mona, Jamaica, Institute of Social and Economic Research, University of the West Indies, Working Paper no. 21.

Broderick, M., 1968. 'Associated Statehood: A New Form of Decolonization', *International and Comparative Law Quarterly*, vol. 17, no. 2.

Caribbean Insight, London: July 1979; December 1980; February 1983; August 1983; September 1983; November 1983.

Caribbean Tourism Research and Development Centre, 1983. *Grenada Visitor Survey*. Barbados, mimeo.

— 1984. *Caribbean Tourism Statistical Report 1983*. Barbados.

Castro, F., 1983. *A Pyrrhic Military Victory and a Profound Moral Defeat*. Havana, Editora Politica.

Chaudin, F., 1975. *The Communist Movement: From Comintern to Cominform*. Harmondsworth, Penguin Books.

Clean, C. A., 1981. 'Reaching Beyond the Grasp. A Revolutionary Approach to Education', *Bulletin of Eastern Caribbean Affairs*, vol. 17, no. 1.

Coard, Bernard, 1984. 'A Letter from Bernard Coard', *Newsletter of the Committee for Human Rights in Grenada*. London, no. 3, October.

Cohen, R., 1985. Review Article, *Journal of Development Studies*, vol. 21, no. 3.

Commission of Inquiry into the Control of Public Expenditure in Grenada during 1961 and Subsequently, 1962. *Report*. London, HMSO, Cmnd. 1735.

'Declaration of St. George's', 1979. *Bulletin of Eastern Caribbean Affairs*, vol. 5, no. 3.

Devas, R. P., 1964. *The History of the Island of Grenada*. St. George's, Careenage Press.

Duncan, W. R., 1979. 'Soviet and Cuban Interests in the Caribbean' in R. Millett and

W. Will (eds), *The Restless Caribbean: Changing Patterns of International Relations*. New York, Praeger.

Emmanuel, P., 1978. *Crown Colony Politics in Grenada, 1917-1951*. Cave Hill, Barbados, Institute of Social and Economic Research (Eastern Caribbean).

— 1983. 'Revolutionary Theory and Political Reality in the Eastern Caribbean', *Journal of InterAmerican Studies and World Affairs*, vol. 25, no. 2.

Enders, T., 1981. *A State of Danger in the Caribbean*. Testimony to Congress, 14 December, Washington D.C., Government Printing Office, mimeo.

EPICA Task Force, 1982. *Grenada: The Peaceful Revolution*. Washington, D.C., Ecumenical Program for Inter-American Communication and Action.

Frucht, R., 1967. 'A Caribbean Social Type: Neither "Peasant" nor "Proletarian" ', *Social and Economic Studies*, vol. 1, no. 3.

Gill, H. S., 1981. 'The Foreign Policy of the Grenadian Revolution', *Bulletin of Eastern Caribbean Affairs*, vol. 7, no. 1.

Gittens Knight, E., 1946. *The Grenada Handbook and Directory 1946*. Bridgetown, Barbados, Advocate Company.

Gonsalves, R. E., 1981. *The Non-Capitalist Path of Development: Africa and the Caribbean*. London, One World Publishers.

Government of Barbados, 1983. *The House of Assembly Debates* (Official Report), 2nd. Session, 1981-86, 15 November.

'Grenada's Airport and Strategic Issues', 1980. *Aviation Week and Space Technology*, 21 December.

Habib, P. C., 1980. 'Address of the US Ambassador-at-Large to the Miami Conference on the Caribbean, 28 November 1979', *Caribbean Contact*, January.

Hart, R., 1984. *In Nobody's Backyard*. London, Zed Books.

Hastings, M., 1983. 'Black Comedy in Grenada', *The Spectator*, London, 29 October.

Henry, P., 1983. 'Decolonization and the Authoritarian Context of Democracy in Antigua', in P. Henry and C. Stone (eds), *The Newer Caribbean*. Philadelphia, Institute for the Study of Human Issues.

Holmes, Jo-Ann., 1982. 'Grenadian Culture: The People Wants to Get Up', *NACLA Report*, September/October.

House of Commons, Foreign Affairs Committee, 1982. *Fifth Report: Caribbean and Central America*. London, HMSO.

Jacobs, R. I., 1974. 'The Movement Towards Independence', in W. R. Jacobs and B. Coard (eds), *Independence for Grenada: Myth or Reality?* St. Augustine, Trinidad, Institute of International Relations.

Jacobs, W. R. and Jacobs, R. I., 1980. *Grenada: The Route to Revolution*. Havana, Casa de las Americas.

Jacobs, W. R., 1981. *The Grenada Revolution at Work*. New York, Pathfinder Press.

James, C. L. R., 1977. *The Future in the Present*. London, Allison and Busby.

Joseph, Rita, 1981. 'The Significance of the Grenada Revolution to Women in Grenada', *Bulletin of Eastern Caribbean Affairs*, vol. 7, no. 1.

Kirkpatrick, J., 1979. *Dictatorships and Double Standards*. Washington D.C., Georgetown University Occasional Paper.

Latin American Political Report, London, 23 March 1979.

Latin America Regional Report: Caribbean. London. RC-83-04, 13 May 1983; RC-83-10, 9 December 1983; RC-84-05, 15 July 1984.

Lenin, V. I., 1962. *Collected Works*, vol. 31. Moscow, Foreign Languages Publishing House.

Levine, B. (ed.), 1983. *The New Cuban Presence in the Caribbean*. Boulder, Westview Press.

Lewis, G. L., 1983. 'On the Limits of the New Cuban Presence in the Caribbean', in B. Levine (ed.), *The New Cuban Presence in the Caribbean*. Boulder, Westview Press.

—— 1984. 'Grenada 1983: The Lessons for the Caribbean Left', *Caribbean Contact*. July.

Lewis, W. A., 1950. 'The Industrialization of the British West Indies', *Caribbean Economic Review*, vol. 2, May.

Looker, R., 1972. *Rosa Luxemburg: Selected Political Writings*. London, Jonathan Cape.

Lowenthal, D., 1972. *West Indian Societies*. London, Oxford University Press for the Institute of Race Relations.

Lowenthal, D. and Clarke, C., 1980. 'Island Orphans: Barbuda and the Rest', *Journal of Commonwealth and Comparative Politics*, vol. 17, no. 3.

McIntyre, A., 1966. 'Some Issues of Trade Policy in the West Indies', *New World Quarterly*, vol. 2, no. 2.

Manning, F. E., 1984. 'Calypso and Politics in Barbados', *Caribbean Chronicle*, vol. 99, no. 1579.

Marcus, B. and Taber M. (eds), 1983. *Maurice Bishop Speaks: The Grenada Revolution, 1979-83*. New York, Pathfinder Press.

Marshall, T. G., 1984. 'Damning Evidence', *The Bajan*, January.

Munroe, T., 1972. *The Politics of Constitutional Decolonization: Jamaica, 1944-62*. Mona, Jamaica, Institute of Social and Economic Research.

—1983. *The Working Class Party: Principles and Practice*. Kingston, Vanguard Publishers.

—— 1984. *Grenada: Revolution, Counter-Revolution*. Kingston, Vanguard Publishers.

Naipaul, V. S., 1984. 'Heavy Manners in Grenada', *Sunday Times Magazine*, London, 12 February.

New Jewel Movement. 1973. *Manifesto of the New Jewel Movement*, St. George's, November.

—— 1983. *Confidential Membership File*.

Obika, N., 1984. *An Introduction to the Life and Times of Uriah 'Buzz' Butler*. Point Fortin, Trinidad, Caribbean Historical Society.

Pastor, R. A., 1983. 'Cuba and the Soviet Union', in B. Levine (ed.), *The New Cuban Presence in the Caribbean*. Boulder, Westview Press.

—— 1984. *The Impact of Grenada on the Caribbean: Ripples from a Revolution*. Paper delivered to the Conference on the Grenada Revolution, Institute of International Relations, St. Augustine, Trinidad, May, mimeo.

Payne, A. P., 1983. 'The Rodney Riots in Jamaica: The Background and Significance of the Events of October 1968', *Journal of Commonwealth and Comparative Politics*, vol. 11, no. 2.

Payne, A. P., 1984. *International Crisis in the Caribbean*. London, Croom Helm.

Payne, A. P., Sutton, P. and Thorndike, T., 1984. *Grenada: Revolution and Invasion*. London, Croom Helm.

Pearce, J., 1982. *Under the Eagle: US Intervention in Central America and the Caribbean*. London, Latin American Bureau.

Public Workers' Union, 1981. 'Statement from the Unions (GUT, TAWU, PWU) re Salaries Negotiations with Government of Grenada'. Tanteen, Grenada, January.

Pye, L., 1965. 'Introduction', in L. Pye and S. Verba (eds), *Political Culture and Political Development*. Princeton, Princeton University Press.

Robinson, C. J., 1983. 'James and the Black Radical Tradition', *Review*, vol. 6, no. 3.

Rodney, W., 1969. *The Groundings with my Brothers*. London, Bogle-L'Ouverture Publications.

Rottenberg, S., 1955. 'Labor Relations in an Underdeveloped Economy', *Caribbean Quarterly*, vol. 4, no. 1.

Searle, C., 1979. 'Grenada's Revolution: An Interview with Bernard Coard', *Race and Class*, vol. 21, no. 2.

— 1983a. *Grenada: The Struggle Against Destabilization*. London, Writers' and Readers' Publishing Cooperative Society.

— 1983b. 'The People's Commentator: Calypso and the Grenada Revolution', *Race and Class*, vol. 25, no. 1.

Singham, A. W., 1965. 'Cuckoo Politics', *New World Quarterly*, vol. 2, no. 1.

— 1968. *The Hero and the Crowd in a Colonial Polity*. New Haven, Yale University Press.

Smith, L., 1979. 'Compulsory Recognition of Trade Unions in Grenada: A Critique of the Trade Unions (Recognition) Act 1979', *Bulletin of Eastern Caribbean Affairs*, vol. 5, no. 3.

Smith, M. G., 1965. *The Plural Society in the British West Indies*. Kingston, University of the West Indies.

Solodivonikov, V. G. and Bogoslovsky, V., 1975. *Non-Capitalist Development: An Historical Outline*. Moscow, Progress Publishers.

Statement by Cuba on the Events in Grenada, 1983. Havana, Editora Politica.

Tawney, R. H., 1931. *Equality*. New York, Capricorn Books.

Thomas, C. Y., 1976. 'Bread and Justice', *Caribbean Contact*, April.

— 1978. '"The Non-Capitalist Path" as Theory and Practice of Decolonization and Social Transformation', *Latin American Perspectives*, vol. V, no. 2.

Thorndike, T., 1974. 'Maxi-Crisis in Mini-State', *The World Today*, vol. 30, no. 10.

Thornton, A. P., 1960. 'Aspects of West Indian Society', *International Journal*, vol. 15.

Tobias, P. M., 1980. 'The Social Content of Grenadian Emigration', *Social and Economic Studies*, vol. 29, no. 1.

Trotsky, L., 1970. *Our Political Tasks* (republished from the 1964 edition). Paris, Denoël–Gunthier.

Ulyanovsky, R. A., 1974. *Socialism and the Newly Independent Nations*. Moscow, Progress Publishers.

West India Royal Commission (1938–9), 1945. *Report*. London, HMSO, Cmd. 6607.

Whitbeck, R. H., 1933. 'The Lesser Antilles—Past and Present', *Annals of the Association of American Geographers*, vol. 23.

Williams, E., 1970. *From Columbus to Castro: A History of the Caribbean, 1492–1969*. London, André Deutsch.

—— 1972. *History of the People of Trinidad and Tobago*, London, André Deutsch.

Working People's Alliance, 1984. *Grenada and the Caribbean*. Georgetown, Guyana, 13 March, mimeo.

World Bank, 1982. *Economic Memorandum on Grenada*. Washington D.C.

Grenada Government Reports and Publications, St. George's

Government of Grenada, 1938. *Report of the Commission Appointed to Enquire into the Economic Condition of Wage Earners*. Agriculture Department.

—— 1969. 'Regional Integration: The Grenada Proposals'. Prime Minister's Office, mimeo.

—— 1970. 'Black Power in Grenada'. Prime Minister's Office, radio broadcast transcript, mimeo.

—— 1974. *Our Independence Prayer*. Government Printery, February.

—— 1978. 'Prime Minister E. M. Gairy's Address to the Assembly of the Organization of American States'. Prime Minister's Office, July, mimeo.

—— 1981. 'Grow More Food!' Ministry of Agriculture, mimeo.

—— 1982. *Final Report on Grenada Agriculture Census, 1981*. Ministry of Planning, 31 August.

—— 1984a. *Economic Memorandum on Grenada*, Vol. 1. Advisory Council, prepared with the assistance of the Caribbean Development Bank.

—— 1984b. 'Grenada Census, 30 April 1981'. Population Census Office, computer printout.

People's Revolutionary Government, 1979. 'Centre for Popular Education: Initiatory Phase'. June, mimeo.

—— 1980. Minutes of Meeting Between Trade Union Representatives and Government Regarding Negotiations for Salaries Increases for Public Workers, 29 December. Grenada Treasury mimeo..

—— 1981a. *Is Freedom We Making*.

—— 1981b. 'Proceedings of Aid Donors' Meeting Held in Brussels at ACP House on 14 and 15 April 1981: International Airport Project—Grenada'. Embassy of Grenada.

—— 1981c. 'Protocol of the Military Collaboration Between the Government of Cuba and the People's Revolutionary Government of Grenada'.

—— 1982a. 'Cultural Agreement Between the People's Revolutionary Government and the Government of the People of Cuba'. 8 December, mimeo.

—— 1982b. *Grenada Is Not Alone*. Fedon Publishers.

—— 1982c. *Report on the National Economy for 1981 and the Prospects for 1982*. Presented by Bro. B. Coard, Government Printing Office.

—— 1982d. *To Construct From Morning: Making the People's Budget in Grenada*. Fedon Publishers.

People's Revolutinary Government, 1983a. 'Report of Detainees Committee Meeting', June.

—— 1983b. *Report on the National Economy for 1982 and the Budget-Plan for 1983 and Beyond*. Presented by Cde. Coard to the National Conference of Delegates of Mass Organizations, Thursday 24 February, Government Printing Office.

Central Committee of the New Jewel Movement, Minutes (mimeo): Meeting, 15–16 April 1981; Meeting, 12–15 October 1982; First Plenary Session 13–19 July 1983; Emergency Meeting, 26 August 1983; Extraordinary Meeting, 14–16 September 1983; Fifth Sitting, Plenary, 19 September 1983; Sixth Sitting, Plenary, 20 September 1983; Seventh Sitting, Plenary, 21 September 1983; Eighth Sitting, Plenary, 22 September 1983; Plenary Meeting, 23 September 1983; Meeting, 28 September 1983; Meeting, 12 October 1983.

Central Committee Reports (mimeo): 'Central Committee Resolution on Agriculture', January 1983; 'On the Possible Establishment of a State Trading Corporation for Effecting Grenada's Trade with the Socialist Countries', June 1983; 'Progress Report of Commission No. 5'.

General Meetings of NJM Members, Minutes (mimeo): 14 September 1982; 25 September 1983; *Why Meeting?* Background document for members on the crisis, 25 September 1983.

Political Bureau Meetings, Minutes (mimeo): 22 June 1983; 10 August 1983.

Political-Economic Bureau Meetings, Minutes (mimeo): 3 August 1983.

National Women's Organization (mimeo): 'National Women's Organization Work Plan for 1982', 15 November 1981; 'The Part the National Women's Organization Must Play in the Development of Women in Grenada, 1983–5', February 1983.

National Youth Organization (mimeo): 'Draft Protocol on Youth: Between the Socialist Youth in Czechoslovakia and the NJM National Youth Organization in Grenada', June 1982; 'Issues to be Raised in Discussions Between the Cuba Union of Young Communists (UJC) and the NJM National Youth Organization', 4 November 1982.

People's Revolutionary Army (mimeo): 'Plan of Action for Security Forces in Armed Force Manoeuvre, 30 January–1 February 1981'; 'Plan of Intelligence Operations, Ministry of Interior' (Major Keith Roberts to Cde. Bishop), February 1983.

Radio Free Grenada, Transcripts (personal communication), 18, 19, 20 and 23 October 1983.

Revolutionary Military Council (mimeo): *Bulletin*, 20 October 1983; 'Emergency Economic Plan', 21 October 1983; 'Emergency Economic Programme', 22 October 1983; Meeting, 20 October 1983.

Correspondence

Austin, General, letter to Commander Andropov, Chairman of Committee of State Security, Moscow, 17 February 1982.

Cornwall, Ambassador Leon, letter to Major Layne and General Austin, November 1982–March 1983.

Husbands, Victor, Memorandum to Maurice Bishop re detainees, 14 December 1982.
— 'Release of Detainees', 20 December 1982.
Jacobs, Ambassador W. R., confidential letter to Foreign Minister U. Whiteman, 11 July 1983, 'Grenada's Relations with the USSR'; January 1983, 'Relations with the CPSU'.
Request for Military Assistance to the People's Revolutionary Armed Forces of the USSR, 2 July 1982.
Roberts, Major Keith, Memorandum to Cde. Bishop, 12 July 1983, 'Analysis of the Church in Grenada'.
Sibblies, Langston, Deputy Director of Prosecutions, Report to Maurice Bishop re detainees, 26 January 1982.

Newspapers

Advocate News, later *Barbados Advocate*
Caribbean Contact (Barbados)
Caribbean Sun (Barbados)
Caribbean Times (London)
Daily Express (London)
Daily Gleaner (Jamaica)
Daily Telegraph (London)
Everybody's Magazine (New York)
Free West Indian (St. George's)
Granma (Havana)
Justice (St. Vincent)
Miami Herald (Miami)
New Chronicle (Dominica)
New York Post (New York)
New York Times (New York)
Newsweek (New York)
Outlet (Antigua)
The Bomb (Trinidad)
The Guardian (London)
The New Jewel (St. George's)
The People's Tribune (St. George's)
The Times (London)
Time (New York)
Trinidad and Tobago Review (Trinidad)
Washington Post (Washington D.C.)

Index

Marxist Regimes
Politics, Economics and Society

A series of 36 multi-disciplinary volumes each examining and evaluating critically the application of Marxist doctrine to the respective societies, assessing its interpretations, its successes and failures. Each book includes: Basic Data, History and Political Traditions, the Social Structure, the Political System, the Economic System, and the Regime's Policies. The series draws upon an international collection of authors, each an expert on the country concerned, thus ensuring a unique depth and breadth of analysis.

GRENADA

The US-led invasion of Grenada in October 1983 followed a bitter ideological struggle within the ruling New Jewel Movement. This had resulted in the deaths of Prime Minister Maurice Bishop and several colleagues and supporters. Bishop led a party which attempted to spearhead a Marxist-Leninist revolution and follow the 'non-capitalist path'. This was, however, largely restricted to a foreign policy centred upon close links with Cuba and the Soviet Union.

The Grenadian revolution was improbable in time and place. Grenada had a peasant-based agricultural economy with a powerful land ownership tradition. The 89,000 Grenadians were strongly influenced by values and assumptions bequeathed by British colonialism, and lived in a region claimed by a resurgent United States as its sphere of interest. Seizing power through a popular insurrection in March 1979 against the dictatorship of Sir Eric Gairy, the NJM sought to surmount these obstacles by applying strict Leninist principles of party organisation and discipline, whereby vacillation from orthodoxy had to be resisted at all costs. But another orthodoxy, that of the USA, was the eventual cost.